Sustainable Entrepreneurship

Sustainable Entrepreneurship

Alan S. Gutterman

BEP BUSINESS EXPERT PRESS

Sustainable Entrepreneurship

First published in 2018 by
Business Expert Press, LLC
222 East 46th Street, New York, NY 10017
www.businessexpertpress.com

ISBN-13: 978-1-94897-657-2 (paperback)
ISBN-13: 978-1-94897-658-9 (e-book)

Business Expert Press Entrepreneurship and Small Business Management Collection

Collection ISSN: 1946-5653 (print)
Collection ISSN: 1946-5661 (electronic)

Cover and interior design by Exeter Premedia Services Private Ltd., Chennai, India

First edition: 2018

10 9 8 7 6 5 4 3 2 1

Printed in the United States of America.

Abstract

Sustainability has become a multidimensional concept that extends beyond environmental protection to economic development and social equity—in other words, entrepreneurship guided and measured by the three pillars of the "triple bottom line." Sustainable entrepreneurship is the continuing commitment by businesses to behave ethically and contribute to economic development while improving the quality of life of the workforce, their families, the local and global community as well as future generations. This definition recognizes that several different stakeholder groups, not just shareholders, must be taken into account when managerial decisions are made and operational activities in furtherance of the organizational purposes are carried out. This book traces the foundations for sustainable entrepreneurship, beginning with sustainability, ecopreneurship, and social entrepreneurship and then continuing with a comprehensive review of the basic principles of sustainable entrepreneurship and how entrepreneurs can integrate sustainability into their business models. This book will be an invaluable resource for entrepreneurs who have chosen to focus their efforts on building a new concept based on the principles of sustainability from the outset. In addition, the book can be used by academics teaching sustainable entrepreneurship, a topic of surging interest to students, and by attorneys and professionals working with sustainable businesses.

Keywords

corporate sustainability, ecopreneurship, entrepreneurship, social entrepreneurship, sustainability, sustainable entrepreneurship

Contents

CHAPTER 1

Introduction to Entrepreneurship

Definitions of Entrepreneurship

Few topics in the business area have attracted more attention among academics and journalists than "entrepreneurship." From an economic perspective, "entrepreneurship" is generally conceptualized as the creation of a new business and the bearing of the risk associated with that business in exchange for profits to be derived from the exploitation of opportunities in the marketplace (e.g., demands of consumers that are not currently being satisfied). Defined in this manner, entrepreneurship can take a variety of different forms. One of the most famous types of entrepreneurship, one that has also become closely aligned with conceptualizations of various forms of entrepreneurship, is Schumpeter's "creative destruction." In Schumpeter's view, the entrepreneur is driven by innovation, which can take the form of a totally new product or process or an innovative change to existing products or processes, which ultimately "destroy," or render obsolete, products and processes that have been used in the past. While entrepreneurship is often discussed in the context of policies for encouraging and supporting small businesses, Graham observed that entrepreneurship differs from small business in four critical ways: amount of wealth creation, speed of wealth accumulation, risk, and innovation.[1]

Entrepreneurship is widely celebrated as an engine for progress that brings growth to the economy, makes the marketplace more competitive, makes individual firms more productive through technological change, and creates jobs and added value and welfare for members of society.

---

[1] Graham, S. September 16, 2010. *What Is Sustainable Entrepreneurship?* http://ezinearticles.com/?What-Is-Sustainable-Entrepreneurship?&id=5045492

However, while entrepreneurship is generally lauded for the positive impacts and benefits it has provided to society, it is also true that entrepreneurial activities can have negative consequences such as environmental degradation or unequal distribution of wealth.[2] Recognizing this situation, there have been calls among researchers for entrepreneurial skills and processes to be applied to mitigate and resolve some of the problems that entrepreneurs may have created, an idea which provides the foundation for ecopreneurship, social entrepreneurship, and sustainable entrepreneurship.[3] For example, Hall et al. argued that "entrepreneurship may be a panacea for many social and environmental concerns" and Pacheco et al. asserted that entrepreneurs can be an important force for social and ecological sustainability.[4]

---

[2] See, for example, Cohen, B., and M. Winn. 2007. "Market Imperfections, Opportunity and Sustainable Entrepreneruship." *Journal of Business Venturing* 22, no. 1, p. 29; and Dean, T., and J. McMullen. 2007. "Toward a Theory of Sustainable Entrepreneurship: Reducing Environmental Degradation through Entrepreneurial Action." *Journal of Business Venturing* 22, no. 1, p. 50.

[3] Hall, J., G. Daneke, and M. Lenox. 2010. "Sustainable Development and Entrepreneurship: Past Contributions and Future Directions." *Journal of Business Venturing* 25, no. 5, p. 439; Hockerts, K., and R. Wüstenhagen. 2010. "Greening Goliaths Versus Emerging Davids: Theorizing about the Role of Incumbents and New Entrants in Sustainable Entrepreneurship." *Journal of Business Venturing* 25, no. 5, p. 481; O'Neil, I., and D. Ucbasaran. February 1–4, 2011. "Sustainable Entrepreneurship and Career Transitions: The Role of Individual Identity." *Conference proceedings in 8th International AGSE Entrepreneurship Research Exchange Conference.* Swinburne University of Technology, Melbourne, Australia; Parrish, B. 2010. "Sustainability-Driven Entrepreneurship: Principles of Organization Design." *Journal of Business Venturing* 25, no. 5, p. 510; and Tilley, F., and W. Young. 2009. "Sustainability Entrepreneurs: Could They be the True Wealth Generators of the Future?" *Green Management International* 55, p. 79.

[4] Majid, I., and W.L. Koe. June 2012. "Sustainable Entrepreneurship (SE): A Revised Model Based on Triple Bottom Line (TBL)." *International Journal of Academic Research in Business and Social Sciences* 2, no. 6, pp. 293, 96 (citing Hall, J., G. Daneke, and M. Lenox. 2010. "Sustainable Development and Entrepreneurship: Past Contributions and Future Directions." *Journal of Business Venturing* 25, no. 5, pp. 439, 440; and Pacheco, D., T. Dean, and D. Payne. 2010. "Escaping the Green Prison: Entrepreneurship and the Creation of Opportunities for Sustainable Development." *Journal of Business Venturing* 25, no. 5, p. 464.

Research regarding "entrepreneurship" has been made challenging by the absence of a consistent definition of the term across the universe of studies on the topic.[5] According to Stokes et al., the concept of entrepreneurship has existed for centuries and has been important to the development of modern economic and social life.[6] The term itself has been linked to the French word "entreprendre," which means "to undertake" or "to do something," and early definitions and descriptions of the concept can be found in works of economists going back as far as the 18th century (e.g., Cantillon, Adam Smith, Say, John Stuart Mill, and Hermann).[7] For example, one of the first uses of the term "entrepreneur" has been attributed to Cantillon, who wrote in the 18th century about individuals who bought materials and means of production at prices that enabled them to combine them into a new product.[8]

Many researchers have focused on the economic function served by the entrepreneur. For example, one of the earliest definitions of entrepreneurship focused on merchants who were willing to assume the risks of purchasing items at certain prices while there was uncertainty about the prices at which those items could eventually be resold. Later definitions began to focus on the risks and challenges associated with combining various factors of production to generate outputs that would be made available for sale in constantly changing markets. Schumpeter was one of the first to include innovation in the definition of entrepreneurship and believed strongly that the proper role of the entrepreneur was creating and responding to economic discontinuities. Others involved in the study of entrepreneurship focus on the personality traits and life experiences

---

[5] Shane. S., E. Locke, and C. Collins. 2003. "Entrepreneurial Motivation." *Human Resource Management Review* 13, no. 2, pp. 257–79, 274.

[6] Stokes, D., N. Wilson, and M. Mador. 2010. *Entrepreneurship.* Hampshire, UK: South-Western Cengage Learning.

[7] Veciana, J. 2007. "Entrepreneurship as a Scientific Research Program." In *Entrepreneurship: Concepts, Theory and Perspective*, eds. A. Cuervo, D. Ribeiro, and S. Roig, 23. Berlin, Heidelberg: Springer-Verlag.

[8] Tilley. F., and W. Young. 2009. "Sustainability Entrepreneurs—Could they be the True Wealth Generators of the Future?" *Greener Management International* 55, no. 79 (citing Hisrich, P., and M. Peters. 1998. *Entrepreneurship.* International Edition Boston: Irwin McGraw-Hill).

of the entrepreneur in an attempt to generate lists of common entrepreneurial characteristics—propensity for "risk taking," need for achievement and childhood deprivation. While these studies are interesting they have generally been far from conclusive and often have generated conflicting results.

Gartner surveyed the landscape of the attempts to define entrepreneurship and concluded that finding a common definition of the entrepreneur remains "elusive."[9] Gartner quoted an observation made by Cole in 1969:

> My own personal experience was that for 10 years we ran a research center in entrepreneurial history, for 10 years we tried to define the entrepreneur. We never succeeded. Each of us had some notion of it—what he thought was, for his purposes, a useful definition. And I don't think you're going to get farther than that.[10]

Gartner also pointed out that Borkchuas and Horwitz, who reviewed the literature on the psychology of the entrepreneur in the mid-1980s, struck a similar note when they reported:

> The literature appears to support the argument that there is no generic definition of the entrepreneur, or if there is we do not have the psychological instruments to discover it at this time. Most of the attempts to distinguish between entrepreneurs and small

[9] Gartner, W. Spring 1988. "'Who is an Entrepreneur?' Is the Wrong Question." *American Journal of Small Business* 12, no. 4, pp. 11–32, 11 (citing, among others, Carsrud, A., K. Olm, and G. Eddy. 1985. "Entrepreneurship: Research in Quest of a Paradigm." In *The Art and Science of Entrepreneurship,* eds. D. Sexton, and R. Smilor. Cambridge, MA: Ballinger; and Sexton, D., and R. Smilor. 1985. "Introduction." In *The Art and Science of Entrepreneurship*, eds. D. Sexton, and R. Smilor. Cambridge, MA: Ballinger).

[10] Id. (quoting Cole, A., and A, Karl. 1969. "Definition of Entrepreneurship." In *Bostrom Seminar in the Study of Enterprise*, ed. J. Komives, 10–22, 17. Milwaukee, WI: Center for Venture Management).

business owners or managers have discovered no significant differentiating features.[11]

Gartner also counseled against the so-called "trait approach" that focuses on identifying "entrepreneurs"[12] and argued that the study of new venture creation must take into account the interaction among several variables or dimensions including not only the personal characteristics of the individual entrepreneur but also competitive entry strategies, "push" and "pull" factors and the actions taken by the entrepreneur during the new venture creation process.[13] Other researchers, including Schumpeter, have added the availability of prospective entrepreneurs with the requisite entrepreneurial orientation (e.g., self-reliance, self-confidence, and perseverance) as a prerequisite to effective new venture creation.[14]

Acknowledging the lack of a universally accepted definition of entrepreneurship, Hessels did comment that "[t]here seems to be agreement … that entrepreneurship involves the creation of something new."[15] For Gartner, that "something new" was a "new organization" and he suggested that the most fruitful path for studying entrepreneurship was to view it as a process that includes a series of behaviors and activities intended to

---

[11] Id. (quoting Brockhaus, R., and P. Horwitz. 1985. "The Psychology of the Entrepreneur." In *The Art and Science of Entrepreneurship*, eds. D. Sexton, and R. Smilor, 42–43. Cambridge, MA: Ballinger).

[12] Id. at p. 26.

[13] Gartner, W. 1985. "A Conceptual Framework for Describing the Phenomenon of New Venture Creation." *Academy of Management Review* 10, no. 4, pp. 696–706.

[14] Mueller, S., and A. Thomas. 2000. "Culture and Entrepreneurial Potential: A Nine Country Study of Locus of Control and Innovativeness." *Journal of Business Venturing* 16, pp. 51–75, 53–54, 62 (citing Schumpeter, J. 1934. *The Theory of Economic Development*, 132. Cambridge, MA: Harvard University Press).

[15] Hessels, J. 2008. *International Entrepreneurship: An Introduction, Framework and Research Agenda*, 6. Zoetermeer, The Netherlands: Scientific Analysis of Entrepreneurship and SMEs (citing Reynolds, P., N. Bosma, E. Autio, S. Hunt, N. De Bono, I. Servais, P. Lopez-Garcia, and N. Chin. 2005. "Global Entrepreneurship Monitor: Data Collection Design and Implementation 1998–2003." *Small Business Economics* 24, no. 3, pp. 205–31).

create organizations.[16] Davidsson et al. referred to entrepreneurship as "the creation of new economic activity" that occurs both through the creation of new ventures and new economic activity of established firms.[17] Use of the concept of "creation of new economic activity" includes not only the creation of new organizations championed by Gartner but also recognition and exploitation of opportunities, conversion of new ideas into innovations and even imitative behavior that is new to a firm.[18] It is not necessary that the same person or entity that discovered an opportunity actually exploit that opportunity and entrepreneurship should be defined broadly enough to include the sale of opportunities to others. For that matter, discovery of a new technology should not be a prerequisite to entrepreneurship with respect to that opportunity and the concept of entrepreneurship should include actions taken to interpret the capabilities of the technology so as to identify applications of the technology that eventually become the foundation of opportunities.

All of the foregoing was taken into account by Shane and Venkataraman when they defined entrepreneurship as "the process by which 'opportunities to create future goods and services are discovered, evaluated and exploited.'"[19] A few years later, Shane, working with Eckhardt, elaborated

---

[16] Gartner, W. Spring 1988. "'Who is an Entrepreneur?' Is the Wrong Question." *American Journal of Small Business* 12, no. 4, pp. 11–32, 26. Gartner argued that all of the different studies of entrepreneurship that can be identified in the field actually begin with the creation of new organizations including research on "psychological characteristics of entrepreneurs, sociological explanations of entrepreneurial cultures, economic and demographic explanations of entrepreneurial locations, and so on." Id.

[17] Davidsson, P., F. Delmar, and J. Wiklund. 2006. "Entrepreneurship as Growth; Growth as Entrepreneurship." In *Entrepreneurship and the Growth of Firms*, eds. P. Davidsson, F. Delmar, and J. Wiklund, 21–38, 27. Cheltenham, UK: Edward Elgar Publisher.

[18] Hessels, J. 2008. *International Entrepreneurship: An Introduction, Framework and Research Agenda*, 6. Zoetermeer, The Netherlands: Scientific Analysis of Entrepreneurship and SMEs.

[19] Shane, S., and S. Venkataraman. 2000. "The Promise of Entrepreneurship as a Field of Research." *Academy of Management Review* 25, no. 1, pp. 217–26, 218 (as cited in Shane, S., E. Locke, and C. Collins. 2003. "Entrepreneurial Motivation." *Human Resource Management Review* 13, no. 2, pp. 257–79, 259).

on the previous definition by describing entrepreneurship as a business process that encompassed several stages and activities including the identification and appraisal of opportunities, the choice to whether to exploit or sell the opportunities, efforts to acquire resources needed to exploit the opportunities, the development of an appropriate strategy for exploiting the opportunity, and the design of the new project or business model relating to the exploitation of the opportunity.[20] Shane et al. highlighted several key points that followed from using these definitions.[21] For example, the definition does not require that the entrepreneur be a firm founder or business owner, a common assumption in the research relating to entrepreneurship, and allows for the fact that new and innovative ideas for goods and services can come from anywhere in the organizational hierarchy and not just from the top, such as sales managers who develop new ways to market products and services to target markets.[22] In addition, it calls for interpreting entrepreneurship as a "process" rather than a one-time event, action, or decision. For example, the decision to form and organize a new firm, while important, is just one of a series of actions that must be taken in order to effectively discover, evaluate, and exploit an opportunity. Finally, the definition recognizes that entrepreneurship is based on "creativity," which can include not only uncovering new ideas and knowledge but also arranging resources in ways that have not been done before. There is no minimum threshold of "creativity" that must be met in order for an activity to qualify as "entrepreneurship" and, as Shane et al. pointed out, "the degree of creativity involved in entrepreneurship varies across the types of resource recombination that occurs."[23]

Later, Oviatt and McDougall acknowledged and added to definition the definition offered by Shane and Venkataraman in the context of their

---

[20] Eckhardt, J., and S. Shane. 2003. "Opportunities and Entrepreneurship." *Journal of Management* 29, no. 3, p. 333.

[21] Shane, S., E. Locke, and C. Collins. 2003. "Entrepreneurial Motivation." *Human Resource Management Review* 13, no. 2, pp. 257–79, 259.

[22] See, for example, McClelland, D. 1961. *The Achieving Society*. Princeton, NJ: Van Nostrand; and Kirzner, I. 1973. *Competition and Entrepreneurship*. Chicago, IL: University of Chicago Press.

[23] Shane, S., E. Locke, and C. Collins. 2003. "Entrepreneurial motivation." *Human Resource Management Review* 13, no. 2, pp. 257–79, 259.

effort to describe "international entrepreneurship" by referring to entrepreneurship as "the discovery, enactment, evaluation, and exploitation of opportunities … to create future goods and services."[24] According to Harper, the opportunities associated with entrepreneurship may call for development of new markets, new products, new methods of production and management, the discovery of new inputs, the establishment of new businesses, and the creation and design of new organizational forms.[25]

Theoretical Underpinnings of Entrepreneurship

Lawai et al. summarized some of the various theories that have been advanced by researchers to explain the field of entrepreneurship, noting that the theories had drawn on principles for a wide array of academic fields including economics, psychology, sociology, anthropology, and management[26]:

- *Economic Entrepreneurship Theories*: Economic theories
  of entrepreneurship highlight the economic factors that
  enhance entrepreneurial behavior. For example, classical
  theory is based on the benefits of free trade, specialization,
  and competition, and sees the entrepreneur as the essential
  director of the production and distribution of goods in a
  competitive marketplace. Classical theory has been criticized
  as failing to take into account the role that entrepreneurs have
  played in disrupting existing markets and economists such
  as Schumpeter have argued that the role of the entrepreneur

---

[24] Oviatt, B., and P. McDougall. 2005. "Defining International Entrepreneurship and Modeling the Speed of Internationalization." *Entrepreneurship Theory and Practice* 29, no. 5, pp. 537–53, 540.

[25] Harper, D.A. 2003. *Foundations of Entrepreneurship and Economic Development*. New York, NY: Routledge.

[26] Lawai, F., R. Worlu, and O. Ayoade. May 2016. "Critical Success Factors for Sustainable Entrepreneurship in SMEs: Nigerian Perspective." *Mediterranean Journal of Social Sciences* 7, no. 3, pp. 340–42, 338; See also Kwabena, N. 2011. "Entrepreneurship Theories and Empirical Research: A Summary Review of the Literature." *European Journal of Business and Management* 3, no. 6.

was to drive market-based systems by creating something new which resulted in processes that transformed the market economy.

- *Psychological Entrepreneurship Theories*: Psychological theories emphasize personal characteristics of individuals who seek to engage in entrepreneurial activities including personality traits, need for achievement and locus of control, ability to take risk, innovativeness, and tolerance for ambiguity. For example, Coon identified the following characteristics or behaviors associated with entrepreneurs: tendency toward being more opportunity driven, demonstration of high level of creativity and innovation, display of high level of management skills and business know-how, optimism, emotional resilience and mental energy, hard-working spirit, intense commitment and perseverance, competitive desire to excel and win, tendency to be dissatisfied with the status quo and desire for improvement, transformational in nature, lifelong learners, and able to use failure as a tool and springboard.[27]

- *Sociological Entrepreneurship Theories*: Sociological entrepreneurship theories focus on the social context for entrepreneurship. For example, Reynolds claimed to have identified four social contexts that relate to entrepreneurial opportunity vis-a-vis: building social relationships and bonds that fosters trust instead of opportunism; ethnic identification where individual's sociological background serve as decisive factor in propelling entrepreneurial affinity; population ecology (in which case environmental factors) determine survival of new ventures; and life course stage context which involves analyzing life situations and characteristic of individuals who have decided to become entrepreneurs.[28]

---

[27] Id. at p. 341 (citing Coon, D. 2004. *Introduction to Psychology*, 9th ed. Minneapolis: West Publishing Company).

[28] Id. at pp. 341–42 (citing Reynolds, P. 1991. "Sociology and Entrepreneurship: Concepts and Contributions." *Entrepreneurship: Theory & Practice* 16, no. 2, p. 47).

- *Anthropological Entrepreneurship Theories*: Related to sociological entrepreneurship theories, anthropological entrepreneurship theories focus on the importance of both social and cultural context as determinants of successful entrepreneurship. Specific issues include cultural attitudes toward entrepreneurship and integration of cultural values and norms into the processes used to launch new ventures.
- *Opportunity-Based Entrepreneurship Theories*: Opportunity-based entrepreneurship theories are based on the premise that entrepreneurs do not necessarily bring about change directly but scan the environment for changes and then seize and exploit the opportunities that create change (e.g., opportunities related to change in technology and/or consumer preferences).
- *Resource-Based Entrepreneurship Theories*: Resource-based entrepreneurship theories are focused on the importance of access to resources (e.g., financial, social, and human resources) as a facilitator and predictor of identifying opportunities suitable for entrepreneurial activities.[29]

Types of Entrepreneurship

Entrepreneurship can take a variety of forms and a number of researchers have suggested that it is important to recognize different "types" of entrepreneurship when analyzing issues such as the characteristics of entrepreneurs, their motives for choosing entrepreneurship, and the contributions of their entrepreneurial activities to economic development.[30] The Global Entrepreneurship Monitor (GEM) researchers acknowledged that entrepreneurship is a process that extends over multiple phases, thus allowing

---

[29] Alvarez, S., and L. Busenitz. 2001. "The Entrepreneurship of Resource Based Theory." *Journal of Management* 27, no. 6, pp. 755–75; and Davidson, P., and B. Honing. 2003. "The Role of Social and Human Capital Among Nascent Entrepreneurs." *Journal of Business Venturing* 20, p. 121.

[30] See, for example, Baumol, W. 1990. "Entrepreneurship—Productive, Unproductive and Destructive." *Journal of Political Economy* 98, no. 5, pp. 893–921.

opportunities for assessing the state of entrepreneurship in a particular society at different phases. Four of the phases are readily identifiable stages of the new venture formation process and each stage has its own "type" of entrepreneur[31]:

- Potential entrepreneurs: These are persons who see opportunities in their areas, believe they have the abilities and resources to start businesses to pursue those opportunities and who are not deterred by fear of failure in pursuing those opportunities. The level of broader societal support for entrepreneurship is also important at this phase. The GEM survey uses a variety of measures of entrepreneurial perceptions, intentions, and societal attitudes including perceived opportunities, perceived capabilities, fear of failure, entrepreneurial intentions, entrepreneurship as a "good career choice" high status to successful entrepreneurs, and media attention for entrepreneurship.

- Expected entrepreneurs: Expected entrepreneurs are those persons who have not yet started a business but who have expressed an expectation that they would start a business within the next three years.

- Nascent entrepreneurs: This phase covers the first three months after the entrepreneur establishes a new business to pursue the identified opportunities.

- New business owners: These are persons who have successfully emerged from the nascent phase and have been in business more than three months but less than three and-half years.

---

[31] Kelley, D., S. Singer, and M. Herrington. 2012. *Global Entrepreneurship Monitor: 2011 Global Report.* Babson Park, MA: Global Entrepreneurship Research Association. The GEM researchers actually identified six phases; the four mentioned in the text and two more: "established businesses" (i.e., businesses that have been operating for more than three and one-half years, thus moving beyond "new business owner" status) and "discontinued businesses," which were factored into the analysis regardless of how long they were operating because they are a source of experienced entrepreneurs who may start new businesses and/or use their expertise and experience to support other entrepreneurs (e.g., by providing financing and/or business advice).

Two other popular methods for classifying entrepreneurs are the distinctions that have been made between "push" and "pull" entrepreneurs[32] and the distinctions between "necessity-based" and "opportunity-based" entrepreneurs. Others, when analyzing conditions in transition economies, have distinguished between "proprietorship," which includes situations where individuals start their own businesses to generate income to sustain their families when no other options are available, and "genuine entrepreneurship," which is a term that describes situations where individuals start businesses with the goal of generating sufficient income so that a portion of it can be reinvested in order to underwrite business growth and development.[33]

A number of researchers have focused on the existence and influence of "push/pull situational factors" in motivating individuals to engage in entrepreneurial activities and the factors identified have included the frustration of the entrepreneur with his or her current lifestyle, childhood influences, family environment, age, education, work history, role models, and support networks.[34] In many instances, entrepreneurs may be literally "pushed" into entrepreneurship, often against their wishes,

---

[32] See, for example, Amit, R., and E. Muller. 1995. "'Push' and 'Pull' Entrepreneurship." *Journal of Small Business and Entrepreneurship* 12, no. 4, pp. 64–80.

[33] Scase, R. 1997. "The Role of Small Businesses in the Economic Transformation of Eastern Europe: Real but Relatively Unimportant." *International Small Business Journal* 16, pp. 113–21; Scase, R. 2003. "Entrepreneurship and Proprietorship in Transition: Policy Implications for the SME Sector." In *Small and Medium Enterprises in Transitional Economies*, eds. R. McIntyre, R. Dallago, and B. Houndsmil, 68–77. Basingstoke: Palgrave Macmillan.

[34] Mueller. S., and A. Thomas. 2000. "Culture and Entrepreneurial Potential: A Nine Country Study of Locus of Control and Innovativeness." *Journal of Business Venturing* 16, no. 1, pp. 51–75, 54 (citing Hisrich, R. 1990. "Entrepreneurship/Intrapreneurship." *American Psychologist* 45, no. 2, pp. 209–22; Martin, M. 1984. *Managing Technological Innovation and Entrepreneurship*. Reston, VA: Prentice-Hall); Moore, C. 1986. *Understanding Entrepreneurial Behavior: A Definition and Model*, 66–70. Proceeding of the National Academy of Management; Krueger, N. 1993. "The Impact of Prior Entrepreneurial Exposure on Perceptions of New Venture Feasibility and Desirability." *Entrepreneurship Theory and Practice* 18, no. 1, pp. 5–21; Scheinberg, S., and I. MacMillan. 1988. **"**An Eleven Country Study of the Motivations to Start a Business." In *Frontiers of Entrepreneurship*

by unanticipated and unwelcome lifecycle developments such as loss of employment, extreme dissatisfaction with a current job, and other career setbacks. Unfortunately, these entrepreneurs are frequently viewed in a somewhat negative fashion by society—"misfits" or "rejects."[35] On the other hand, entrepreneurs may be "pulled" into creating a new venture by factors viewed more positively in most societies including training and exposure to business that creates interest and confidence in looking for new opportunities to exploit.[36] Some researchers have viewed either a "push" or a "pull" as a prerequisite to new venture formation since it triggers a state of general readiness to take action once a suitable opportunity and the necessary resources can be identified.[37]

The terms "opportunity-based" and "necessity-based" entrepreneurship have been popularized by their use in the GEM.[38] The questions asked of entrepreneurs included seeking information about why they

Research, eds. B. Kirchhoff, W. Long, W. McMullan, K.H. Vesper, and W. Wetzel. Wellesley, MA: Babson College.

[35] Brockhaus, R. 1980. "The Effect of Job Dissatisfaction on the Decision to Start a Business." *Journal of Small Business Management* 18, no. 1, pp. 37–43; Shapero, A. 1975. "The Displaced, Uncomfortable Entrepreneur." *Psychology Today* 9, no. 6, pp. 83–88; Kets de Vries, M. 1977. "The Entrepreneurial Personality: A Person at the Crossroads." *Journal of Management Studies* 14, no. 1, pp. 34–57; Giladm, B., and P. Levine. 1986. "A Behavioral Model of Entrepreneurial Supply." *Journal of Small Business Management* 24, no. 4, pp. 44–53.

[36] Krueger, N. 1993. "The Impact of Prior Entrepreneurial Exposure on Perceptions of New Venture Feasibility and Desirability." *Entrepreneurship Theory and Practice* 18, no. 1, pp. 5–21; Mancuso, J. 1973. *Fun and Guts: The Entrepreneur's Philosophy*. Reading, MA: Addison-Wesley; Gilad, B., and P. Levine. 1986. "A Behavioral Model of Entrepreneurial Supply." *Journal of Small Business Management* 24, no. 4, pp. 44–53; Scheinberg, S., and I. MacMillan. 1988. "An Eleven Country Study Of the Motivations to Start a Business." In *Frontiers of Entrepreneurship Research*, eds. B. Kirchhoff, W. Long, W. McMullan, K.H. Vesper, and W. Wetzel. Wellesley, MA: Babson College.

[37] See also Shapero, A. 1975. "The Displaced, Uncomfortable Entrepreneur." *Psychology Today* 9, no. 6, pp. 83–88.

[38] For further discussion of the GEM surveys, see "Research on Entrepreneurship." In "Entrepreneurship: A Library of Resources for Sustainable Entrepreneurs" prepared and distributed by the Sustainable Entrepreneurship Project (www.seproject.org).

decided to start and grow their businesses. Respondents who indicated that they chose entrepreneurship to "take advantage of a business opportunity" or "seek better opportunities" were practicing opportunity-based entrepreneurship while respondents starting businesses "because [they had] no better choices for work" were identified as necessity-based entrepreneurs.[39] The key characteristic among opportunity-based entrepreneurs is their acknowledgment that they made a voluntary career choice to pursue an entrepreneurial path. The GEM also recognizes another type of entrepreneurship, referred to as "improvement-driven," that includes persons interested in pursuing an opportunity and who do so in order to improve their incomes and/or independence in their work, as opposed to "necessity."

In contrast, necessity-based entrepreneurs choose entrepreneurship only because other options were not available or were considered to be unsatisfactory. The term "reluctant entrepreneurship" is sometimes used to describe these persons and it is common to find that they have been pushed to start their own businesses because they have either lost the jobs they had with their employers or had been placed in the path of what appears to be an inevitable elimination of their positions. In either instance, entrepreneurship was, at least initially, a means of survival. It should be noted, however, that there appears to be some debate about whether problems in the overall economy that lead to increased unemployment will lead to higher levels of necessity-based entrepreneurship and one researcher has summarized the findings of various researchers as follows: "It does seem then that there is some disagreement in the literature on whether high unemployment acts to discourage self-employment because of the lack of available opportunities or encourage it because of the lack of viable alternatives."[40]

The GEM research confirms that it is more likely than not that persons start a new business in order to take advantage of a perceived business opportunity, so-called "opportunity entrepreneurship"; however,

[39] For further discussion, see Reynolds, P., W. Bygrave, E. Autio, L. Cox, and M. Hay. 2002. *Global Entrepreneurship Monitor: 2002 Executive Report*, 12. London: Global Entrepreneurship Monitor.

[40] Blanchflower, D. 2004. *Self-Employment: More May Not Be Better*. Cambridge MA: National Bureau of Economic Research.

the existence of "necessity entrepreneurship" must be acknowledged and considered when researching entrepreneurship. It is not surprising to find that there are differences among countries, particularly groups of countries with similar cultural characteristics, with regard to the prevalence of specific types of entrepreneurs. For example, differences between countries with respect to the incidence of entrepreneurial activity have been attributed to differences in "risk tolerance" since there are significant variations among countries with respect to the level of risk (and possibility of failure) that persons are willing to assume before they start a new business. Even within countries, however, variations in the incidence of entrepreneurial activity can be seen when one looks at different characteristics such as age, education, industry, and location. Several studies have confirmed what would appear to be fairly obvious: necessity-based entrepreneurship in a country tends to decline as the level of economic development in that country increases and the overall business environment in the country stabilizes.[41] In addition, one sees lower levels of necessity-based entrepreneurship in "innovation-driven countries."[42]

Categories of Entrepreneurship

The development of thought on the consequences and purposes and goals of entrepreneurship have led to an expansion of the field based on new and different ideas about the processes, behaviors, and outcomes associated with entrepreneurship. Among other things, the recent growing recognition of social and environmental issues, and the accompanying opportunities to develop innovation solutions to problems in each of those areas, has led to the emergence of several new types or categories of entrepreneurs in addition to traditional commercial entrepreneurs: environmental entrepreneurs, or ecopreneurs; social entrepreneurs; and sustainable entrepreneurs.[43]

---

[41] See, for example, Bosma, N., and J. Levie. 2010. *Global Entrepreneurship Monitor: 2009 Global Executive Report.* London: Global Entrepreneurship Monitor.

[42] Id.

[43] Crals, E., and L. Vereeck. February 2004. "Sustainable Entrepreneurship in SMEs. Theory and Practice." *Copenhagen: 3rd Global Conference in Environmental Justice and Global Citizenship*; Dees, G. 2001. *The Meaning of Social Entrepreneurship.* Stanford: Stanford University—Graduate School of Business;

Majid and Koe explained that the study of entrepreneurship has been broken out into several subfields or categories which simultaneously overlap (e.g., each category of entrepreneurship includes a need to survive economically at some level in order to remain viable) yet also have their own distinctive characteristics or primacies[44]:

- Regular/economic/commercial: Being economically orientated by discovering and exploiting opportunities to make profit, through processes of venture start-up, risk assumption, product or process innovation, and resources management. Primary focus is on economic performance, although activities may also general environmental and/or social benefits.
- Green/environmental/ecopreneurship: Being environmentally or ecologically embedded by preserving natural resources and creating economic development. Focus is on addressing environmental or ecological problems and issues.[45]

Schaper, M. 2002. "The Essence of Ecopreneurship." *Greener Management International* 38, p. 26; Young, W., and F. Tilley. 2006. "Can Businesses Move Beyond Efficiency? The Shift toward Effectiveness and Equity in the Corporate Sustainability Debate." *Business Strategy and the Environment*; and Isaak, R. 1998. "Green Logic: Ecopreneurship." *Theory and Ethics*. Sheffield, UK: Greenleaf Publishing.
[44] Majid. I., and W L. Koe. June 2012. "Sustainable Entrepreneurship (SE): A Revised Model Based on Triple Bottom Line (TBL)." *International Journal of Academic Research in Business and Social Sciences* 2, no. 6, pp. 296–97, 293 (citing Richomme-Huet. K., and J. Freyman. June 15–18, 2011. "What Sustainable Entrepreneurship Looks Like: An Exploratory Study from a Student Perspective." *Conference proceedings in 56th Annual International Council for Small Business (ICSB) World Conference*, Stockholm, Sweden; and Tilley, F., and W. Young. 2009. "Sustainability Entrepreneurs: Could They be the True Wealth Generators of the Future?" *Green Management International* 55, p. 79).
[45] Chick, A. 2009. "Green Entrepreneurship: A Sustainable Development Challenge." In *Entrepreneurship for Everyone: A Student Textbook*, eds. R. Mellor, G. Coulton, A. Chick, A. Bifulco, N. Mellor, and A. Fisher, 139. London: SAGE Publications; and Dean, T., and J. McMullen. 2007. "Toward a Theory of Sustainable Entrepreneurship: Reducing Environmental Degradation through Entrepreneurial Action." *Journal of Business Venturing* 22, no. 1, p. 50.

- Social: Being socially embedded by complementing social and profit goals. Focus is on contributing to social or public welfare and creating social values.[46]
- Sustainable: Being future orientated by balancing the efforts in making contributions to produce economic prosperity; social justice and social cohesion; as well as environmental protection. Focus is "holistic" and includes and attempts to equally balance economic, environmental, and social contributions.[47]

Majid and Koe noted that the emergence of the subfields described earlier and the expanded focus of entrepreneurs beyond economic considerations represents a significant transition in entrepreneurship from the early 1970s when Friedman, one of the leading economists of his day, went on record as saying that "the social responsibility of business is to increase its profits."[48]

Lam created a classification scheme for different types of nontraditional entrepreneurs based on comparing their core motivations, main goals, and the role of non-market goals in the activities of the entrepreneur.[49] The first type was ecopreneurship, which was described as having

---

[46] Austin, J., H. Stevenson, and J. Wei-Skillern. January 2006. "Social and Commercial Entrepreneurship: Same, Different or Both?" *Entrepreneurship Theory and Practice* 30, no. 1, pp. 1–22.

[47] O'Neill, G., J. Hershauer, and J. Golden. 2009. "The Cultural Context of Sustainability Entrepreneurship." *Green Management International* 55, p. 33; and Tilley, F., and W. Young. 2009. "Sustainability Entrepreneurs: Could They Be the True Wealth Generators of the Future?" *Green Management International*, 55, p. 79.

[48] Majid, I., and W.L. Koe. June 2012. "Sustainable Entrepreneurship (SE): A Revised Model Based on Triple Bottom Line (TBL)." *International Journal of Academic Research in Business and Social Sciences* 2, no. 6, pp. 293–97 (citing Friedman, M. September 13, 1970. "The Social Responsibility of Business is to Increase its Profits." *The New York Times Magazine*).

[49] *What Is Sustainable Entrepreneurship?* Amsterdam: Sustainable Entrepreneurship Research Platform, 2015 (citing Lam, T. Spring 2014. Bachelor Thesis for International Business School, AUAS).

a core motivation of contributing to solving environmental problems and creating economic value. The main goal of ecopreneurship was to earn money by solving environmental problems and environmental issues were an integrated core element of the activities. The next type was social entrepreneurship, which was described as having a core motivation of contributing to solving societal problems and creating value for society. The main purpose of social entrepreneurship was to achieve societal goals and securing funding to achieve this and the societal goals were the ends for the activities. Finally, sustainable entrepreneurship was described as having a core motivation of contributing to solving environmental and social problems through the realization of a successful business. The main goal of the sustainable entrepreneur was to create sustainable development through entrepreneurial business activities and contributing to sustainable development was a core and integrated element.

Entrepreneurship and Innovation

Any attempt at starting a new business, regardless of the size of the firm or the sophistication of its products or services, falls squarely within the definition of entrepreneurship and generally carries the same levels of risk and stress for the persons involved in the process. Entrepreneurship programs launched and administered by governmental agencies and non-profit organizations are primarily geared toward "small businesses" that often rely on readily available technologies and their goal is to ensure that interested persons have access to basic information about starting a business, complying with applicable laws and locating financing sources. Proprietorships and small firms with less than 20 employees have always been an important part of the economic landscape and this should continue in the future as technology, such as the Internet, makes it easier for entrepreneurs to put their business ideas into practice and quickly and efficiently reach prospective customers and other business partners.

An important niche within the entrepreneurial community, which has been readily filled by universities, focuses on new business formation for the purpose of identifying, developing, and commercializing relatively risky and unproven technologies and business processes. The study of entrepreneurs and their firms that are involved in these sorts of activities is referred to as "entrepreneurship and innovation." A number of different definitions and explanations of "innovation" have been offered by academicians and commentators. For our purposes, it is useful to think of innovation as the process of successfully acquiring and implementing new ideas within a business organization. As suggested by this formulation, new ideas can be developed and created internally, or can be borrowed or purchased from other organizations. New ideas are not confined to new products and services, but also include new or improved processes that enhance productivity or reduce costs associated with manufacturing or distributing existing products. Put another way, innovation involves firms doing new things in new ways to increase productivity, product development, sales, and profitability, including finding new ways of identifying the needs of new and existing clients and making and marketing products that satisfy those needs.

Drucker forcefully promoted the interrelatedness of entrepreneurship and innovation and the need for entrepreneurs to recognize and learn the disciplines and principals of innovation and practice them in the planning for their ventures:

> Innovation is the specific tool of entrepreneurs, the means by which they exploit change as an opportunity for a different business or a different service. It is capable of being presented as a discipline, capable of being learned, capable of being practiced. Entrepreneurs need to search purposefully for the sources of innovation, the changes and their symptoms that indicate opportunities for successful innovation. And they need to know and apply the principles of successful innovation.

Drucker believed that entrepreneurship could be understood as a systematic process and that opportunities for successful entrepreneurship could be uncovered through purposeful innovation and exploration of identified sources of innovation including incongruities, process needs, industry and market structures, demographics, changes in perception, new knowledge, and unforeseen events.[50]

---

[50] Drucker, P. 1993. *Innovation and Entrepreneurship*. New York, NY: Collins.

Certainly there are important and obvious differences between launching a small shoe repair shop and developing and commercializing a cutting-edge pharmaceutical product to fend off cancer; however, those who link entrepreneurship and innovation believe that any new venture, be it a separate start up business or a product development project within a large company, can increase its chances for success by understanding and applying the principles that have been gleaned from studies of what has been referred to as the "innovation process." Of course, while opinions vary on exactly what that process might be it has traditionally flowed sequentially through the following phases: idea generation, concept development, resource acquisition, ramp up, and launch. Studies have shown that many of the elements required for successful innovation are constant across industries and business activities and include an emphasis on product innovation, a strong customer orientation, and a firm commitment to high quality reliable service. Presumably these findings can be effectively deployed by all entrepreneurial ventures; however, it is should be understood that additional innovation strategies may be required in response to specific competitive factors in particular industries.

Research on Entrepreneurship

Entrepreneurship has become a popular career path all over the world and there has been intense interest in the subject shown by researchers and policymakers in both developed and developing countries. Research relating to entrepreneurship has been expanding rapidly and has touched upon a diverse range of issues. In 2003, for example, Richtermeyer published the results of her review of 77 abstracts of articles that had then been recently published in academic journals and compiled the following extensive list of the areas of emerging research on entrepreneurship at that time: culture/ethnicity; economic growth; education/learning; entrepreneurship theory and practice; ethics; family-owned businesses; finance; firm performance/planning; gender; human resources; intepreneurship versus entrepreneurship; international entrepreneurship, cross-national comparisons and individual country studies; internationalization, exporting and small business; motivation/firm creation or dissolution/founder characteristics; quality systems; resource-based views of the firm; social networks/business groups/alliances; strategic planning and product development; supply chain management/distribution; teams; technology, and technology-based firms; and venture capital.[51] In addition, the interest in entrepreneurship is no longer confined to developing countries and it is now well established that encouragement of entrepreneurial activities, including new venture formation, can and should be an important policy tool for governments in emerging markets looking to stimulate economic growth and development.[52]

According to Austin et al., it is possible to identify three streams of research relating to entrepreneurship that focus on the results of entrepreneurship, the causes of entrepreneurship, and entrepreneurial management.[53] A well-known example of research on the results and impact of entrepreneurship is Schumpeter's theory of the entrepreneur as a "change agent" who identifies and attacks opportunities to harness innovation to engage "creative destruction" that overturns the way business has been

---

[51] Richtermeyer, G. 2003. *Emerging Themes in Entrepreneurship Research*, 2. University of Missouri, Business Research and Information Development Group. Richtermeyer also included a comprehensive list of the articles that were reviewed.
[52] See, for example, Harper, M. 1991. "The Role of Enterprise in Poor Countries." *Entrepreneurship Theory and Practice* 15, no. 4, pp. 7–11; Gibb, A. 1993. "Small Business Development in Central and Eastern Europe—Opportunity for a rethink?" *Journal of Business Venturing* 8, no. 6, pp. 461–86; Audretsch, D. 1991. *The Role of Small Business in Restructuring Eastern Europe*. Vaxjo, Sweden: 5th Workshop for Research in Entrepreneurship. Other studies that have identified entrepreneurship as a critical factor in national economic development include Birley, S. 1987. "New Ventures and Employment Growth." *Journal of Business Venturing* 2, no. 2, pp. 155–65; Reynolds, P. 1987. "New Firms: Societal Contributions Versus Survival Potential." *Journal of Business Venturing* 2, no. 3, pp. 231–46; Morris, M., and P. Lewis. 1991. "Entrepreneurship as a Significant Factor in Societal Quality of Life." *Journal of Business Research* 23, no. 1, pp. 21–36; and Shane, S., L. Kolvereid, and P. Westhead. 1991. "An Exploratory Examination of the Reasons Leading to New Firm Formation Across Country and Gender (Part 1)." *Journal of Business Venturing* 6, no. 6, pp. 431–46.
[53] Stevenson, H., and J. Jarillo. 1991. "A New Entrepreneurial Paradigm." In *Socio-Economics: Toward a New Synthesis*, eds. A. Etzioni, and P. Lawrence, 185. Armonk, NY: M.E. Sharpe.

done in entire industries and markets.[54] Research on the causes of entrepreneurship includes work on understanding the personal drives and motivations of entrepreneurs themselves and relies heavily on psychology and sociology.[55] Research on entrepreneurial management focuses on the practical steps that must be taken to execute exploitation of opportunities in an entrepreneurial manner and includes research on the dynamics of start-ups and venture capital,[56] intrapreneurship (i.e., entrepreneurial innovation inside established companies),[57] organizational life cycles,[58] and predictors of entrepreneurial success.[59]

Mueller and Thomas have observed that while entrepreneurship has clearly become a popular topic around the world a number of interesting and important questions regarding entrepreneurial activities and formation of new ventures remain to be answered with respect to countries other than the United States.[60] In fact, one of the most interesting and promising areas of entrepreneurship research is "international entrepreneurship,"

---

[54] Schumpeter, J. 1934. *The Theory of Economic Development*. Cambridge, MA: Harvard University Press.

[55] See, for example, Collins, O., and D. Moore. 1964. *The Enterprising Man*. East Lansing, MI: Michigan State University; and McClelland, D. 1961. *The Achieving Story*. Princeton, NJ: D. Van Nostrand.

[56] See, for example, Timmons, J., and W. Bygrave. 1986. "Venture Capital's Role in Financing Innovation for Economic Growth." *Journal of Business Venturing* 1, no. 2, p. 161.

[57] See, for example, Burgelman, R. 1983. "Corporate Entrepreneurship and Strategic Management: Insights from a Process Study." *Management Science* 29, p. 1349; and Burgelman, R. 1984. "Designs for Corporate Entrepreneurship in Established Firms." *California Management Review* 26, p. 154.

[58] See, for example, Quinn, R., and K. Cameron. 1983. "Organizational Life Cycles and Shifting Criteria of Effectiveness." *Management Science* 29, p. 33.

[59] See, for example, Cooper, A., and A. Bruno. August 1975. "Predicting Performance in New High-Technology Firms." *Academy of Management,* Proceedings of the 35th Annual Meeting, 426; and Dollinger, M. 1984. "Environmental Boundary Spanning and Information Processing Effects on Organizational Performance." *Academy of Management Journal* 27, p. 351.

[60] Mueller, S., and A. Thomas. 2000. "Culture and Entrepreneurial Potential: A Nine Country Study of Locus of Control and Innovativeness." *Journal of Business Venturing* 16, pp. 51–75, 53.

which Oviatt and McDougall defined as "(…) the discovery, enactment, evaluation, and exploitation of opportunities—across national borders—to create future goods and services."[61] Hessels has explained that, as a field of research, international entrepreneurship involves "research into entrepreneurship in multiple countries (cross-country comparisons of the nature and extent of entrepreneurial activity) and research into cross-border entrepreneurship (international activity of SMEs and new ventures)."[62]

It is believed that international entrepreneurship first appeared in the literature in the late 1980s and began as a response to evidence that technological advances and cultural awareness were driving new ventures beyond their more familiar domestic environments toward entering previously untapped foreign markets.[63] McDougall and Oviatt noted research activities under the umbrella of international entrepreneurship

---

[61] Oviatt, B., and P. McDougall. 2005. "Defining International Entrepreneurship and Modeling the Speed of Internationalization." *Entrepreneurship Theory and Practice* 29, no. 5, pp. 537–53, 540.

[62] Hessels, J. 2008. "International Entrepreneurship: An Introduction." *Framework and Research Agenda*, 4. Zoetermeer, The Netherlands: Scientific Analysis of Entrepreneurship and SMEs (citing Lu, J., and P. Beamish. 2001. "The Internationalization and Performance of SMEs." *Strategic Management Journal* 22, nos. 6/7, pp. 565–86; Coviello, N., and M. Jones. 2004. "Methodological Issues in International Entrepreneurship Research." *Journal of Business Venturing* 19, no. 4, pp. 485–508; and Oviatt, B., and P. McDougall. 2005. "Defining International Entrepreneurship and Modeling the Speed of Internationalization." *Entrepreneurship Theory and Practice* 29, no. 5, pp. 537–53). McDougall and Oviatt explained that "the scholarly field of international entrepreneurship examines and compares—across national borders--how, by whom, and with what effects those opportunities are acted upon." McDougall, P., and B. Oviatt. March 31, 2012. "Some Fundamental Issues in International Entrepreneurship." *United States Association for Small Business and Entrepreneurship*, http://usasbe.org/knowledge/whitepapers/mcdougall2003.pdf (accessed March 31, 2012).

[63] Morrow. 1988. "International Entrepreneurship: A New Growth Opportunity." *New Management* 3, no. 5, pp. 59–61; Zahra, S., and G. George. 2002. "International Entrepreneurship: The Current Status of the Field and Future Research Agenda." In *Strategic Entrepreneurship: Creating a New* Mindset, eds. M. Hitt, R. Ireland, S. Camp, and D. Sexton.

expanded beyond "new venture internationalization" to include topics such as national culture,[64] alliances and cooperative strategies,[65] small and medium-sized company internationalization,[66] top management teams,[67] entry modes, cognition,[68] country profiles,[69] corporate entrepreneurship,[70] exporting,[71] knowledge management,[72] venture financing,[73]

---

[64] McGrath, R., and I. MacMillan. 1992. "More Like Each Other than Anyone Else? A Cross-Cultural Study of Entrepreneurial Perceptions." *Journal of Business Venturing* 7, p. 419; Thomas, A., and S. Mueller. 2000. "A Case for Comparative Entrepreneurship: Assessing the Relevance of Culture." *Journal of International Business Studies* 31, no. 2, pp. 287–301.

[65] Steensma, H.K., L. Marino, M. Weaver, and P. Dickson. 2000. "The Influence of National Culture in the Formation of Technology Alliances by Entrepreneurial Firms." *Academy of Management Journal* 43, no. 6, pp. 951–57; Li, H., and K. Atuahene-Gima. 2001. "Product Innovation Strategy and the Performance of New Technology Ventures in China." *Academy of Management Journal* 44, no. 6, pp. 1123–34.

[66] Lu, J.W., and P.W. Beamish. 2001. "The Internationalization and Performance of SMEs." *Strategic Management Journal* 22, nos. 6–7, pp. 565–86.

[67] Reuber, A., and E. Fischer. 1997. "The Influence of the Management Team's International Experience on the Internationalization Behavior of SMEs." *Journal of International Business Studies* 28, no. 4, pp. 807–25.

[68] Mitchell, R.K., B. Smith, K.W. Seawright, and E.A. Morse. 2000. "Cross-Cultural Cognitions and the Venture Creation Decision." *Academy of Management Journal* 43, no. 5, pp. 974–93.

[69] Busenitz, L.W., C. Gomez, and J.W. Spencer. 2000. "Country Institutional Profiles: Unlocking Entrepreneurial Phenomena." *Academy of Management Journal* 43, no. 5, pp. 994–1003.

[70] Birkinshaw, J. 1997. "Entrepreneurship in Multinational Corporations: The Characteristics of Subsidiary Initiatives." *Strategic Management Journal*, pp. 207–29.

[71] Bilkey, W., and G. Tesar. 1977. "The Export Behavior of Smaller-Sized Wisconsin Manufacturing Firms." *Journal of International Business Studies* 8, no. 1, pp. 93–98.

[72] Kuemmerle, W. 2002. "Home Base and Knowledge Management in International Ventures." *Journal of Business venturing* 17, no. 2, pp. 99–122.

[73] Roure, J., R. Keeley, and T. Keller. 1992. "Venture Capital Strategies in Europe and the U.S. Adapting to the 1990's." In *Frontiers of Entrepreneurship Research*, eds. N. Churchill et al., 345.

technological learning[74] and entrepreneurship in developing countries. They also reported that international entrepreneurship research had quickly become multidisciplinary and attracted the interest and resources of researchers in the areas of international business, entrepreneurship, anthropology, economics, psychology, finance, marketing, and sociology. Another indicator of growing interest in international entrepreneurship has been the increased coverage of the topic in leading academic journals and the launch of a completely new journal, the *Journal of International Entrepreneurship,* dedicated specifically to the field.[75] In any event, international entrepreneurship is a field that remains relatively new and immature from a research perspective and holds great promise for informing policymakers and educators about how best to encourage meaningful new business formation that contributes to economic growth and development.

Factors Influencing Entrepreneurial Activities

Shane et al. were particularly interested in improving the quality and conciseness of research on how human motivations influence entrepreneurship; however, they suggested a model that may well have broader application in the design of an analytical framework for studying the various factors that influence entrepreneurship.[76] Shane et al. believed that entrepreneurship was best viewed as a "process" that occurred over an extended period of time, rather than an isolated event or moment in time

---

[74] Zahra, S., R. Ireland, and M. Hitt. 2000. "International Expansion by New Venture Firms: International Diversity, Mode of Market Entry, Technological Learning and Performance." *Academy of Management Journal* 43, no. 2 pp. 925–50.
[75] For useful reviews of international entrepreneurship literature and research issues, see McDougall, P., and B. Oviatt. 1997. "International Entrepreneurship Literature in the 1990s and Directions for Future Research." In *Entrepreneurship 2000*, eds. D. Sexton and R. Smilor, 291; Zahra, S., and G. George. 2002. "International Entrepreneurship: The Current Status of the Field and Future Research Agenda." In *Strategic Entrepreneurship: Creating a New Mindset*, eds. M. Hitt, R. Ireland, S. Camp, and D. Sexton.
[76] Shane, S., E. Locke, and C. Collins. 2003. "Entrepreneurial Motivation." *Human Resource Management Review* 13, no. 2, pp. 257–79, 274–76.

when a person decides whether he or she should become an "entrepreneur." This process included a number of stages, including recognition of opportunities, development of ideas about how to pursue the opportunity by turning it into new products or services and, finally, execution of the activities required to harvest the desired profits from the opportunities. The execution phase involved array of tasks and activities such as evaluating the feasibility of the opportunity, product/service development, assembly of human and financial resources, organizational design, and "market making" (i.e., identification and pursuit of customers). In their model, the success or failure of the entire entrepreneurial process, and the decisions made along the way, are influenced by several important factors. The motivational traits of the prospective entrepreneur is one of them; however, in order to get a complete picture it is necessary to also take into account other factors that Shane et al. felt had been ignored by previous researchers such as cognitive factors, the nature of the opportunity, and environmental conditions.[77]

In order to address the concerns described earlier regarding the inadequacies of prior research on the relationship of human motivation to entrepreneurship, Shane et al. devised their own "model of entrepreneurial motivation and the entrepreneurial process" that focused on the factors that came into play at the various points where individuals (i.e., "entrepreneurs") transitioned from one stage of the entrepreneurial process to the next. It was assumed that at each "transition point," such as moving from "opportunity recognition" to "idea development," influences might come from one or more categories of factors: entrepreneurial motivations, entrepreneurial opportunities, and conditions and cognitive factors.[78] However, the mix of influences in play at a particular stage was

---

[77] Id. at p. 258 ("In our arguments, we explicitly assume that all human action is the result of both motivational and cognitive factors, the latter including ability, intelligence and skills. We also assume that entrepreneurship is not solely the result of human action; external factors also play a role …").

[78] This view was consistent with the observations of others such as Aldrich and Zimmer, who wrote that entrepreneurial activity "can be conceptualized as a function of opportunity structures and motivated entrepreneurs with access to resources." See Aldrich, H., and C. Zimmer. 1986. "Entrepreneurship Through

not fixed, nor was the relative importance of specific factors. Interestingly, the model did not attempt to identify relationships between any of the factors and traditional measures of "success" or "performance," such as profitability or growth rates, but simply focused on sensitizing researchers to the influences on the actions that entrepreneurs must take as they pursue development and commercialization of their ideas. In other words, in contrast to earlier models and assumptions Shane et al. recognized that the most relevant effects of factors such as "entrepreneurial motivations" on venture performance and growth may actually be more "indirect" than "direct."[79]

Entrepreneurial Motivations

The "entrepreneurial motivations" that Shane et al. included in their model were similar to those that they had identified and analyzed in their survey of prior research discussed earlier and were separated into "general" and "task-specific." Motivations classified as "general" included need for achievement, locus of control, "vision," desire for independence, passion, and drive. The motivations classified as "task-specific" included "goal-setting" and "self-efficacy" and were similar to those analyzed in the "situation-specific motivation" domain of the Baum et al. study.[80] Once again, it is important to emphasize that Shane et al. believed that the influence of any of these motivations varied depending upon the stage of the entrepreneurial process:

In some cases, all of the motivations might matter. In other cases, only some of the motivations might matter. The relative

Social Networks." In *The Art and Science of Entrepreneurship*, eds. D. Sexton, and R. Smilor, 3–23, 3. Cambridge, MA: Ballinger.
[79] Shane, S., E. Locke, and C. Collins. 2003. "Entrepreneurial Motivation." *Human Resource Management Review* 13, pp. 257–79, 276. ("Motivations might be more or less stronger than these other factors in the degree that they influence particular transitions points. In addition, there might be important and interesting interaction effects between motivations and opportunities, [knowledge, skills and abilities] and environmental factors.")
[80] Shane, S., E. Locke, and C. Collins. 2003. "Entrepreneurial Motivation." *Human Resource Management Review* 13, no. 2, pp. 257–79, 274.

magnitudes of how much each motivation matters will likely vary, depending on the part of the process under investigation. In fact, it is quite plausible that motivations that influence one part of the process have all of their effects at that stage in the process and have no effects on later stages in the process.[81]

Baum et al. tested for the influence of traits and motives of entrepreneurs on venture success.[82] They noted that several important personality theorists, such as McClelland, had argued that personality predispositions were important predictors of the success of entrepreneurial ventures[83] and observed that venture capitalists, whose job it is to "pick winners" among all the proposals and opportunities presented to them by would-be entrepreneurs, had consistently emphasized how much weight they gave to "entrepreneur characteristics" as key indicators of profitable investments.[84] The problem, from a research perspective, was that studies had shown a relatively weak relationship between the traits and motives of entrepreneurs and venture performance and that traits and motives were not nearly as important to venture success as organizational and industry variables.[85] Baum et al. believed that the influence of individual-level traits and motives of entrepreneurs had not been properly recognized

---

[81] Id. at p. 275.

[82] Baum, J., E. Locke, and K. Smith. 2001. "A Multi-Dimensional Model of Venture Growth." *Academy of Management Journal* 44, no. 2, pp. 292–303.

[83] Hollenbeck, J., and E. Whitener. 1988. "Reclaiming Personality Traits for Personnel Selection." *Journal of Management* 14, pp. 81–91; and McClelland, D. 1965. "N-Achievement and Entrepreneurship: A Longitudinal Study." *Journal of Personality and Social Psychology* 1, pp. 389–92.

[84] MacMillan, I., R. Siegel, and P. SubbaNarisimha. 1985. "Criteria Used by Venture Capitalists to Evaluate New Venture Proposals." *Journal of Business Venturing* 1, pp. 119–28.

[85] Begley, T., and D. Boyd. 1987 ."Psychological Characteristics Associated with Performance in Entrepreneurial Firms and Smaller Businesses." *Journal of Business Venturing* 2, pp. 79–93; Low, M., and I. MacMillan. 1988. "Entrepreneurship: Past Research and Future Challenges." *Journal of Management* 14, pp. 139–51; Sandberg, W., and C. Hofer. 1987. "Improving New Venture Performance: The Role of Strategy, Industry Structure and the Entrepreneur." *Entrepreneurship Theory and Practice* 16, pp. 73–90.

because they did not work in isolation from other factors and prior studies had not included the proper traits.[86] In their study they supplemented the pool of entrepreneurial traits by adding tenacity, proactivity, and passion and tested not only for a direct relationship of traits and motives on venture growth but also for the relationship that traits and motives had on other influencers of venture growth (i.e., "indirect effects"). While they did not find support for the hypothesis that, with all other antecedents of venture growth controlled, the greater the tenacity, proactivity, and passion for work of a venture's CEO, the greater the venture's growth, they did find evidence that these individual-level traits and motives *did* have a strong influence on several other factors relevant to venture growth, including general competencies, situation-specific motivation, and competitive strategies.[87]

As mentioned earlier, Baum et al. created and tested a separate dimension for several situational-specific motivations, including "vision," growth goals, and self-efficacy.[88] These motivations were distinguished from the other entrepreneurial traits and motives because they had previously demonstrated "significant empirical relationships with business performance" and had been celebrated by researchers as important for planning and venture performance.[89] Baum et al. did indeed find confirmation for the hypothesis that "[t]he greater the situationally specific motivation of a venture's CEO with respect to vision, growth goals, and self-efficacy, the greater the venture's growth."[90] Apparently, these traits

---

[86] Baum, J., E. Locke, and K. Smith. 2001. "A Multi-Dimensional Model of Venture Growth." *Academy of Management Journal* 44, no. 2, pp. 292–303, 292.

[87] Id. at pp. 299–300.

[88] Id. at p. 293.

[89] Low, M., and I. MacMillan. 1988. "Entrepreneurship: Past Research and Future Challenges." *Journal of Management* 14, pp. 139–51; and Bird, B. 1989. *Entrepreneurial Behavior.* Glenview, IL: Scott, Foresman. Also, one of the core elements of motivation in charismatic leadership theory is "vision." See Bass, B. 1990. *Handbook of Leadership.* New York, NY: Free Press.

[90] Baum, J., E. Locke, and K. Smith. 2001. "A Multi-Dimensional Model of Venture Growth." *Academy of Management Journal* 44, no. 2, pp. 292–303, 293, 297, 301 (citing Bandura, A. 1997. *Self-efficacy: The Exercise of Control.* New York, NY: W.H. Freeman); and Locke, E., and G. Latham. 1990. *A Theory of Goal Setting and Task Performance.* Englewood Cliffs, NJ: Prentice-Hall.

and motivations had a much greater direct effect on venture growth than the more "general" traits and motives tested by Baum et al.; however, those general traits and motives did have a significant influence on the strength of the situational-specific motivations.[91] The general competencies of entrepreneurs also had a large influence on their situational-specific motivations. Situational-specific motivations also had a significant influence on elements of the competitive strategies selected by entrepreneurs which, in turn, ultimately influenced venture growth. Specifically, Baum et al. argued that organizations led by highly motivated entrepreneurs often reflected the character of these entrepreneurs as evidenced by the choices made regarding organizational structures and processes and the bias toward recruiting goal-oriented employees.[92]

Cognitive Factors

According to Locke, all action is a result of the integration or combination of motivational and cognitive factors and thus it was necessary and appropriate for Shane et al. to include certain cognitive factors—knowledge, skills, and abilities ("KSAs")—in their analytical framework.[93] They explained that entrepreneurs must have "some knowledge," particularly knowledge about the industry and markets in which they are involved and the technology that is relevant to the projected success of the entrepreneurial activities. In addition, entrepreneurs must have certain skills, the range of which depends on the circumstances, which can be called upon during the various stages of the entrepreneurial process. Shane et al. listed skills such as "selling and bargaining, leadership, planning, decision making, problem solving, team building, communication and conflict management." Shane et al. mentioned that entrepreneurs can hire

---

[91] Id. at pp. 294–99 (confirming hypothesis that "[t]he greater the tenacity, proactivity, and passion for work of a venture's CEO, the greater his or her situationally specific motivation with respect to vision, goals, and self-efficacy").

[92] Id. at p. 301 (citing Hambrick, D., and P. Mason. 1984. "Upper Echelons: The Organization as a Reflection of its Top Managers." *Academy of Management Review* 9, no. 2, pp. 193–206).

[93] Id. at p. 275.

persons to fill in gaps in their own "skill set"; however, they believed that entrepreneurs cannot rely on others for the knowledge about the industry and technology that is crucial for setting the right course during the entrepreneurial process. Finally, entrepreneurs needed certain abilities, such as intelligence, in order to acquire and process the knowledge and develop and use the skills referred earlier.

As with the "entrepreneurial motivations," the KSAs are needed in order for entrepreneurs to navigate the entrepreneurship process and Shane et al. noted that not only did the KSAs come into play in making the best decisions at each stage of the process but also in the development of an overriding "vision" for entrepreneurial activities, including formulation of a viable strategy for the firm.[94] Inclusion of these cognitive factors in the model was consistent with the findings of other researchers that have highlighted the importance of certain types of knowledge and skills on various phases of the entrepreneurial process, particularly the start-up and resource assembly and organization stages.[95] Motivations are linked to cognitive factors in that motivations provide entrepreneurs with the incentive and drive to acquire the necessary KSAs and take the actions necessary to implement the vision and associated strategies.

KSAs were also part of the foundational principles for the "individual competencies" domain in the Baum et al. model.[96] Baum et al. actually broke out this domain into two categories: "general" competencies, which included an array of so-called "organizational competencies" such as oral

---

[94] Locke referred to "vision" as the "capacity of the human mind to discover, through creative thought, solutions that had not existed before" and noted that vision often stepped in when traditional financial methods of assessing and mapping an opportunity would not be helpful (e.g., when Jobs first developed the mass market for personal computers or Walton planted the seeds for discount retailing). Id. at p. 263 (citing Locke, E. 2000. *The Prime Movers: Traits of the Great Wealth Creators*. New York, NY: AMACOM).

[95] Id. at p. 275 (citing Bates, T. 1990. "Entrepreneur Human Capital Inputs and Small Business Longevity." *Review of Economics and Statistics* 72, no. 4, pp. 551–59; and Schoonhoven, C., K. Eisenhardt, and K. Lyman. 1990. "Speeding Products to Market: Waiting Time to First Product Introduction in New Firms." *Administrative Science Quarterly* 35, pp. 177–207).

[96] Id. at p. 293.

presentation skills, decision-making ability, conceptualization ability, diagnostic use of concepts, use of power and "opportunity recognition"; and "specific competencies," which included technical skills and industry skills.[97] They found that the general competencies of a venture's CEO, particularly with respect to organizational skills and opportunity recognition, did not have a material positive relationship on venture growth; however, they did influence situation-specific motivations and the selection process for competitive strategies. On the other hand, specific competencies were found to have a direct positive relationship with, and effect on, venture growth.[98] In their own words, Baum et al. explained:

> We speculate that an entrepreneur's technical and industry competencies are an important form of expert power that facilitates the implementation of the entrepreneur's vision and strategy. We can further hypothesize that these entrepreneurial skills may serve as sources of competitive advantage that rivals find difficult to identify and imitate.[99]

Notice should be taken of the work of Nassif et al., who studied entrepreneurship from a dynamic perspective in order to gain a better understanding of the values, characteristics, and actions over time as they launch and develop their businesses.[100] Based on their analysis of work by various researchers on the types and characteristics of Brazilian small business entrepreneurs, Nassif et al. developed an entrepreneurial process dynamics framework that included and distinguished "affective aspects,"

[97] Id. (citing Bird, B. 1989. *Entrepreneurial Behavior*. Glenview, IL: Scott, Foresman); Boyatzis, R. 1982. *The Competent Manager*. New York, NY: Wiley; Chandler, G., and E. Jansen. 1992. "The Founder's Self-Assessed Competence and Venture Performance." *Journal of Business Venturing* 7, no. 3, pp. 223–36; and Herron, L., and R. Robinson. 1990. "Entrepreneurship Skills: An Empirical Study of the Missing Link Connecting the Entrepreneur with Venture Performance." Paper presented at the Annual Meeting of the Academy of Management, San Francisco.
[98] Id. at pp. 299–301.
[99] Id. at pp. 300–01.
[100] Nassif, V., A. Ghobril, and N. Siqueira da Silva. April/June 2010. "Understanding the Entrepreneurial Process: A Dynamic Approach." *Brazilian Administrative Review* 7, no. 2.

which were most important during the earliest stages of the entrepreneurial process, and "cognitive aspects," which became more important relative to the affective aspects as time went on and the business matured. Affective aspects included perseverance, courage, willpower, initiative, willingness to take risks, personal motivation, facing challenges, passion for the business, autonomy, self-confidence, and independence. Cognitive aspects included assumption of calculated risks, ability to establish partnerships, defining goals and planning skills, knowing one's limits, and eloquent communication skills.

Entrepreneurial Opportunities

Shane et al. argue that the nature of entrepreneurship, including the decisions made with regard to entrepreneurial actions and even deciding whether or not entrepreneurship is an appropriate and desired path, depends upon the specific "opportunity" confronting the would-be entrepreneur.[101] They defined "entrepreneurial opportunities" as "situations in which new goods, services, raw materials, and organizing methods can be introduced and sold at greater than the cost of their production."[102] The problem, of course, is coming up with a reasonable estimate of the "expected value" of an opportunity since, by definition, an opportunity is all about potential rather than guarantees. One issue, of course, is that there is wide range of activities that would fit within this definition of opportunity: grand and bold initiatives that seek to establish whole new industries (e.g., the early biotechnology firms) as well as more modest undertakings such as starting a new business in an established industry to exploit a small, yet potential profitable, market niche.[103] In addition,

---

[101] Shane, S., E. Locke, and C. Collins. 2003. "Entrepreneurial Motivation." *Human Resource Management Review* 13, no. 2, pp. 257–79, 269.

[102] Id. at pp. 260–61 (citing Shane. S., and S. Venkataraman. 2000. "The Promise of Entrepreneurship as a Field of Research." *Academy of Management Review* 25, no. 1, pp. 217–26, 220).

[103] Established industries may also be reenergized and transformed by entrepreneurs testing new business models, such as Sam Walton's disruptive activities in the retail sector and the new organizing models in that same sector deployed by a wide array of "e-tailors." Id. at pp. 261–62.

the value of opportunities not only varies across industries but one also finds variations in opportunity values within industries. Still another factor that must be considered is how the entrepreneur "interprets" the opportunity. The Internet, for example, has generated a wide array of new business models from e-tailing targeting millions of potential customers to sole proprietors looking to make their mark through website design or consulting on online advertising. Finally, "solutions" clearly matter—if an entrepreneur develops a product, service, or method that creates more sales and/or lower production costs then he or she can rightly assign a high value to that opportunity.

It is assumed that an individual will generally not pursue opportunities unless they have value to the individual and a "valuable opportunity for an individual is one that generates a level of profit that exceeds the entrepreneur's opportunity cost, a premium for the illiquidity of money, time and effort expended, and a premium for bearing risk and uncertainty."[104] Obviously, this formulation allows that some opportunities will have more value than others for a particular entrepreneur and that the same opportunity may be valued differently by different entrepreneurs.[105] It does not necessarily mean that entrepreneurs will always choose the opportunity that has the highest "value" since that decision will be influenced by the motivations that are most important in the entrepreneur's decision-making process at the particular time; however, studies have shown that entrepreneurs are more likely

---

[104] Id. (citing Venkataraman, S. 1997. "The Distinctive Domain of Entrepreneurship Research: An Editor's Perspective." In *Advances in Entrepreneurship, Firm Emergence and Growth*, eds. J. Katz and R. Brockhaus, 119–38. 3 vols. Greenwich, CT: JAI Press).

[105] Shane et al. observed that variations in the opportunities that various entrepreneurs might pursue were not being taken into account by researchers studying the effects of motivation on entrepreneurial decisions. They suggested, among other things, that "researchers could explore settings in which potential entrepreneurs pursue reasonably identical opportunities," such as comparing the motivations of persons interested in purchasing a McDonald's franchise against those of persons preferring to tapped to manage a company-owned McDonald's outlet. Id. at p. 270.

to pursue an opportunity based on a condition or asset that is likely to generate extraordinary returns (e.g., patented technology, large market opportunity, and/or high margins).[106]

Ultimately, the value of entrepreneurial opportunities only becomes clear in hindsight once the entrepreneurial process has played out and each of the stages in that process have been navigated and completed. At each point along the way information is gathered, and decisions are made, that influence the assessment of the value of the opportunity and there may come a point where an opportunity ceases to be "valuable" for the entrepreneur because, for example, the anticipated level of profits no longer exceeds the entrepreneur's estimate of the opportunity costs that will need to be borne over the remaining stages of the entrepreneurial process. All of this does necessarily dissuade the boldest of innovators from moving forward in situations where it is impossible to quantify the value of an opportunity simply because what is being attempted has never been done before. Shane et al. reminded that Jobs in the PC industry and Walton in retailing were able to take advantage of opportunities through entrepreneurial actions that turning nothing more than a potential market for a product or service that had not been created into tangible industries in which values could eventually be assigned to the anticipated outputs of their actions. For Jobs, he not only had to develop the technical solution (i.e., a computer with a reasonable design cost) he also had to create a new "mass market" through a combination of design features, easy-to-use software, pricing, and marketing. Walton had to test and prove the viability of his "discounting" strategy and fend off the responses of his existing competitors as well as new competitors that entered the market after Walton took the first steps.[107]

---

[106] Shane, S. 2001. "Technology Opportunities and New Firm Creation." *Management Science* 47, no. 9, pp. 1173–81. For further discussion of the "characteristics of entrepreneurial opportunities," see Christiansen, C. 1997. *The Innovators Dilemma*. Cambridge, MA: Harvard Business School Press.

[107] Shane, S., E. Locke, and C. Collins. 2003. "Entrepreneurial Motivation." *Human Resource Management Review* 13, no. 2, pp. 257–79, 261–62.

Environmental Conditions

There has been a large amount of research on the impact of environmental conditions on entrepreneurship and many of these studies have found indications that the success of an entrepreneurial activity, as measured by the firm growth, is influenced by things such "(1) political factors (e.g., legal restrictions, quality of law enforcement, political stability and currency stability); (2) market forces (e.g., structure of the industry, technology regime, potential barriers to entry, market size and population demographics); and (3) resources (e.g., availability of investment capital, labor market including skill availability, transportation infrastructure and complimentary technology)."[108] Shane et al. argued that it would be interesting and useful to study whether the motivations of entrepreneurs led to different types of entrepreneurial actions and decisions under different environmental conditions.[109] They also noted that in order to gain a clearer understanding of the influence on motivations on the entrepreneurial process the impact of environmental conditions would need to be controlled, perhaps by limiting sampling to firms in the same industry pursuing comparable market and technological opportunities.

Baum et al. also analyzed environmental conditions and focused on three dimensions relating to the environment: dynamism, which is the level of environmental predictability, including the rate of market and industry change and the level of uncertainty that firms must endure due to forces that are out of their control; munificence, which refers to the support provided by the environment for organizational growth; and complexity, which is measured by the concentration or dispersion of

---

[108] Id. at pp. 260, 275–76. Other environmental factors mentioned by Shane et al. included the age of the industry, the condition of capital markets and the overall health of the economy. See also, for example, Aldrich, H., and G. Wiedenmayer. 1993. "From Traits to Rates: An Ecological Perspective on Organizational Foundings." In *Advances in Entrepreneurship, Firm Emergence, and Growth*, eds. J. Katz, and R. Brockhaus, Sr., 145–95. 1 vols. Greenwich, CT: JAI Press; and Aldrich, H. 2000. *Organizations Evolving*. Beverly Hills, CA: Sage.
[109] Id.

organizations in the environment.[110] Somewhat surprisingly, Baum et al. did not find sufficient evidence to support their hypothesis that a firm's environment is related to venture growth. Specifically, operating in a stable, munificent, and simple environment did not guarantee that a firm would achieve the highest growth.[111] Environmental factors did have a significant, positive influence on competitive strategies but not as much as the traits, general competencies, and situation-specific motivations of the entrepreneurs leading the firms.[112] Baum et al., noting the somewhat surprising "relatively low impact of the environmental domain on venture growth," suggested that perhaps CEOs of smaller firms have more control over the growth and performance of their firms than had previously been suggested by several "macro theories" such as those posited by Hannan and Freeman and Pfeffer and Salancik.[113]

---

[110] Id. at pp. 293–94 (citing Dess, G., and P. Davis. 1984. "Porter's Generic Strategies as Determinants of Strategic Group Membership and Organizational Performance." *Academy of Management Journal* 27, no. 3, pp. 467–88; and Aldrich, H., and G. Wiedenmayer. 1993. "From Traits to Rates: An Ecological Perspective on Organizational Foundings." In *Advances in Entrepreneurship, Firm Emergence and Growth*, eds. J. Katz and R. Brockhaus, Sr., 145–95. 1 vols. Greenwich, CT: JAI Press).

[111] Id. at p. 301.

[112] Id. at p. 299.

[113] Id. at p. 301 (citing Hannan, M., and J. Freeman. 1977. "The Population Ecology of Organizations." *American Journal of Sociology* 82, no. 5, pp. 929–64; and Pfeffer, J., and G. Salancik. 1978. *The External Control of Organizations*. New York, NY: Harper & Row).

CHAPTER 2

Sustainability

Introduction

While debate continues regarding the appropriate level of government intervention via regulation in the marketplace, one area in which government involvement appears to be steadily increasing is social conduct. At the same time, consumers are demanding greater transparency on environmental and social matters from the companies asking them to purchase their products and services, and investors are incorporating social responsibly into their assessments of the overall performance of portfolio companies.[1] These trends have served as the catalyst for interest in "sustainable entrepreneurship," which has been described as the continuing commitment by businesses to behave ethically and contribute to economic development (e.g., job creation that increases disposable income that generates tax revenues that can be invested in projects focused on sustainable development) while improving the quality of life of the workforce, their families, the local and global community as well as future generations.[2] Sustainable entrepreneurship should be carried out using a sustainable business model that does not deplete resources,

---

[1] Van Beurden, P., and T. Gössling. 2008. "The Worth of Values: A Literature Review on the Relation Between Corporate Social and Financial Performance." *Journal of Business Ethics* 82, no. 2, p. 407; and Shane, S., and S. Venkataraman. 2000. "The Promise of Entrepreneurship as a Field of Research." *The Academy of Management Review* 25, p. 217.

[2] Based on a variety of sources including Di Maio, P. September 16, 2010. *Sustainable Entrepreneurship.*
http://slideshare.net/PaolaDIM/sustainable-entrepreneurship and Graham, S. September 16. 2010. "What Is Sustainable Entrepreneurship?" http://ezinearticles.com/?What-Is-Sustainable-Entrepreneurship?&id=5045492

but rather replenishes them (e.g., natural resources, human resources, knowledge, and technology foundations), and creates value and material and nonmaterial wealth (i.e., well-being and happiness) for all stakeholders through actions which are ethical and just. Sustainable entrepreneurship, and any sustainable business model, is based on acceptance of the principle that long-term environmental and social outcomes and impact are just as important as short-term economic objectives.

In order to understand the particular definition and description of "sustainable entrepreneurship" used in this publication, it is necessary to work through the evolution of the concept of sustainability that has occurred over the last several decades. Writers and activists from the 1970s and 1980s brought attention to concerns about the impact that economic growth would have on the Earth's finite natural resources. Proponents of what was often referred to as the "limits of growth" theory argued that unchecked consumption and economic growth would eventually lead to the planet's downfall and disaster.[3] Specific problems included accelerating industrialization, rapid population growth, widespread malnutrition, depletion of nonrenewable resources and a deteriorating environment. Opponents countered with faith in the ability that technological change and market signals would allow economic growth to continue without the predicted dire consequences (e.g., as natural resources became scarce, market prices would increase to the point where demand would decrease, thus preserving the scarce resources). While the two sides could not reach agreement—opponents also issued scathing critiques of the data and methodology used to support the theory, the issue of the boundaries of the maximum sustainable scale of usage of natural resources came into sharper focus and the debate has led to several different types and conceptualizations of "sustainability" that have become the basis for fields of academic research and organizational activities.

---

[3] Bell, J., and J. Stellingwerf. 2012. *Sustainable Entrepreneurship: The Motivations & Challenges of Sustainable Entrepreneurs in the Renewable Energy Industry Jonkoping*, 3. Sweden: Jonkoping International Business School Master Thesis in Business Administration (citing Meadows, D., D. Meadows, J. Randers, and W. Behrens. 1972. *Limits of Growth*. New York, NY: Universe Books).

Principles for Sustainable Business

According to the authors of *Sustainable Business: A Handbook for Starting a Business*, published and distributed by New Zealand Trade and Enterprise, there are two types of principles for sustainable business: operational and strategic. Operational principles were described as being practical and addressing the questions of what organizations do and how they do business on a day-to-day basis. In contrast, strategic principles are used as guidance in setting the overall direction of the business of the organization and should be used to help make decisions about operational principles.

The key operational principles were described as follows:

- **Good Employer:** The organization is committed to employee satisfaction, development, and well-being. The organization, from the most senior management level display and model fairness and equity in all aspects of employee relations and show no tolerance for discrimination, bullying, or harassment. Workplaces are safe and healthy and employees are encouraged to provide input and participate.
- **Environmental Responsibility:** The organization is respectful of environmental limits and operates in an environmentally efficient way in the design and delivery of its products/services. For example, material/resource use is minimized, products are designed and manufactured considering the full life cycle of the materials and waste products. Environmental technology is invested in and/or used, for example, using solar panels to generate electricity.
- **Community Contribution and Fairness:** The organization contributes to making the communities in which it operates better places to live and do business (e.g., sourcing materials locally) and employees are encouraged to become involved in achieving this goal. Often this will be at a local level, but there may also be opportunities to apply this at the national and/or global level. All employees demonstrate honesty and fairness when dealing with stakeholders, including working closely with local community constituencies and empowering them in decisions that affect them.
- **Influencing Others:** The organization actively encourages others such as suppliers, customers, and its employees to improve their own sustainability performance. For example, making it easy for customers to recycle the product and requiring that foreign material manufacturers must implement internationally accepted labor standards to ensure that forced or child labor is not used in the manufacture of materials or parts.

The key strategic principles were described as follows:

- **Integration of Sustainability into the Organization:** Sustainability is a business priority for the organization and is reflected in all aspects of the organization, including business processes (i.e., decision making, vision, and performance management) to ensure that decisions are made with their sustainability effects in mind. In addition, there is clear evidence of management commitment to sustainability.
- **Minimizing Risks and Maximizing Opportunities:** The organization addresses risks and uncertainty when making choices and takes a precautionary approach when making decisions that may cause serious or irreversible damage. Organizations that adopt this approach do not lean on the alleged lack of full scientific certainty about climate change as a reason for postponing measures to prevent environmental degradation.

- **Transparency and Accountability:** The organization is transparent and accountable about its performance in matters that are important to others.
- **Meeting the Needs of Tomorrow with Innovation:** Considering the long-term (intergenerational) implications of all decisions and seeking solutions that are mutually reinforcing rather than accepting that a gain in one area, such as reduction of environmental degradation, will necessarily be achieved at the expense of another, such as profitability. For example, recycling was material is not only good for the environment it will also save money for the organization by reducing the costs of removing rubbish.

The principles of sustainability outlined earlier, like many recommendations from the sustainability community, call on organizations to integrate sustainability into all aspects of their business processes to ensure that decisions are made with their sustainability effects in mind and ensure that there is clear and visible evidence of management commitment to sustainability. The following questions can be helpful in assessing whether sustainability has been integrated into the business of an organization:

- What norms or policies exist to ensure integration? For example, does the organization have a volunteering policy (i.e., providing employees with a certain amount of time off work to volunteer), environmental policy/goals and/or fair trade policy?
- What certification systems are available for the organization's business (e.g., an environmental management system or an industry-specific standard)?
- What membership organizations are available to join to increase the organization's learning and profile in sustainability?
- How do staff members know that sustainability is important to the business of the organization and how are they rewarded for integrating it into their roles?
- What are the sustainability goals of the organization? Do the stakeholders know what the goals are? Is the actual performance being measured? How does the actual performance compare with the goals and how is the business communicating its performance to its stakeholders?
- How does the organization encourage its supply chain (e.g., suppliers, customers) to make sustainable choices and/or improve their sustainability performance?

Source: Sustainable Business: A Handbook for Starting a Business (New Zealand Trade and Enterprise).

Sustainability had its beginnings at the level of the "household" and its ability to produce and reproduce everything that was needed in order to sustain the livelihood of its members.[4] Leal Filho observed that the term "sustainability" has been traditionally used as synonyms for "long-term,"

---

[4] Stankeviciute, Z., and A. Savaneviciene. 2013. "Sustainability as a Concept for Human Resource Management." *Economics and Management* 18, no. 4, pp. 837–39 (citing Ehnert, I. 2009. "Sustainability and Human Resource Management: Reasoning and Applications on Corporate Websites." *European Journal of International Management* 3, no. 4, p. 419).

"durable," "sound," or "systematic."[5] Rey provided several basic definitions of "sustainability":

> In the literal sense, sustainable refers to, "*of relation to, or being*
> *a method of harvesting or using a resource so that the resource is not*
> *depleted or permanently damaged.*" Alternatively, it is "*of relating to*
> *a lifestyle involving the use of sustainable methods,*" both according
> to the Webster's dictionary. The Chambers Concise Dictionary
> defines the root word of sustainability—*sustain*—among other
> things, as "*to hold up, to bear, to support, to provide for, to maintain,*
> *to prolong, to support the life of*"—selecting the definitions that
> fundamentally define sustainability at its core (emphasis added by
> original author).[6]

In recent decades, the understanding of sustainability in both theory
and practice has been influenced by three main groups: ecologists, the
United Nation's World Commission on Environment and Development,
often referred to as the "Brundtland Commission," and business strate-
gists.[7] In the 1970s and 1980s, sustainability was embraced by various
ecological movements interested in balancing consumption and regener-
ation in nature and ensuring that natural resources were not abused and
overused such that they were not as abundant for future citizens of the
world, a cause that ultimately led to the emergence of interest in "sustainable development." Ecologists have traditionally focused on the ecological
dimension of sustainability, generally recognized as a desire to protect the
natural environment and prevent over-exploitation of natural and environmental resources. In 1987, the Brundtland Commission convened by
the United Nations added a social dimension to the discussion of sustainability by defining sustainable development as development that meets

---

[5] Leal Filho, W. 2000. "Dealing with Misconceptions on the Context of Sustainability." *International Journal of Sustainability in Higher Education* 1, no. 1, p. 9.
[6] Rey, L. December 2011. *Sustainable Entrepreneurship and its Viability*, 11.
Rotterdam: Master Thesis for MS in Entrepreneurship, Strategy and Organizations Economics from Erasmus School of Economics.
[7] Mazur, B. January 2014. "Sustainable Human Resource Management in
Theory and Practice." *Economics and Management*, pp. 158–59.

the needs of the present without compromising the ability of future generations to meet their own needs. In general, definitions of sustainability introduced during this period stressed justice in and between generations with respect to use and stewardship of natural resources.[8]

Sustainability first entered the realm of strategic management in 1980s when it was proposed that organizations could achieve a "sustainable competitive advantage" by employing valuable, rare, imperfectly imitable, and difficult to substitute resources in a manner that would enhance their economic sustainability.[9] A more radical infusion of sustainability at the corporate business level began to take shape in the late 1990s and early 2000s with the popularization of the "triple-bottom-line," which was based on the proposition that the long-term success of businesses (i.e., their sustainable growth and development) depended on satisfaction of three conditions, all of which needed to be given equal consideration by management: environmental integrity, economic prosperity, and social equity.[10] This concept evolved into "corporate sustainability" and "corporate social responsibility" based on purposeful selection and use of sustainable business practices that mixed the traditional pursuit of economic profits with simultaneous attention to identify and meeting the demands and concerns of a wide range of stakeholders beyond the owners of the corporation.[11] Daly argued that while there was no single universally accepted definition of sustainability, there should be little dispute that it

---

[8] See Ehnert, I. 2009. "Sustainability and Human Resource Management: Reasoning and Applications on Corporate Websites." *European Journal of International Management* 3, no. 4, p. 419.

[9] See Kazlauskaite, R., and I. Buciuniene. 2008. "The Role of Human Resources and their Management in the Establishment of Sustainable Competitive Advantage." *Engineering Economics* 5, p. 78; and Barney, J. 1991. "Firm Resources and Sustained Competitive Advantage." *Journal of Management* 17, no. 1, p. 99.

[10] See Elkington, J. 1997. *Cannibals with Forks: The Triple Bottom Line of 21st Century Business.* Oxford: Capstone; and Bansal, P. 2005. "Evolving Sustainability: Longitudinal Study of Corporate Sustainable Development." *Strategic Management Journal* 26, no. 3, p. 197.

[11] Kiron, D., N. Kruschwitz, K. Haanaes, and I. von Streng Velken. 2012. "Sustainability Nears a Tipping Point." *MIT Sloan Management Review* 53, no. 2, p. 69 (noting six criteria for "corporate sustainability": eco-efficiency, eco-effectiveness, sufficiency, ecological equity, socio-effectiveness, and socio-efficiency).

is "both morally and economically wrong to treat the world as a business in liquidation" when engaging in commercial activities.[12]

In summary, "sustainability" has taken on a number of different meanings and has become a widely used term in a wide array of scientific, social, economic, and political contexts. Stankeviciute and Savaneviciene noted that sustainability is regularly used to describe each of the following[13]:

- The systematic, long-term use of natural resources so that they are available for future generations, the concept famously defined by the Brundtland Commission in the late 1980s (i.e., development is "sustainable" when it meets the needs of the present without compromising the ability of future generations to meet their own needs);
- The modality of development that enables countries to progress economically and socially, without destroying their environmental resources (i.e., "sustainable development");
- The type of development which is ethically acceptable, morally fair, socially just, and economically sound; and
- The type of development where environmental and social indicators are as important as economic indicators.

The term is also often used in contexts that combine two or more of the concepts mentioned earlier. For example, Schuler and Jackson integrated the Brundtland Commission definition into the business world by arguing that an organization's success requires meeting the present demands of multiple stakeholders while also anticipating their future needs.[14] In addition, sustainability is transforming thinking in a number

---

[12] Daly, H. 1991. *Steady-State Economics*. Washington, D.C.: Island Press.

[13] Stankeviciute, Z., and A. Savaneviciene. 2013. "Sustainability as a Concept for Human Resource Management." *Economics and Management* 18, no. 4, pp. 837, 839 (citing Leal Filho, W. 2000. "Dealing with Misconceptions on the Context of Sustainability." *International Journal of Sustainability in Higher Education* 1, no. 1, p. 9).

[14] Schuler, R., and S. Jackson. 2005. "A Quarter-Century Review of Human Resource Management in the U.S." *The Growth in the Importance of the International Perspective* 16, no. 1, p. 11; See also Boudreau, J. 2003. "Sustainability

of management fields such as human resources management (HRM), where employees are no longer seen as simply tools to be used to achieve financial goals but also as resources to be valued and preserved so that they can continue to make contributions to their companies, families, and the general community. As a result, HRM professionals are beginning to see HRM as both a "means" for achieving an organization's sustainability-based strategic objectives and an "end," or objective, in its own right. Specifically, HRM professionals are expected to train and direct employees in carrying out their individual roles and responsibilities with respect to sustainability (i.e., HRM as a "means") and initiate and administer programs and practices that enhance the long-term physical, social, and economic well-being of employees (i.e., HRM as an "end").[15]

Definitions of Sustainable Development

Sustainability is often associated with the concept of "sustainable development." One of the first, and still among the most commonly cited, definitions of "sustainable development" was proposed in 1987 by the World Commission on Environment and Development of the United Nations (generally referred to simply as the Brundtland Commission), which described sustainable development as "a process in which the exploitation of natural resources, the allocation of investments and the process

---

and the Talentship Paradigm: Strategic Human Resource Management Beyond the Bottom Line." CAHRS Working Paper Series (Sustainability is "An Alternative Definition of Organizational Success"), and Boudreau, J., and P. Ramstad. 2005. "Talentship, Talent Segmentation and Sustainability: A New HR Decision Science Paradigm for a New Strategy Definition." *Human Resource Management* 44, no. 2, p. 129 (sustainability is "achieving success today without compromising the needs of the future").

[15] See Huselid, M., B. Becker, and R. Beatty. 2005. *The Workforce Scorecard: Managing Human Capital to Execute Strategy*. Boston, MA: Harvard Business School Press; and Taylor, S., J. Osland, and C. Egri. 2012. "Guest Editor's Introduction: Introduction to HRM's Role in Sustainability: Systems, Strategies and Practices." *Human Resources Management* 51, no. 6, p. 789. For further discussion of human resources management (HRM) and the relationship of sustainability to HRM, see "Human Resources: A Library of Resources for Sustainable Entrepreneurs" prepared and distributed by the Sustainable Entrepreneurship Project (www.seproject.org).

of technological development and organizational change are in harmony with each other for both current and future generations."[16] The Commission also described sustainable development as "development that meets the needs of the present generation without compromising the ability of future generations to meet their own needs." In the context of entrepreneurial opportunities and activities, the concept of sustainable development brings into focus the need to preserve a sufficient amount of limited resources to ensure that entrepreneurs in future generations will have the same opportunities as current entrepreneurs to tap into those resources.

At the macro-level, the definitions offered by the Commission cautioned that the pursuit of economic growth must be tempered by consideration of social and environmental concerns. The lesson for companies was that managers seeking to act in a sustainable manner need to confront a fundamental challenge and conflict: popular and heavily entrenched short-term goals, such as profit maximization for the benefit of one group of stakeholders—the shareholders—must be balanced against protecting the long-term needs and opportunities of future generations. Twenty years later, an updated perspective on sustainable development explicitly highlighted the need to balance social equity, including business practices that sustain and value employees and other workers in the supply chain, alongside economic health and environmental resilience.[17] That period also saw the emergence of sentiment that the pursuit of sustainable development, albeit challenging to existing ways of doing business, also offered opportunities for new forms of entrepreneurship and that sustainable entrepreneurs could be recognized as persons who created business enterprises that were based on the pursuit of business strategies and activities that simultaneously met the current needs of the enterprise and its stakeholders while also protecting, sustaining, and enhancing the human and natural resources that would be needed in the future.[18]

---

[16] United Nations World Commission on Environment and Development. 1987. *Our Common Future*. New York, NY: Oxford University Press.
[17] Cohen, B., and M. Winn. 2007. "Market Imperfections, Opportunity and Sustainable Entrepreneurship." *Journal of Business Venturing* 22, no. 1, p. 29.
[18] Business Strategy for Sustainable Development: Leadership and Accountability for the 90s (International Institute for Sustainable Development. 1992. Deloitte & Touche and the World Business Council for Sustainable Development).

Business and Sustainable Development

The International Institute for Sustainable Development (www.iisd.org) (IISD) was established in 1990 as an independent nonprofit organization dedicated to promoting human development and environmental sustainability through innovative research, communication, and partnerships. The strategic plan for the IISD includes the following programs and core strategic goals:

- Economic Law and Policy: Reform economic policies to advance sustainable and equitable development.
- Energy: Shift energy systems and policies to support universal access to clean, low-carbon energy.
- Water: Advance science-based solutions for universal access to water and healthy ecosystems.
- Resilience: Strengthen capacities to manage climate- and conflict-related risks.
- Knowledge: Transform data and information into knowledge that supports sustainable development.
- Reporting Services: Provide accurate, neutral, high-quality analysis that informs decision making about multilateral environmental negotiations.

Content available on the IISD website includes materials on Business and Sustainable Development collected and presented on their own site (https://iisd.org/business/) which includes six sections covering the following:

- Key Issues: Briefings on specific sustainable development topics from a business perspective including corporate social responsibility, corporate reporting, integrated product policy, climate change, and trade
- Strategies and Tools: How to incorporate the principle of sustainability into everyday business activities, illustrated by real-life examples
- Markets: Business opportunities arising from sustainable development
- Banking and Investment: Spotlight on how sustainable development is being approached by the financial services industry
- Working with NGOs: How businesses are forging working partnerships with lobby groups
- Training Opportunities: How universities and professional training providers can help industry leaders incorporate sustainability into their business strategies

Among the strategies and tools are guiding principles (i.e., the CERES principles, the International Chamber of Commerce Business Charter, the GoodCorporation accreditation scheme, IISD's checklist of sustainable business practices, "factor four" and the "triple bottom line); business tools (i.e., by-product synergy and industrial ecology, cleaner production, design for environment, eco-efficiency, energy efficiency, environmentally-conscious manufacturing, the "four R's," green procurement, performance contracting, pollution prevention, and zero-emission processes); and systems and standards (i.e., environmental management systems, ISO 14001, EMAS, EH&S programs, SA 8000, life-cycle assessment, reporting, total cost assessment, and total quality environment).

The IISD, in collaboration with Deloitte & Touche and the World Business Council for Sustainable Development, published "Business Strategy for Sustainable Development: Leadership and Accountability for the 90s" in 1992, and that publication included a number of steps for managing an enterprise according to sustainable development principles:

- Perform a stakeholder analysis to identify all the parties that are directly or indirectly affected by the enterprise's operations and set out the issues, concerns, and information needs of the stakeholders with respect to the organization's sustainable development activities.
- Assess the current position to determine the degree to which the company's activities line up with sustainable development principles, a process that requires evaluating the company's overall strategy, the performance of specific operations, and the effect of particular activities. This process should compare the company's current performance with the expectations of the stakeholders, review management philosophies and systems, analyze the scope of public disclosures on sustainability topics, and evaluate the ability of current information systems to produce the required data should be evaluated.
- Set sustainable development policies and objectives including articulating the basic values that the enterprise expects its employees to follow with respect to sustainable development, incorporating sustainable development objectives as an additional dimension of business strategy, setting targets for operating performance, and establishing an effective external monitoring system that gathers information on new and proposed legislation; industry practices and standards, competitors' strategies, community and special interest group policies and activities, trade union concerns and technical developments (e.g., new process technologies).
- Establish a social responsibility committee of the board of directors with responsibility for setting corporate policies on sustainable development and monitoring their implementation and for dealing with issues such as health and safety, personnel policies, environmental protection, and codes of business conduct.
- Decide on a strategy taking into account the performance of other comparable organizations and with a focus on narrowing the gap between the current state of the corporation's performance and its objectives for the future. The strategy should be supported by a plan that describes how and when management expects to achieve the stated goals and the various milestones that must be reached along the way. Once the strategy and the general plan have been approved, detailed plans should be prepared indicating how the new strategy will affect operations, management systems, information systems, and reporting. Plans should be reviewed and approved by senior management following consultation with employees throughout the organization.
- Design and execute an implementation plan for the management system changes that are needed in order to achieve sustainable development objectives, a process that normally includes changing the corporate culture and employee attitudes, defining responsibilities and accountability, and establishing organizational structures, information reporting systems and operational practices.
- Develop a supportive corporate culture to ensure that the organization and its people give their backing to the sustainable development policies. In most cases, managers will need to be retrained to change attitudes that have traditionally emphasized wealth management for the owners of the enterprise. An effort should also be made to develop a culture that emphasizes employee participation, continuous learning, and improvement.
- Develop appropriate measures and standards of performance taking into account the company's sustainable development objectives and standards that have been established by government and other public agencies.

- Develop meaningful reports for internal management and stakeholders, outlining the enterprise's sustainable development objectives and comparing performance against them. Directors and senior executives use internal reports to measure performance, make decisions, and monitor the implementation of their policies and strategies. Shareholders, creditors, employees, and customers, as well as the public at large, use external corporate reports to evaluate the performance of a corporation, and to hold the directors and senior executives accountable for achieving financial, social, and environmental objectives.
- Enhance internal monitoring processes to help directors and senior managers ensure that the sustainable development policies are being implemented. Monitoring can take many forms, such as reviewing reports submitted by middle managers, touring operating sites, and observing employees performing their duties, holding regular meetings with subordinates to review reports and to seek input on how the procedures and reporting systems might be improved, and implementing an environmental auditing program.

Other resources and references relating to sustainable business are available from the Sustainable Business and Entrepreneurship Platform (http://susent.org/), which is a research group from the International Business School and the Centre of Applied Research of Economics and Management at the Amsterdam University of Applied Science. The Platform was developed as a resource for professionals, primarily in the fashion, apparel, and textile industries, to learn more about sustainability in practice and includes case studies and tools that can be used for assessment of sustainability and development and implementation of strategies for achieving sustainability change.

Dimensions of Sustainability

In many ways, the definition of sustainable development proposed by the Brundtland Commission was vague and ambiguous; however, commentators eventually began to focus on what became known as the three pillars, or dimensions, of sustainable development: environmental protection, economic development, and social equity.[19] Many of them argued that environmentally conscious, or sustainable, businesses should pursue environmental, economic, and social objectives simultaneously and conduct their operations ethically with sustainable environmental, economic, and social dimensions embedded within their products, processes, and services.[20] From time to time, others have

---

[19] Choi, D., and E. Gray. 2008. "The Venture Development Process of 'sustainable' Entrepreneurs." *Management Research News* 31, no. 8, p. 558.

[20] Bell. J., and J. Stellingwerf. 2012. *Sustainable Entrepreneurship: The Motivations & Challenges of Sustainable Entrepreneurs in the Renewable Energy Industry*, 4. Jonkoping, Sweden: Jonkoping International Business School Master Thesis in Business Administration.

suggested that additional dimensions of sustainability should be recognized and integrated into a model along with the first three dimensions. For example, a cultural dimension would take into account the need for sustainable businesses to sustain traditional or indigenous knowledge, maintain cultural diversity, and prevent the loss of personal and community identify.[21] Racelis argued that sustainable development was, by its very nature, an ethically motivated normative concept and thus it was essential to include an ethical domain in any framework or model of sustainable entrepreneurship.[22]

The "Triple Bottom-Line"

In the 1990s, Elkington proposed a framework for measuring and quantifying an organization's economic activities that had a direct impact on society and the environment, thus moving beyond traditional performance measures such as profit, return on investment and shareholder value to incorporate creation of social and environmental value and the impact of operations on all of the organization's stakeholders (i.e., shareholders, customers, employees, business partners, governments, and local communities).[23] Elkington referred to his framework as the "triple bottom-line," described by others as an expansion of the "traditional accounting and performance framework to encompass its ecological and social impact,

---

[21] See Nurse, K. 2006. "Culture as the Fourth Pillar of Sustainable Development." *Small States: Economic Review and Basic Statistics* 11, p. 28; Shepherd, D., and H. Patzelt. January 2011. "The New Field of Sustainable Entrepreneurship: Studying Entrepreneurial Action Linking 'What is to be Sustained' With 'What is to be Developed.'" *Entrepreneurship Theory and Practice*, p. 137; and Shepherd, D., and H. Patzelt. February 5–8, 2008. "Sustainable Entrepreneurship: Entrepreneurial Mechanisms Linking What is to be Sustained With What is to be Developed." *Conference Proceedings in 5th International AGSE Entrepreneurship Research Exchange*, Swinburne University of Technology, Melbourne, Australia.
[22] Racelis, A. 2014. "Sustainable Entrepreneurship in Asia: A Proposed Theoretical Framework Based on Literature Review." *Journal of Management for Global Sustainability* 2, no. 6.
[23] Elkington, J. 1998. *Cannibals with Forks: the Triple Bottom-Line of 21st Century Business*. Oxford: Capstone.

in addition to its financial impact."[24] The constituent aspects of the triple bottom-line have become known as the "3 P's" (i.e., People, Planet, and Profit), and can be briefly described as follows[25]:

- *People:* This aspect focuses on how companies behave with respect to addressing social and ethical issues such as fair treatment for employees and promotion of social cohesion. Issues that need to be addressed include, job creation, protection of human rights, non-indulgence toward fraud and corruption, use of child labor, gender relationships and discrimination in the workplace, workplace safety, labor participation in management and profits, implementation and enforcement of behavior codes and social cohesion (i.e., fulfilling individual and community needs). Companies must not only adhere to formal labor regulations but also must voluntarily and purposely adopt self-imposed systems to manage these issues. Companies should provide fair salaries, tolerable working hours and conditions, and meaningful benefits such as health care and insurance, and should also demonstrate their understanding of the value of their workforce through hiring,

---

[24] Green Marketing TV: empowering green & Social Entrepreneurs. 2011 (as cited in Bell, J., and J. Stellingwerf. 2012. *Sustainable Entrepreneurship: The Motivations & Challenges of Sustainable Entrepreneurs in the Renewable Energy Industry,* 4. Jonkoping, Sweden: Jonkoping International Business School Master Thesis in Business Administration).

[25] The descriptions of the 3 P's are adapted from Crals, E., and L. Vereeck. July 18, 2016. "Sustainable Entrepreneurship in SMEs—Theory and Practice." http://. inter-disciplinary.net/ptb/ejgc/ejgc3/cralsvereeck%20paper.pdf (accessed July 18, 2016), pp. 3–4; Bell, J., and J. Stellingwerf. 2012. *Sustainable Entrepreneurship: The Motivations & Challenges of Sustainable Entrepreneurs in the Renewable Energy Industry Jonkoping,* 4–5. Sweden: Jonkoping International Business School Master Thesis in Business Administration; and Rey, L. December 2011. *Sustainable Entrepreneurship and its Viability,* 19–20. Rotterdam: Master Thesis for MS in Entrepreneurship, Strategy and Organizations Economics from Erasmus School of Economics. See also Crals, E., and L. Vereeck. 2004. *Sustainable Entrepreneurship in SMEs. Theory and Practice.* Belgium: Limburgs Universitair Centrum.

developing, and training the "right" people that complement
their sustainable business objectives. Training should not
only meet the current needs of the company but also include
a "knowledge" component that strengthens the ability of
employees to survive in a competitive labor marketplace.

- *Planet:* The second aspect recognizes that sustainability is crucial to the longevity of the planet and its inhabitants and calls
on companies to measure and manage the impact of its activities on natural resources and the landscape. Unsustainable use
and abuse of natural resources will ultimately cause companies to lose their people, employees, and customers, and
destroy their profitability and economic viability.[26] Among
the specific issues that need to be considered are environmental care, supply chain management, eco-efficiency, clean
products, sustainable technology development, sustainable
industry fields, and eco-design. In many instances, protecting
the environment is a real and substantial constraint on profit
maximization for companies; however, the triple bottom-line
places environmental integrity side-by-side with profit seeking
as overall goals and purposes for the organization. As is the
case with the People aspect, companies must not only deal
with environmental laws and regulations but also a broad and
continuously growing array of self-regulatory standards.

- *Profit:* The third aspect, profit, is certainly not new to
commercial ventures and it can be expected that companies will be concerned about the financial results of their
business activities. Simply put, companies cannot achieve
the long-term value for Planet and People described earlier
unless they are financially viable and sustainable and thus
able to survive and ultimately achieve the goals and purposes

[26] Langdon, K. 2010. *The 3 P's of Sustainability* (as cited in Bell, J., and
J. Stellingwerf. 2012. *Sustainable Entrepreneurship: The Motivations & Challenges
of Sustainable Entrepreneurs in the Renewable Energy Industry*, 5. Jonkoping,
Sweden: Jonkoping International Business School Master Thesis in Business
Administration).

originally stabled by the entrepreneurs who founded the venture.[27] However, success with regard to profitability in the triple bottom-line framework is gauged by additional factors such as allocating excess funds away from self-gratification and into meaningful, helpful ways such as investments in machines and infrastructure, sponsoring and donating, and equitable distribution of financial profits (e.g., labor participation). In addition, the framework also takes into account the economic benefits that society in general enjoys from the business activities of the company including profits realized by supply chain members and other business partners which must be understood and valued as social benefits.

While each of the 3 P's can be understood and appreciated in isolation, the challenge for companies lies in achieving and maintaining the appropriate balance among the three areas, a task that is particularly difficult given that companies operate in a turbulent and evolving external market that is constantly changing and thus requires a series of twists and turns in business strategy and the areas of immediate focus. For example, the need to generate revenues to maintain operations and invest in new equipment and personnel required to grow the business may lead to temptations to cut corners on using eco-friendly materials that may be more costly. Sustainable entrepreneurs may also find that their desire to protect and reward their employees threatens the long-term viability of the business during recessionary times when sales are down due to factors outside the control of the company. Similarly, donations and sponsorships may need to be cut back during times that excess capital needs to be diverted to

---

[27] Crals, E., and L. Vereeck. February 12–14, 2004. *Sustainable Entrepreneurship in SMEs: Theory and Practice. Conference proceedings in 3rd Global Conference on Environmental Justice and Global Citizenship.* Copenhagen, Denmark; Austin, J., H. Stevenson, and J. Wei-Skillern. January 2006. "Social and Commercial Entrepreneurship: Same, Different or Both?" *Entrepreneurship Theory and Practice* 1; and Hall, J., G. Daneke, and M. Lenox. 2010. "Sustainable Development and Entrepreneurship: Past Contributions and Future Directions." *Journal of Business Venturing* 25, no. 5, p. 439.

upgrading products to address changing customer requirements. In all of these instances, the impact of changes in strategy and tactics needs to be analyzed and communicated to the involved stakeholders

While the "triple bottom-line" has been well known and recognized, a strong perception remains that financial and social returns are mutually exclusive and that improvements on one of these dimensions will be accompanied by reductions on the other dimension. Commentators have argued that it should not be a question of whether to focus on creating financial wealth or social change but rather on conceptualizing the path of the organization as concurrently pursuing both economic and social value. Bergh described that "blended value proposition" developed by Emerson et al., which is based on the belief that "the nature of value is integrated and non-divisible; that value attained as an outcome of an activity has financial, social and environmental elements integrated at the core of the value proposition."[28] What this means is that the focus of analysis should be on whole value created for all of the stakeholders, not just investors but also other impacted groups and society in general. Richomme-Huet and De Freyman have also stressed that sustainable entrepreneurs should create values that produces economic prosperity, together with social justice and environmental protection. In other words, there should not be a zero-sum game or tradeoff between profit and other non-profit aspects, such as environmental well-being or social welfare.[29]

One issue that makes it difficult for companies to simultaneously manage People, Planet, and Profits is that while there are accepted and

[28] Bergh, L. July 2013. *Sustainability-Driven Entrepreneurship: Perceptions of Challenges and Obstacles in a South African Context*, 6. Cambridge, UK: Master Thesis for MS in Sustainability Leadership (citing Emerson, J., S. Bonini, and K. Brehm. 2003. *The Blended Value Map: Tracking the Intersects and Opportunities of Economic, Social and Environmental Value Creation*).

[29] Majid, I., and W.L. Koe. June 2012. "Sustainable Entrepreneurship (SE): A Revised Model Based on Triple Bottom Line (TBL)." *International Journal of Academic Research in Business and Social Sciences* 2, no. 6, pp. 293–303 (citing Richomme-Huet, K., and J. Freyman. June 15–18, 2011. "What Sustainable Entrepreneurship Looks Like: An Exploratory Study from a Student Perspective." *Conference Proceedings in 56th Annual International Council for Small Business (ICSB) World Conference*, Stockholm, Sweden).

reasonably objective ways to measure financial performance it is problematic to gauge the actual impact of a company's behavior on nature and the communities in which it operates and thus assess the company's overall performance along all included dimensions. Racelis cited an example provided by Sir Partha Dasgupta, who was involved in the development of the Inclusive Wealth Index:

> If a national accountant claims the savings ratio of a country like Brazil or Costa Rica is 15 percent, but doesn't take into account the natural capital, the forests being razed, then it is not a true indication of the accumulation of wealth. If depreciation of forests is deducted from savings, the picture looks significantly different.[30]

An obvious problem is that there is no common unit of measurement, which makes it difficult to afford equal weight to each of the three dimensions.[31] While there have been suggestions that social welfare and environmental damage can and should be measured using monetary values, the reality it is problematic, if not impossible, to put a price on social and environmental issues such as endangered species, nuclear disasters, and soil degradation.[32] Critics have claimed that companies have taken advantage of the lack of measurement tools to inaccurately report their triple bottom-line performances, with Pojasek arguing that while many companies have made a great public show of embracing the triple bottom-line, they often have used it in ways that have "provided a smokescreen behind

---

[30] Racelis, A. 2014. "Sustainable Entrepreneurship in Asia: A Proposed Theoretical Framework Based on Literature Review." *Journal of Management for Global Sustainability* 2, p. 16 (citing UN Environment Programme. 2012. *Inclusive Wealth Report 2012: Measuring Progress Toward Sustainability.* Bonn: United Nations University-International Human Dimensions Programme).

[31] Slaper, T., and T. Hall. 2011. "The Triple Bottom Line: What is it and How Does it Work?" *Indiana Business Review* 4.

[32] Bell, J., and J. Stellingwerf. 2012. *Sustainable Entrepreneurship: The Motivations & Challenges of Sustainable Entrepreneurs in the Renewable Energy Industry*, 5. Jonkoping, Sweden: Jonkoping International Business School Master Thesis in Business Administration.

which firms can avoid truly effective and environmental reporting and performance."[33]

In 2006, Savitz and Weber proposed a menu of economic, environmental, and social performance measures based on information drawn from different functions within the company—accounting, marketing, and human resources—that could provide a clear picture of a company's management of the triple bottom-line and opportunities for reporting and assessing results[34]:

- *Economic*: Traditional economic measures such as sales, profits, and return on investment should be supplemented by taxes paid, monetary flows, and jobs created (e.g., job growth and cost of underemployment).
- *Environmental*: Objective/quantitative measures can be obtained for air and water quality, energy usage (e.g., electricity and fossil fuel consumption), and waste production (e.g., hazardous and solid waste management).
- *Social*: Labor practices (e.g., unemployment rate and female labor force participation rate), community impacts (e.g., relative poverty, health adjusted life expectancy, and violent crimes per capita), human rights, and product safety and responsibility.

Majid and Koe observed that the use of the triple bottom line, often referred to as the "TBL," had been extended beyond being a means for explaining or describing sustainable development to being recognized as a "tool or device for sustainable reporting under the headings of

---

[33] Pojasek, R. 2012. *Debunking the Notion of a Triple Bottom Line* (as cited in Bell, J., and J. Stellingwerf. 2012. *Sustainable Entrepreneurship: The Motivations & Challenges of Sustainable Entrepreneurs in the Renewable Energy Industry*, 5. Jonkoping, Sweden: Jonkoping International Business School Master Thesis in Business Administration).

[34] Savitz, A., and K. Weber. 2006. *The Triple Bottom Line: How Today's Best-Run Companies are Achieving Economic, Social, and Environmental Success—and How You can you too*. San Francisco: Jossey-Bass.

environmental quality, social justice, and economic prosperity by organizations; due to its ease in monitoring the effects of business activities on the three dimensions in TBL."[35]

Many businesses, nonprofit organizations, and government agencies have cited the triple bottom line as the foundation for their measurement and reporting of sustainability performance; however, many have complained that significant shortcomings remain in developing reliable, objective, and widely accepted standards for measuring performance on the environmental and social dimensions of the triple bottom line and simultaneously integrating the performance on each of the dimensions to arrive at a viable measure of overall return on investment.[36] Racelis criticized the efficacy of the "triple bottom line" as a measurement tool for sustainable entrepreneurship due to its failure to clearly mention the degree of emphasis that should be given to the domains identified in the model. Others have attempted to solve the puzzle of how to balance the domains by maintaining that equal priority should be given to each of the domains in the model, a stance taken by Majid and Koe for their model, discussed in the following texts, that includes four domains: economic, social, ecological, and cultural.[37]

---

[35] Majid, I., and W.L. Koe. June 2012. "Sustainable Entrepreneurship (SE): A Revised Model Based on Triple Bottom Line (TBL)." *International Journal of Academic Research in Business and Social Sciences* 2, no. 6, pp. 293–300 (citing McCartney, J., and P. Rouse. July 4–6, 2004. "A Framework for Sustainability, Strategy and Management Control." *Conference Proceedings in 4th Asia Pacific Interdisciplinary Research in Accounting Conference*, Singapore); and Mitchell, M., A. Curtis, and P. Davidson. May 21–25, 2007. "Can the 'Triple Bottom Line' Concept Help Organizations Respond to Sustainability Issues?" *Conference Proceedings in 5th Australian Stream Management Conference*, New South Wales, Australia.

[36] See Mitchell, M., A. Curtis, and P. Davidson. May 21–25, 2007. "Can the 'Triple Bottom Line' Concept Help Organizations Respond to Sustainability Issues?" *Conference Proceedings in 5th Australian Stream Management Conference*, New South Wales, Australia; and Slaper, T., and T. Hall. Spring 2011. "The Triple Bottom Line: What Is It and How Does It Work?" *Indiana Business Review* 4.

[37] Majid, I., and W.L. Koe. June 2012. "Sustainable Entrepreneurship (SE): A Revised Model Based on Triple Bottom Line (TBL)." *International Journal of Academic Research in Business and Social Sciences* 2, no. 6, p. 293.

Cultural Dimension

Majid and Koe surveyed definitions of sustainable entrepreneurship that served as the foundation for suggesting that "culture" should be added to the three original dimensions of the triple bottom line and recognized as a context for entrepreneurship that should be sustained. They noted that O'Neill et al. described sustainable entrepreneurship as "a process of venture creation that links the activities of entrepreneurs to the emergence of value-creating enterprises that contribute to the sustainable development of the social-ecological system" and the characteristics of the cultural environment in which the entrepreneurial activities are being carried out play a significant role in influencing the "values" that sustainable enterprises seek to create.[38] Earlier, Nurse had argued that culture should be integrated into sustainable entrepreneurship in the same manner as economic viability, environmental responsibility, and social equity.[39] In fact, Nurse proposed that not only should culture be the "fourth pillar of sustainable development, but should be central to it in order help the people to deal with sustainability issues in one's own way," because "culture shapes what we mean by development and determines how people act in the world."[40]

Majid and Koe relied upon and endorsed these definitions when proposing their own definition of sustainable entrepreneurship: "A process in which entrepreneurs exploit the opportunities in an innovative manner for economic gains, society equity, environmental quality and cultural

---

[38] Id. at p. 299 (citing O'Neill, G., J. Hershauer, and J. Golden. 2009. "The Cultural Context of Sustainability Entrepreneurship." *Green Management International* 55, pp. 33–34).

[39] Id. at p. 306 (citing Nurse, K. 2006. "Culture as the Fourth Pillar of Sustainable Development." *Small States: Economic Review and Basic Statistics* 11, p. 28). While arguing that culture should be included in any comprehensive model of sustainable entrepreneurship, Nurse did not advocate that "cultural entrepreneurs" should be recognized as sustainable entrepreneurs as they typically focused their activities on the art sector or cultural industries which could be not-for-profit and non-entrepreneurial oriented. Id.

[40] Id. at p. 302 (citing Nurse, K. 2006. "Culture as the Fourth Pillar of Sustainable Development." *Small States: Economic Review and Basic Statistics* 11, pp. 28–37).

preservation on an equal footing."[41] They then continued to propose a revised model of sustainable entrepreneurship based on analysis of four domains: the economic, environmental, and social domains in the traditional TBL, and a cultural domain that specifically recognized preservation of the community and cultural values as an obligation of sustainable entrepreneurs and their activities. Majid and Koe noted that explicitly including culture in the model was consistent with the significant role that culture played in setting the context for sustainable entrepreneurship, particularly the social impact of entrepreneurship.

In the same vein, Racelis pointed out that in many areas of the world, sustainable entrepreneurship must be understood to include addressing concerns about damage to traditional or indigenous knowledge or culture and over-dependence on Western culture arising from economic progress and development as defined by Western standards. Racelis noted that measurement and assessment tools relating to sustainability entrepreneurship must take into account cultural factors including those aspects related to learning, education, awareness, and marketing.[42]

Ethical Dimension

An important element of sustainable entrepreneurship is ensuring that the businesses launched and operated by the entrepreneurs conduct their affairs in a sustainable manner and demonstrate ethical behavior. Many commentators have stressed that the pursuit of the various types of economic and noneconomic entrepreneurship described in this Guide cannot be sustainable unless the entrepreneurs conduct their operations ethically. Building on this, Racelis argued for consideration of the ethical environment created within an entrepreneurial firm, the mechanisms put in place by the entrepreneur to ensure ethical standards are observed, and the ways in which unethical behaviors on the part of employees are

---

[41] Id. at pp. 300–301.

[42] Racelis, A. 2014. "Sustainable Entrepreneurship in Asia: A Proposed Theoretical Framework Based on Literature Review." *Journal of Management for Global Sustainability* 2, no. 1, p. 16.

addressed.[43] According to Racelis, "*sustainable development* is, by its very nature, an *ethically motivated normative concept* referring to a form of economics and lifestyle that does not endanger our future" and that it is therefore essential to include an ethical domain in any framework or model of sustainable entrepreneurship.[44]

Racelis argued that "entrepreneurship is an ethical activity of pressing importance as it significantly influences the sort of lives we will lead in the future" and noted, in particular, that "the very process of creating new products, services, and markets is a journey with its own enormous ethical impact on the stakeholders immediately affected by the entrepreneur's actions." For example, there are strong ethical dimensions at play in the relationship between the entrepreneur and the supporters of the new venture who put themselves in a position of great vulnerability to the entrepreneur and place much at stake in anticipation of the success of the entrepreneur.[45]

Racelis mentioned several important and complex moral and ethical issues and problems that all entrepreneurs must confront with respect to basic fairness, personnel and customer relationships, distribution dilemmas, and other challenges.[46] Illustrations of major ethical concerns and issues with respect to entrepreneurship include[47]:

---

[43] Id. at p. 14 (citing Morris, M., M. Schindehutte, J. Walton, and J. Allen. 2002. "The Ethical Context of Entrepreneurship: Proposing and Testing a Developmental Framework." *Journal of Business Ethics* 40, no. 4, p. 331).

[44] Id. at p. 6.

[45] Id. at p. 11 (citing Dunham, L. 2005. *Entrepreneurship and Ethics*).

[46] Id. (citing Hannafey, F. 2003. "Entrepreneurship and Ethics: a Literature Review." *Journal of Business Ethics* 46, no. 2, p. 99).

[47] Id. (citing Garriga, E., and D. Melé. 2004. "Corporate Social Responsibility Theories: Mapping the Territory." *Journal of Business Ethics* 53, nos. 1–2, p. 51; Morris, M., M. Schindehutte, J. Walton, and J. Allen. 2002. "The Ethical Context of Entrepreneurship: Proposing and Testing a Developmental Framework." *Journal of Business Ethics* 40, no. 4, 331; and Raeesi, R., M. Dastrang, S. Mohammadi, and E. Rasouli. 2013. "Understanding the Interactions Among the Barriers to Entrepreneurship using Interpretive Structural Modeling." *International Journal of Business and Management* 8, no. 13, pp. 56.

- *Human dignity and human rights issues*: Racelis argued that "a normative approach to entrepreneurial ethics calls for the application of social norms to business and management since social norms serve as the foundation for rules of behavior within a community." Racelis suggested that organizations, including sustainable entrepreneurial ventures, need to treat members of their community with dignity and respect and must be mindful of: (1) maltreatment (i.e., blatant injustice through abuse of power or mistreatment); (2) indifference (i.e., disrespectful treatment through lack of recognition of people's personhood and concern); (3) justice (i.e., respect for persons and their rights), (4) care (i.e., concern for people's legitimate interests and support for them in resolving their problems); and (5) development (i.e., favoring human flourishing, mutual esteem, and friendship-based reciprocity).[48]
- *Contributing to a harmonious way of living together in just, peaceful, and friendly conditions*: Racelis observed that humans are also social beings; they possess "sociability" and want to live together in an established order, with harmony, justice, and peace. These traits and needs should be demonstrated by feelings of care, trust, concern, and interest for others, including those who are vulnerable to the choices of others and those who deserve extra consideration.[49]
- *Corruption, especially in the supply and customer chains*: Hefty fines, damaged reputations, and jail sentences—recent scandals prove that corruption in business does not always bring profits, yet bribery persists.

---

[48] Id. at p. 12 (citing Melé, D. 2014. "Human Quality Treatment: Five Organizational Levels." *Journal of Business Ethics* 120, p. 457; and Morris, M., M. Schindehutte, J. Walton, and J. Allen. 2002. "The Ethical Context of Entrepreneurship: Proposing and Testing a Developmental Framework." *Journal of Business Ethics* 40, 331).

[49] Id. at pp. 12–13 (citing Melé, D. 2014. "'Human Quality Treatment': Five Organizational Levels." *Journal of Business Ethics* 120, p. 457).

- *Financial and operational pressures which heighten the incentives for entrepreneurs to engage in expedient behavior (including dishonesty)*: Rising incidents of corruption, piracy, terrorism, and human and drug trafficking. Legal and reputational issues (i.e., penalties for willful infringement and having unlicensed software reduces credibility and can be seen as being very unprofessional).

Other unethical practices include violations of union rights, use of child labor, dangerous working conditions, race and gender discrimination, and underhanded influence on people to gain benefit or power by way of lies, deceit, or the creation of false expectations.[50]

Racelis argued that "a strong case for our moral responsibility to future generations can be established on the grounds of fiduciary duties, virtue ethics, stewardship and accountability, respect for human dignity and human rights, promoting the common good, and so on." and that the job of leaders such as sustainable entrepreneurs should include caring and taking responsibility for their followers.[51] Ethical missteps will cause sustainable entrepreneurs to lose their existing funds and resources due to corruption and make it more difficult for them to obtain new financial resources and recruit and retain the human capital needed for the venture to be successful.[52] As to some of the actual steps that sustainable entrepreneurs can take in order to fulfill their ethical obligations, a survey described by Morris et al. mentioned implementing penalties for unethical behavior and communicating them to employees; drafting and adopting a formal code of conduct that provided guidance for resolving specific on-the-job

---

[50] Id. at p. 14 (citing Andersen, M., and T. Skjoett-Larsen. 2009. "Corporate Social Responsibility in Global Supply Chains." *Supply Chain Management: An International Journal* 14, no. 2, p. 75; and Melé, D. 2014. "Human Quality Treatment: Five Organizational Levels." *Journal of Business Ethics* 120, p. 457).

[51] Id. at pp. 16–17 (citing Ciulla, J. 2009. "Leadership and the Ethics of Care." *Journal of Business Ethics* 88, no. 1, p. 3).

[52] Id. at p. 18 (citing Raeesi, R., M. Dastrang, S. Mohammadi, and E. Rasouli. 2013. "Understanding the Interactions Among the Barriers to Entrepreneurship using Interpretive Structural Modeling." *International Journal of Business and Management* 8, no. 13, p. 56).

ethical dilemmas; implementing ongoing ethics-related training; preparing and circulating among employees a company policy manual covering ethics was accessible to employees; designating an officer or manager who is assigned direct responsibility for ethical issues; and launching and maintaining a program regularly scheduled discussions with employees regarding ethical issues.[53] The ideal is for the business as a whole and each of its managers and employees to embrace and practice ethical values and adopt and live the simple premise that "Good Ethics is Good Business."[54]

---

[53] Morris, M., M. Schindehutte, J. Walton, and J. Allen. 2002. "The Ethical Context of Entrepreneurship: Proposing and Testing a Developmental Framework." *Journal of Business Ethics* 40, no. 4, p. 331.

[54] Racelis, A. 2014. "Sustainable Entrepreneurship in Asia: A Proposed Theoretical Framework Based on Literature Review." *Journal of Management for Global Sustainability* 2, no. 1, p. 18 (citing Van Beurden, P., and T. Gössling. 2008. "The Worth of Values: a Literature Review on the Relation Between Corporate Social and Financial Performance." *Journal of Business Ethics* 82, no. 2, p. 407).

CHAPTER 3

Ecopreneurship

Introduction

Interest in sustainable development began with concerns about the impact that economic growth would have on the Earth's finite natural resources and some of the parties involved in that debate argued that while overuse was an issue it would eventually be addressed through market forces. According the York and Venkataraman, there are several different ways that environmental degradation can be addressed[1]:

- Government regulation and control, the so-called "visible hand"; however, while the government has promulgated an expansive portfolio of regulations over the last several decades environmental degradation has continued to occur;
- Stakeholder activism, such as lobbying action by non-governmental organizations focusing on perseveration of natural resources;
- Corporate social responsibility initiatives launched by individual corporations on their own initiative as ethics-based programs to address environmental problems they are responsible for or have association with—initiatives that have been critiqued as being more about doing "less bad" than doing good; and
- Other forms of corporate action which include cost savings and differentiation with an important goal of gaining a competitive advantage by implementing environmentally friendly practices (e.g., creating a positive public image by being perceived as a "green business").

[1] York, J., and S. Venkataraman. 2010. "The Entrepreneur-Environment Nexus: Uncertainty, Innovation, and Allocation." *Journal of Business Venturing* 25, no. 5, p. 449.

Going down a path on which market forces would eventually address the environmental problems that the market itself created, Gibbs explained the concept of "ecological modernization," which he described as a process of the progressive transformation and modernization of the institutions of modern society in order to avoid ecological crisis.[2] In this view, it was not just market forces that would "save the Earth," but also the inert drive of capitalism for innovation that would be harnessed to realize environmental improvements, thus allowing the world to continue forward with "modernization" undeterred by environmental crises.[3] According to Roberts and Colwell: "ecological modernization suggests that it is possible to integrate the goals of economic development, social welfare and environmental protection, and that through this reconciliation synergies will be generated which can be harnessed and put to good use."[4]

While appealing, there is not sufficient evidence to conclude that ecological modernization is inevitable and it would certainly require cooperation and participation by various actors. Incumbent businesses in the private sector would presumably consider acting in order to gain various advantages: through greater business efficiency due to reduced pollution and waste production; avoiding future financial liabilities, such as the potential cost of contaminated land clean-up; through improved recruitment and retention of the workforce due to the creation of a better work environment; from the potential for increased sales of more "environmentally friendly" products and services; and through the sale of pollution prevention and abatement technologies.[5] As for political institutions, several measures would seem to be appropriate: restructuring

---

[2] Gibbs, D. September 2006. "Sustainability Entrepreneurs, Ecopreneurs and the Development of a Sustainable Economy." *Greener Management International* 55, pp. 63–66.

[3] Beveridge, R., and S. Guy. 2005. "The Rise of the Eco-preneur and the Messy World of Environmental Innovation." *Local Environment* 10, no. 6, pp. 665–66.

[4] Roberts, P., and A. Colwell. 2001. "Moving the Environment to Centre Stage: A New Approach to Planning and Development at European and Regional Levels." *Local Environment* 6, no. 4, pp. 421–24.

[5] Drysek, J. 1997. *The Politics of the Earth: Environmental Discourses.* Oxford, UK: Oxford University Press (as cited in Gibbs, D. September 2006. "Sustainability Entrepreneurs, Ecopreneurs and the Development of a Sustainable Economy." *Greener Management International* 55, pp. 63–67).

of production and consumption toward ecological goals, including the development and diffusion of clean production technologies; decoupling economic development from the relevant resource inputs, resource use, and emissions; exploring alternative and innovative approaches to environmental policy, such as "economizing ecology" by placing an economic value on nature and introducing structural tax reform; and integrating environmental policy goals into other policy areas; and the invention, adoption, and diffusion of new technologies and production processes.[6]

The publication of the report by the Brundtland Commission mentioned earlier fueled what quickly became a comprehensive dialogue on the impact that economic growth was having on the global environment and biodiversity. The early 1990s saw the adoption of extensive new environmental regulations and the emergence of what was referred to as the "green agenda."[7] Corporate social responsibility was also becoming more important and businesses were beginning to see that integrating ecological concerns into their business models could not only be popular with consumers but also help them reduce costs and the risks associated with operations that might be harmful to surrounding communities and the world generally. Given these changes in behavioral patterns and the rise of social institutions concerned with protecting the environment, the scene was set for the emergence of environmental entrepreneurship, or "ecopreneurship," which often took the form of start-ups based on more sustainable business models and deploying processes reflecting greater concern for environmental, and latterly more social issues.[8] Like traditional

[6] Gouldson, A., and J. Murphy. 1997. "Ecological Modernisation: Restructuring Industrial Economies." In *Greening the Millennium? The New Politics of the Environment*, ed. M. Jacobs, 74. Oxford, UK: Blackwell, (as cited in Gibbs, D. September 2006. "Sustainability Entrepreneurs, Ecopreneurs and the Development of a Sustainable Economy." *Greener Management International* 55, pp. 63–66).
[7] Holt, D. 2010. "Where are They Now? Tracking the Longitudinal Evolution of Environmental Businesses from the 1990s." *Business Strategy and the Environment* 20, no. 4, p. 238.
[8] See Holt, D. 2010 ."Where are They Now? Tracking the Longitudinal Evolution of Environmental Businesses from the 1990s." *Business Strategy and the Environment* 20, no. 4, p. 238; and Randjelovic, J., A. O'Rourke, and R. Orsato. 2003. "The Emergence of Green Venture Capital." *Business Strategy and the Environment* 12, no. 4, pp. 240–41.

entrepreneurs, ecopreneurs sought to satisfy unmet needs or identify an unresolved problem in the marketplace; however, while traditional entrepreneurs focused on generating economic value, with creating social value being ancillary, an ecopreneur is a mission-driven individual "who starts up a business with 'green' initiatives from day one, with strong commitment to transforming a sector of the economy toward becoming more sustainable and environmentally responsible."[9] Ecopreneurship offered another path to addressing issues of environmental degradation and ecopreneurs did not just run a "green business" but incorporated innovation into a mission that focused on creating value for sustainable development with products and services that not only generated economic growth but also created societal benefits.

Researchers noted that ecological modernization was arguably an area particularly well suited to entrepreneurial action by ecopreneurs.[10] While ecopreneurs have been described as "social activists, who aspire to restructure the corporate culture and social relations of their business sectors through proactive, ecologically oriented business strategies,"[11] they are also able to attack and address environmental issues using the Schumpeterian "process of creative destruction" that includes creating new products, services, processes, and "ways of doing work" that challenge, and eventually overturn, conventional methods.[12] As explained by Schaltegger: "ecopreneurs destroy existing conventional production methods, products, market structures and consumption patterns and replace them with superior environmental products and services ... [and] ... create the market

[9] Bell, J., and J. Stellingwerf. 2012. *Sustainable Entrepreneurship: The Motivations & Challenges of Sustainable Entrepreneurs in the Renewable Energy Industry Jonkoping*, 7. Sweden: Jonkoping International Business School Master Thesis in Business Administration (citing Isaak, R. 2002. "The Making of the Ecopreneur." *Greener Management International* 38, p. 81).

[10] Schaper, M. 2005. *Making Ecopreneurs: Developing Sustainable Entrepreneurship*. Aldershot, UK: Ashgate.

[11] Isaak, R. 1998. *Green Logic: Ecopreneurship, Theory and Ethics*, 88. Sheffield, UK: Greenleaf Publishing.

[12] Schumpeter, J. 1934. *The Theory of Economic Development*. Cambridge, MA: Harvard University Press.

dynamics of environmental progress."[13] The businesses that they form have been referred to by Isaak as "green-green businesses," firms that have been founded from the outset on an environmentally friendly basis and with a focused mission on achieving social and ethical transformation of their specific business sectors.[14]

It has been argued that the emergence and success of ecopreneur-ship has turned on the ability of ecopreneurs to exploit sources of opportunity such as uncertainty and market failure. There is significant uncertainty with respect to the environment and multiple stakeholders continuously struggle to find solutions for problems such as environmental degradation, pollution, waste and contamination, and resource depletion. While incumbent companies recognize these problems, they are often reluctant to invest in the development of innovative solutions due to the opportunity costs of their current investments. In contrast, ecoentrepreneurs are willing and eager to accept uncertainty in exchange for the possibility of being rewarded with a premium and also do not have to worry about diminishing the value of their previous investments. Environmental degradation is also a form of market failure: government regulations, subsidies, and incentives have proven to be inappropriate and ineffective interventions in many cases and traditional commercial entrepreneurs have struggled to appropriate the gains emanating from their investments in new environmental technology and convince consumers to pay for the related products and services. Ecopreneurs have been successful where the government and commercial entrepreneurs have struggled by engaging customer-focused entrepreneurship that emphasizes identifying specific customer needs for environmental products and services and then addressing another form of market failure, imperfect information, by informing customers about the environmental attributes of products and services and the health and environment

---

[13] Schaltegger, S. 2002. "A Framework for Ecopreneurship: Leading Bioneers and Environmental Managers to Ecopreneurship." *Greener Management International* 38, pp. 45–46.

[14] Isaak, R. 1998. *Green Logic: Ecopreneurship, Theory and Ethics*, 87. Sheffield, UK: Greenleaf Publishing.

effect of methods of production, product contents, product use, and post-consumption disposal.[15]

Definitions and Conceptualizations of Environmental Entrepreneurship

Bell and Stellingwerf noted that a variety of terms have been used to describe "entrepreneurship behavior conducted through an environmental lens" including eco-entrepreneurship, environmental entrepreneurship, Enviropreneurship, green entrepreneurship, and green–green businesses.[16] They preferred "ecopreneurship" and included the following examples of definitions and conceptualizations of that term[17]:

- "A person who seeks to transform a sector of the economy toward sustainability by starting up a business in that sector with a green design, with green processes, and with a life-long commitment to sustainability."[18]
- "Entrepreneurs who found new businesses based on the principle of sustainability—Ecopreneurs are those entrepreneurs

---

[15] van Eijck, P. January 2012. *Sustainable Entrepreneurship: Institutional Profile and Cross-Country Comparison Denmark & US and its Viability*, 10. Rotterdam: Bachelor Thesis in Entrepreneurship, Strategy and Organizations Economics from Erasmus School of Economics.

[16] Bell, J., and J. Stellingwerf. 2012. *Sustainable Entrepreneurship: The Motivations & Challenges of Sustainable Entrepreneurs in the Renewable Energy Industry*, 7. Jonkoping, Sweden: Jonkoping International Business School Master Thesis in Business Administration (citing Schaltegger, S. 2005. "Chapter 4: A Framework and Typology of Ecopreneurship: Leading Bioneers and Environmental Managers to Ecopreneurship." In *Making Ecopreneurs: Developing Sustainable Entrepreneurship*, ed. M. Shaper, 43. Burlington: Ashgate Publishing Company). For a brief summary and critique of research on ecopreneurship, see Gibbs, D. September 2006. "Sustainability Entrepreneurs, Ecopreneurs and the Development of a Sustainable Economy." *Greener Management International* 55, pp. 73–74, 63.

[17] Id. at pp. 7–8.

[18] Isaak, R. 2002. "The Making of the Ecopreneur." *Greener Management International* 38, p. 81.

who start for-profit businesses with strong underlying green values and who sell green products or services."[19]

- "Individuals or institutions that attempt to popularize eco-friendly ideas and innovations either through the market or nonmarket routes may be referred to as Ecopreneurs."[20]

- "Usually the Ecopreneur has a 'raison d'ˆetre' that exceeds their desire for profits and often this is associated with making the world a better place to live."[21]

- "Ecopreneurs can be classified according to two criteria: (1) their desire to change the world and improve the quality of the environment and life; and (2) their desire to make money and grow as a business venture."[22]

- Ecopreneurs are visionaries, with the ability to foresee a "demand for fundamental innovations in traditional markets. The challenge is to be economically successful with the supply of products and services that change—on a purely voluntary basis—consumption patterns and market structures, leading to an absolute reduction of environmental impacts."[23]

- Ecopreneurs are effectively decisive change agents, enabling the world to change its path, are highly motivated in making a difference and displacing unsustainable means, an important transitional role in sustainability.[24]

---

[19] Kirkwood, J., and S. Walkton. 2010. "What Motivates Ecopreneurs to Start a Business?" *International Journal of Entrepreneurial Behaviour & Research* 16, no. 3, p. 204.

[20] Pastakia, A. 1998. "Grassroots Ecopreneurs." *Journal of Organisational Change Management* 11, no. 2, p. 157.

[21] Linnanen, L. 2002. "An Insider's Experiences with Environmental Entrepreneurship." *Greener Management International* 38, p. 71.

[22] Id. (cited in Rogers, C. 2010. "Sustainable Entrepreneurship in SMEs: A Case Study Analysis." *Corporate Social Responsibility and Environmental Management* 17, p. 125).

[23] Schaltegger, S., and M. Wagner. 2011. "Sustainable Entrepreneurship and Sustainability Innovation: Categories and Interactions." *Business Strategy and the Environment* 20, p. 222.

[24] Cohen, B., and M. Winn. 2007. "Market Imperfections, Opportunity and Sustainable Entrepreneurship." *Journal of Business Venturing* 22, no. 1, p. 29.

Bell and Stellingwerf argued that ecopreneurs filled gaps in the marketplace that could not be effectively addressed by large incumbent firms or traditional entrepreneurs. While many established companies appreciate the importance of taking steps to operate in a more environmentally friendly manner, many feel that the sustainability strategies of these companies are "push" strategies driven by their need to comply with the demands of external regulatory bodies and other stakeholders. In contrast, ecopreneurs act to implement "pull" strategies based on actively taking a stance toward becoming "greener" and building a competitive advantage over less "green" firms.[25] As for distinctions between traditional entrepreneurship and ecopreneurship, the following words of Bell and Stellingwerf are instructive:

> Entrepreneurs may effectively bring new combinations to the economy—that is, new products, methods and markets. However, it is the Ecopreneur who plays a critical role in the development process, constructing environmentally friendly products, processes, and services toward the sustainable development objective—"development that meets the needs of the present generation without compromising the ability of future generations to meet their own needs."[26]

While their small size and relative lack of resources appeared to make ecopreneurial start-ups unlikely candidates for transforming business sectors, many researchers believed that these start-ups were actually well positioned to identify and exploit innovative technological strategic niches that can not only bring about technological change but also challenge and pressure existing institutions, rules, and norms.[27] As explained by Smith, ecopreneurs are

---

[25] Bell, J., and J. Stellingwerf. 2012. *Sustainable Entrepreneurship: The Motivations & Challenges of Sustainable Entrepreneurs in the Renewable Energy Industry*, 8. Jonkoping, Sweden: Jonkoping International Business School Master Thesis in Business Administration.

[26] Id. at pp. 8–9.

[27] Gibbs, D. September 2006. "Sustainability Entrepreneurs, Ecopreneurs and the Development of a Sustainable Economy." *Greener Management International* 55, pp. 63–68.

Table 3.1 Corporate environmental management-related definitions

References	Definitions
Kneese (1973)	Quality of the Environment: Discharges into the environmental media—air and water.
Shrivastava (1995b)	Total Environmental Quality Management (TQEM): Combines two ideas of environmentally oriented product design: design for disassembly and manufacturing for the environment. TQEM applies a total systems perspective and quality management principles to environmental problems.
Klassen and McLaughlin (1996)	Environmental Management: All efforts to minimize the negative environmental impact of the firm's products throughout their life cycle (p. 1199).
Judge and Douglas (1998)	Environmental Issues Integration Capability: Organization's capability to incorporate issues related to the environment into the strategic planning process (p. 243).
Bansal and Roth (2000)	Ecological responsibility: Motivation that stems from the concern that a firm has for its social obligations and values.
Christmann (2000)	Best Practices of Environmental Management: Practices that simultaneously reduce the negative impact of firm's activities on the natural environment and contribute to competitive advantage in product markets (p. 664).
Winn and Angell (2000)	Corporate Greening: Overall organizational response to the natural environment as a type of social issue.
Whiteman and Cooper (2000)	Ecological Embeddedness: Extent to which a manager is rooted in the land. To be ecologically embedded is to personally identify with the land, to adhere to beliefs of ecological respect and caretaking, to actively gather ecological information, and to be physically located in the ecosystem (p. 1265).
Ramus and Steger (2000)	Eco-initiative: Any action taken by an employee that he or she thought would improve the company's environmental performance (p. 606).
Lewis and Harvey (2001)	Perceived Environmental Uncertainty (PEU): A measurement of PEU based on Miller's (1993) and grounded in environmental management literature.
Christmann and Taylor (2001)	Environmental Compliance: Related to compliance with national environmental regulations.
Halme (2002)	Environmental Management Paradigms: A shared worldview consisting of the core beliefs, basic assumptions, and values of the firm's managers regarding the relationship of its activities to the natural environment (p. 1088).
Rothenberg (2003)	Environmental Management: Considers management of firm's pollution and waste.

Table 3.1 Continued

References	Definitions
Sharma and Vredenburg (1998)	Corporate Environmental Responsiveness: Defines 11 dimensions to examine corporate environmental strategies on the basis of the areas in which the oil and gas industry substantially affects the natural environment (species habitat preservation, environmental soil restoration, risk reduction of environmental accidents and wastes, waste reduction, or reuse).
Prasad and Elmes (2005)	Corporate Environmentalism: Directed by little more than direct instrumental concerns about green practices (p. 847). Reform Environmentalism: Influenced by both systems theory and sustainable development; organizations and the biospheric environment are reciprocally interconnected (p. 848).

Source: Montiel, I. September 2008. "Corporate Social Responsibility and Corporate Sustainability: Separate Pasts, Common Futures," *Organization and Environment* 21, no. 3, pp. 245, 258. The article reported the results of the author's extensive survey of the evolution of management literature in both general management and specialized journals with respect to CSR and corporate sustainability (CS). The article quantifies the research work and summarizes the different CSR- and CS-related definitions to identify the definitional differences between CSR and corporate sustainability. This table, adapted from the article, lists different environmental management-related definitions used in the general management articles reviewed and full citations for the references can be found in the "References" section of the article.

the "idealists (producers and supportive users) who initiate a sustainable niche [and] are later joined by entrepreneurial 'system builders' who open the niche out to a wider set of users) and, eventually, by serious amounts of capital seeking to profit from the proto-regime."[28]

Factors Driving and Influencing Ecopreneurship

It is important to remember that ecopreneurship may be driven by several factors. Three main drivers of ecopreneurship identified by Post and Altman included[29]:

---

[28] Smith, A. 2003. "Transforming Technological Regimes for Sustainable Development: A Role for Alternative Technology Niches?" *Science and Public Policy* 30. no. 2, pp. 127–30.

[29] Post, J., and B. Altman. 1994. "Managing the Environmental Change Process: Barriers and Opportunities." *Journal of Organizational Change Management* 7, no. 4, p. 64.

- Compliance-based, with environmental improvement emerging as an outcome of government regulation and legislation;
- Market-driven, with environmentally beneficial behavior coming through positive incentives; and
- Value-driven, with environmental change coming in response to consumer demands as they act on their environmental values.

Walley and Taylor noted that these drivers were not mutually exclusive and that ecopreneurs may, at any given moment, be responding to two, or even all three, drivers. For example, it is not uncommon for consumer demands to lead to regulatory activities, which means that ecopreneurs will be engaged in developing products, services, and processes that are not only commercially viable but also conform to the standards that may be established by lawmakers and government bureaucrats.[30]

However, regardless of the forces that drive a particular ecopreneur, he or she can almost certainly count on having to overcome certain challenges that generally pose less significant issues for traditional entrepreneurs. Gibbs noted that all entrepreneurs, including ecopreneurs, share the same burden of creating new markets or expanding existing markets,

> market creation is even more difficult for environmental business ideas than it is for nonenvironmental business ideas, because the financial community may not yet be mature enough to finance environmental innovations, and the role of ethical reasoning creates confusion within the mainstream business community.[31]

---

[30] Walley, E., and D. Taylor. 2002. "Opportunists, Champions, Mavericks? A Typology of Green Entrepreneurs." *Greener Management International* 38, p. 31.
[31] Gibbs, D. September 2006. "Sustainability Entrepreneurs, Ecopreneurs and the Development of a Sustainable Economy." *Greener Management International* 55, pp. 63–70 (citing Linnanen, L. 2002. "An Insider's Experiences with Environmental Entrepreneurship." *Greener Management International* 38, pp. 79–80, 71).

In the finance arena, ecopreneurs often have difficulties due to a short-age of investors with knowledge about the ecopreneurial market, and eco-preneurs themselves may not have as much experience with fund raising as conventional entrepreneurs.[32] Certain types of start-up financing, such as venture capital, may not be available to ecopreneurial firms because their timetable to achieving market breakthroughs and profitability may be much longer than the capital provider is willing to wait.[33] In addition, while ecopreneurship is attractive to many because of the opportunity to pursue a commitment to achieving environmental and social purposes, as opposed to simply focusing of profits, ecopreneurs must nonetheless make difficult managerial decisions when ethical considerations such as providing long-term employment clash with the need to keep their firms afloat by laying off workers to reduce costs.[34]

Regulations and the availability of capital are just two of many factors in an ecopreneur's socioeconomic environment that will have an impact on his or her actions and the success of the ventures that they launch. Walley and Taylor explained that ecopreneurs "will be influenced by the evolving economic and social structures around them and, in turn, are influencing those structures."[35] Pastakia argued that there must be con-gruence between personal ideals and context for ecopreneurs to emerge.[36]

---

[32] See O'Rourke, A. 2005. "Venture Capital as a Tool for Sustainable Entrepre-neurship." In *Making Ecopreneurs: Developing Sustainable Entrepreneurship*, ed. M Schaper, 122. Aldershot, UK: Ashgate;, and Randjelovic, J., A. O'Rourke, and R. Orsato. 2003. "The Emergence of Green Venture Capital." *Business Strategy and the Environment* 12, no. 4, p. 240.

[33] See Cohen, B. 2006. "Sustainable Valley Entrepreneurial Ecosystems," *Business Strategy and the Environment* 15, no. 1, p. 1; and Randjelovic, J., A. O'Rourke, and R. Orsato. 2003. "The Emergence of Green Venture Capital." *Business Strat-egy and the Environment* 12, no. 4, p. 240.

[34] Lahdesmaki, M. 2005. "When Ethics Matters: Interpreting the Ethical Discourse of Small Nature-Based Entrepreneurs." *Journal of Business Ethics* 61, no. 1, p. 55.

[35] Walley, E., and D. Taylor. 2002. "Opportunists, Champions, Mavericks? A Typology of Green Entrepreneurs." *Greener Management International* 38, pp. 31–33.

[36] Pastakia, A. 2002. "Assessing Ecopreneurship in the Context of a Developing Country: The Case of India." *Greener Management International* 38, p. 93.

At the same time, however, opportunities in the environment will not be exploited unless there are persons that have the internal motivations to invest the necessary time and effort.[37]

Research indicates that the weight that businesses assign to environmental issues depends, at least in part, on the nature of their products and services and the industries and markets in which they are engaged. For example, Brand and Dam and Perrini et al. found a positive relationship between the degree of tangibility in the goods produced by a company and the emphasis that the company placed on environmental management activities and "environmentally friendly" behavior, presumably because the operations of these companies involved more raw materials, generated more waste, and created more potential for pollution.[38]

Typologies of Ecopreneurs

Gibbs noted that the interplay between external factors and the personal motivations of ecopreneurs had been used to suggest various typologies of ecopreneurs.[39] The typology proposed by Walley and Taylor was based on two axes: structural influences and personal orientation/motivation. The structural dimension ranged from "hard" (e.g., regulation and economic incentives) to "soft" (e.g., past experiences, family and friends), and the poles of the personal dimension were economic and sustainability. Gibbs described the resulting four ideal types of ecopreneurs as follows[40]:

[37] Beveridge, R., and S. Guy. 2005. "The Rise of the Eco-preneur and the Messy World of Environmental Innovation." *Local Environment* 10, no. 6, p. 665.

[38] Brand, M., and L. Dam. 2009. "Corporate Social Responsibility in Small Firms—Illusion or Big Business? Empirical Evidence from the Netherlands." RENT Conference, Budapest, Hungary; and Perrini, F., A. Russo, and A. Tencati. 2007. "CSR Strategies of SMEs and Large Firms. Evidence from Italy." *Journal of Business Ethics* 74, no. 3, p. 285.

[39] Gibbs, D. September 2006. "Sustainability Entrepreneurs, Ecopreneurs and the Development of a Sustainable Economy." *Greener Management International* 55, pp. 71–73, 63.

[40] Id. at p. 72 (citing Walley, E., and D. Taylor. 2002. "Opportunists, Champions, Mavericks? A Typology of Green Entrepreneurs." *Greener Management International* 38, p. 31).

- *Innovative opportunists.* Those who identify a green niche for economic exploitation and who are mainly influenced by hard structural factors, such as regulation
- *Visionary champions.* Champions of sustainability who seek to transform the world and whose business is founded on the basis of sustainability
- *Ethical mavericks.* Influenced by soft structural drivers (e.g., past experience, networks, or friends) and a sustainability orientation. These may be alternative-style businesses
- *Ad hoc enviropreneurs.* These are financially driven, but influenced by soft structural drivers. They may be "accidental green entrepreneurs"

The typology suggested by Schaltegger was also based on two dimensions that measured the priority given to environmental issues on the one hand and the projected market effect of the activities on the other hand. The spectrum on the attention to environmental issues dimension ran from "high" to "low," and the spectrum on the market effect of the business spanned from "alternative scene" to "econ-niche" and then to "mass market." Schaltegger was not interested in companies that were founded mainly to engage in environmental management or administration but instead focused companies with environmental goals that were core to their business purpose and strategy. This process led to the identification of three main types of actors, which were described by Gibbs as follows[41]:

- *Alternative actors.* Market goals are not important and the business may exist to support a lifestyle. These may be counter-cultural in type and engage in nonmarket transactions. While the wider impact on environmental improvement is (deliberately) limited, this group may provide a seedbed for the next two types.

---

[41] Id. (citing Schaltegger, S. 2002. "A Framework for Ecopreneurship: Leading Bioneers and Environmental Managers to Ecopreneurship." *Greener Management International* 38, p. 45).

- *Bioneers.* Occupy medium-sized niche markets with customer-focused eco-products. These are often inventors with a strong R&D focus and can be found in high technology sectors, such as alternative energy sources. The markets served are big enough for economic success, but small enough to be neglected by larger suppliers, such that their direct impact is limited.
- *Ecopreneurs.* Actors aim to possess a large market share and to engage with mass markets. These are rarely inventors, but aim "to search for business ideas with products and services that solve environmental problems, to identify the market potential of inventions and to realize market success with them."[42]

Another approach to developing a typology was taken by Linnanen who identified the following four types of ecopreneurs based on high to low measures on two dimensions of internal motivators ("desire to change the world" and "financial drive")[43]:

- *Non-profit business.* High desire to change the world, low financial drive
- *Self-employer.* Low desire to change the world, low financial drive
- *Opportunist.* Low desire to change the world, high financial drive
- *Successful idealist.* High desire to change the world and high financial drive

[42] Schaltegger, S. 2002. "A Framework for Ecopreneurship: Leading Bioneers and Environmental Managers to Ecopreneurship." *Greener Management International* 38, pp. 45–51.
[43] Gibbs, D. September 2006. "Sustainability Entrepreneurs, Ecopreneurs and the Development of a Sustainable Economy." *Greener Management International* 55, pp. 63–72 (citing Linnanen, L. 2002. "An Insider's Experiences with Environmental Entrepreneurship." *Greener Management International* 38, p. 71).

While the typologies were based on different criteria, Gill noted a number of similarities across the models. For example, ethical mavericks are similar to self-employers, opportunists are similar to accidental green entrepreneurs, and successful idealists are similar to visionary champions.[44]

Tilley and Young explained that environmental entrepreneurs are different from economic entrepreneurs in that they "place the principal of environmental protection and/or restoration at the center of their organization" and also noted that Volery has observed that the rationale for environmental responsibility in entrepreneurship is that "there are limits to resources but none to human creativity."[45] Tilley and Young noted that researchers have attempted to distinguish and describe two types of environmental entrepreneurs. The first type was described by Volery as "environment-conscious entrepreneurs" and by Isaak as "green businesses."[46] Environment-conscious entrepreneurs "are aware of the issues but are they do not operate in the environmental marketplace … [and] … more typically follow a business case for their environmental activities by striving for eco-efficiency in the use of resources." Isaak described green businesses as organizations in which entrepreneurs discover and attempt to implement the advantages of environmental innovation or marketing after their businesses have already been launched and established. Tilley and Young noted that examples of this first type of environmental entrepreneurship could be found in all industry sectors and were actually more common than the second type described in the following texts; however,

---

[44] Id. at p. 73.

[45] Tilley, F., and W. Young. 2009. "Sustainability Entrepreneurs—Could they be the True Wealth Generators of the Future?" *Greener Management International* 55, p. 79 (citing Volery, T. 2002. "Ecopreneurship: Rationale, Current Issues and Future Challenges." In *Radical Changes in the World—will SMEs Soar or Crash?* eds. U. Fugistaller, H. Pleitner, T. Volery, and W. Weber. St. Gallen, 541. Switzerland, Rencontres Conferences).

[46] Volery, T. 2002. "Ecopreneurship: Rationale, Current Issues and Future Challenges." In *Radical Changes in the World—will SMEs Soar or Crash?* eds. U. Fugistaller, H. Pleitner, T. Volery, and W. Weber, St. Gallen, Switzerland, Rencontres Conferences; and Isaak, R. 2002. "The Making of Ecopreneurship." *Greener Management International* 38, p. 81.

Tilley and Young argued that this group of environmental entrepreneurs has generally had limited success moving toward sustainability.[47]

The second type of environmental entrepreneur was described by Volery as "green entrepreneurs" and by Isaak as "green-green businesses." Tilley and Young observed that entrepreneurs falling into this type were more radical in their approach and personal value and were not only aware of the environmental issues in the environmental marketplace in which their organizations would be operating but also sought to create new businesses that from the very beginning possessed a potential for economic success (i.e., profitability). As explained by Isaak in describing a green-green business, these types of ecopreneurs have the intention from the very beginning to design products and processes that are "green" and seek not only to make money but also to be environmentally responsible while socially transforming the industrial sector toward a model of sustainable development.[48]

Characteristics of the Ecopreneurship Business Model

Schlange conducted field studies involving 10 start-up firms in Switzerland in order to gain a better understanding of the nature, motivation and drivers of "ecopreneurs" or "green entrepreneurs." He found that the main characteristic of these types of entrepreneurs was a strong emphasis on ecological aspects in their business vision as opposed to the traditional entrepreneurial aspiration to grow and create profits. In addition, the methodology that he designed to select companies to be part of the field studies provided interesting insights into the preferred characteristics for the business models that are most amenable to effective ecopreneurship. Schlange began with the traditional three stage "input-transformation-output" view of the firm and then identified indicators for each stage that reflected not only economics but also the other two dimensions of sustainability (i.e., ecology and social/ethics), a step that he believed was necessary given that "green startups" are different than other entrepreneurial ventures because of their ecological and social–ethical aspects:

- *Economics:* The main indicator for the input stage was procurement, specifically the use of input factors from regional suppliers. The indicators for the transformation stage included persistence (i.e., a clear perspective for long-term development of

---

[47] Tilley, F., and W. Young. 2009. "Sustainability Entrepreneurs—Could they be the True Wealth Generators of the Future?" *Greener Management International* 55, p. 79.

[48] Isaak, R. 1998. *Green Logic: Ecopreneurship, Theory and Ethics.* Sheffield, UK: Greenleaf Publishing; and Isaak, R. 2002. "The Making of Ecopreneurship." *Greener Management International* 38, p. 81.

the company); growth potential (i.e., economic growth objectives that demonstrated an orientation toward investment in innovation); mission (i.e., a clear orientation toward sustainability orientation that had become embedded as an integral part of company's value system); and identification (i.e., all members of the organization shared a common understanding of sustainability objectives). The main indicator for the output stage was cooperation as evidenced by lasting relationships with local and regional partners that supported the company's credibility as an agent of sustainability.

- *Ecology:* The main indicator for the input stage was transport, specifically the use of ecologically sound transport systems. The indicators for the transformation stage included energy (i.e., selection and use of alternative sources of energy and efficient use of energy consumed); residuals (i.e., minimizing resource throughput, avoidance of residual and waste materials); emissions (i.e., minimizing emission levels and exclusivity of toxicity); and production processes (i.e., the methods of production management used by the company are environmentally sound). The main indicator for the output stage was the degree to which the company's products demonstrated that an ecological product life cycle perspective had been adopted during the product development process.

- *Social/Ethics:* The main indicator for the input stage was equality of rights, specifically recruitment and hiring processes that addressed gender and generational issues and provided opportunities for disabled workers. The indicators for the transformation stage included participation (i.e., providing employees and other stakeholder a voice in establishing of business objectives and company support of community activities); personnel (i.e., active development of employee's competences and implementation of fair rewards programs); workplace (i.e., offering safe and hazard-free jobs and health programs for employees); and regional integration (i.e., proactive exchanges with the regional economy and participation/support of local/regional cultural activities). The main indicator for the output stage was communication to stakeholders included honest and transparent reporting about the company's business activities and progress toward sustainability goals.

One of things that stands out the from the framework outlined earlier is the dependence of ecopreneurs on regional actors and the important part that relationships and communications with local and regional parts and other stakeholders plays in assessing the output of the company's business activities. In fact, Schlange argued that the results of his field studies confirmed that ecopreneurs "are social activists who promote and conduct activities which generate social and economic values at the regional level."

Sources: Schlange, L. 2006. "What Drives Sustainable Entrepreneurs?" *ABEAI*, https://researchgate.net/publication/255570580_Topic_area_9_Entrepreneurship_and_Small_Business_Management

Ecological Economics

Related to ecopreneurship is the emerging field of "ecological economics" popularized by Costanza and which Graham described as being focused on the need for economic activities to adapt to changes in environmental conditions and accepts as a goal the improvement of human well-being through economic development that occurs through thoughtful planning for the sustainable development of ecosystems and societies.[49] Ecological economics was actually conceived as being a subfield of ecology: ecology deals with the energy and matter transactions of life and the Earth and the economic activities of human take place within the broader ecological system. The ecological system includes both "natural capital" (i.e., non-renewable resources such as oil, coal, gas, and minerals) and "renewable resources" (i.e., ecosystems that comprise the planet). Ecological economists are concerned with nature's "carrying capacity," which refers to its ability to support human activities, and thus provides a theoretical foundation for sustainable entrepreneurship and its focused on conducting economic activities in a manner that is consistent with the limits and requirements of sustainable development.

The website of the International Society for Ecological Economists (ISEE) (http://isecoeco.org/) includes a list of the fundamental questions and issues that ecological economics seek to address through cross-disciplinary collaboration of economists and ecologists:

- **Modeling**: How can we better integrate economic and ecological models to address management of local biodiversity, an ocean fishery, or the climate services of the global atmosphere?
- **Equity**: How does equity between individual people, nations, and over generations relate to sustainability?
- **Indicators**: Can we redirect development by augmenting traditional indicators such as GDP (gross domestic product) with biophysical indicators such as ecological footprint and social indicators such as the education of women?
- **Limits**: What properties of ecological and social systems act as "limits" to development and to what extent can human-produced capital substitute for natural capital?
- **Trade and Development**: How do current policies to promote development through capital mobility affect the

---

[49] Graham, S. September 16, 2010. *What Is Sustainable Entrepreneurship?* http://ezinearticles.com/?What-Is-Sustainable-Entrepreneurship?&id=5045492

control of natural resources, the ability of nations to manage environmental systems, and the distribution of well-being?

- **Valuation**: To what extent can we measure the value of nonmarket services provided by ecosystems and how can we promote public discourse on environmental and social values that significantly enriches economic measures?
- **Policy Instruments**: How should systems of tradable environmental permits and obligations, combined with environmental tax reform, be implemented?

Measuring Environmental Management Performance

As with any strategic initiative, there needs to be a way to measure performance with respect to any environmental management initiative. Table 3.2 summarizes some environmental management performance measures that have been cited in a selection of studies that were reviewed by Montiel.[50] A variety of metrics have been used include the steps taken to integrate environmental issues into decision making regarding the company's strategies and operations; the scope of environmental policies; and selection and use of various strategies based on environmental management initiatives.

Table 3.2 Examples of environmental management performance measures

Measures	Selected studies
Environmental Management (Corporate Environmental Strategies)	
10 dimensions (practices to reduce impact on animal and natural habitats, voluntary actions for environmental restoration, modification of business practices to reduce wastes and emissions from operations, modification of business practices to reduce purchase of nonrenewable materials, use of reduction of traditional fuels by the substitution of some less polluted energy sources, reduction of energy consumption, reduction of environmental impact of products, reduction of risk of environmental accidents, partnerships to reduce environmental impact, environmental audits)	Sharma and Vredenburg (1998); Chan (2005)

[50] Montiel, I. September 2008. "Corporate Social Responsibility and Corporate Sustainability: Separate Pasts, Common Futures." *Organization and Environment* 21, no. 3, pp. 262–63, 245.

Environmental Issues (Integration Capability)	
Survey items about environmental issues explicitly considered, consideration for the natural environment within the company's mission statement, top management team makes proactive thinking decisions, environmental personnel participate in the company's strategic planning process	Judge and Douglas (1998)
Best Practices in Environmental Management	
8 survey items on cost advantage, use of pollution prevention technologies, innovation of proprietary pollution, and timing of environmental strategies	Christmann (2000)
Eco-Initiatives	
13 environmental policies: policy publication, environmental performance targets, annual environmental report, environmental management system, environmental purchasing, environmental training, environmental responsibilities, life-cycle assessment, sustainable development understanding, fossil fuel use reduction, toxic chemical use reduction, sustainable products use, practices abroad	Ramus and Steger (2000)

Source: Montiel, I. September 2008. "Corporate Social Responsibility and Corporate Sustainability: Separate Pasts, Common Futures," *Organization and Environment* 21, no. 3, pp. 245, 262–63. The article reported the results of the author's extensive survey of the evolution of management literature in both general management and specialized journals with respect to CSR and corporate sustainability (CS). The article quantifies the research work and summarizes the different CSR- and CS-related definitions to identify the definitional differences between CSR and CS. This table, adapted from the article, lists examples of measurement instruments used by scholars to operationalize environmental management in the general management articles reviewed and full citations for the references can be found in the "References" section of the article.

CHAPTER 4

Social Entrepreneurship

Introduction

According to Daft and Marcic, "social entrepreneurship" seeks to launch and build companies that are entirely focused on combining good business with good citizen and the leaders of these companies, the "social entrepreneurs," are primarily interested in improving society rather than maximizing profits while nonetheless demanding high performance standards and accountability for results.[1] Examples of "for profit" social entrepreneurship run the gambit of commercial activities from partnering with traditional banks to offer microloans to small businesses in developing countries to launching manufacturing facilities in poor areas to provide jobs and produce products that can be distributed at no costs to community members to improve their lives. While many of these businesses are not started with the intent to generate significant profits, a number of them have achieved impressive profits margins and market shares. In addition, Tilley and Young observed that

> the concept of social entrepreneur is very broadly interpreted to mean any organization that is operating in a not-for-profit capacity ... [including] ... community-based organizations tackling education, poverty, health, welfare and well-being issues as well as organizations attempting to address environmental concerns relating to renewable energy, waste minimization, pollution abatement and water quality (to name a few).[2]

---

[1] Daft, R., and D. Marcic. 2006. *Understanding Management*, 147–48. 5th ed. Mason, OH: South-Western Publishing Co.

[2] Tilley, F., and W. Young. 2009. "Sustainability Entrepreneurs—Could they be the True Wealth Generators of the Future?" *Greener Management International* 55, p. 79.

Austin et al. defined social entrepreneurship as an "innovative, social value creating business activity that can occur within or across the non-profit, business, or government sectors"[3] and van Eijck observed that the "organizational form is usually based on the most attractive form to gain resources for the social mission."[4] Dees described social entrepreneurs as companies who play the role of change agents in the social sector by adopting a mission to create and sustain value (not just private value); recognizing and relentlessly pursuing new opportunities to serve that mission; engaging in a process of continuous innovation, adaptation, and learning; acting boldly without being limited by resources currently in hand, and exhibiting a heightened sense of accountability to the constituencies served and for the outcomes created.[5]

When writing about social entrepreneurship, some researchers have largely ignored the economic outcomes associated with the entrepreneurial activities while other researchers do acknowledge that economic performance is relevant but cannot be more important than the social goals and objectives.[6] When social entrepreneurship was first recognized it was typically associated with nonprofit organizations; however, as time has gone by, the conceptualization has broadened and even nonprofits have participated in commercial activities to access financial resources for the social activities that would have otherwise been difficult to obtain.[7] Social entrepreneurship can also create competitive advantages similar to those

---

[3] Austin, J., H. Stevenson, and J. Wei-Skillern. 2006. "Social and Commercial Entrepreneurship: Same, Different, or Both?" *Entrepreneurship Theory and Practice* 30, no. 1, pp. 1–2.

[4] van Eijck, P. January 2012. "Sustainable Entrepreneurship: Institutional profile and Cross-Country Comparison Denmark & US and its Viability." Rotterdam: Bachelor Thesis in Entrepreneurship, Strategy and Organizations Economics from Erasmus School of Economics, 7.

[5] Dees, J. 1998. *The Meaning of Social Entrepreneurship.* Stanford: Stanford University Graduate School of Business.

[6] Dacin, P., M. Dacin, and M. Matear. 2010. "Social Entrepreneurship: Why We Don't Need a New Theory and How We Move Forward from Here." *Academy of Management Perspectives* 24, no. 2, p. 36.

[7] Dees, J. 1998. "Enterprising NonProfits." *Harvard Business Review* 76, no. 1, p. 54.

sought by traditional entrepreneurs (e.g., developing and offering innovation solutions to environmental degradation or a social justice problem) that allow social entrepreneurs to enjoy economic returns without impairing or interfering with their social objectives. As such, it is no longer taboo to profit from satisfying humanitarian and ecological needs so long as the profits are reinvested in activities that further the social objectives (e.g., distribute and add value to employment, investments in machines, infrastructure, sponsoring, and labor participation).[8] These elements appear in the definition of sustainable, not social, entrepreneurship offered by Crais and Vereeck: "the continuing commitment by business to behave ethically and contribute to economic development while improving the quality of life of the workforce."[9]

Social entrepreneurship was first investigated in the 1990s and emerged naturally with the popularization of ecopreneurship, no surprise given that it was impossible for ecopreneurs to achieve their goal of "changing the world" and improving the overall quality of life without also acting in a socially responsible fashion.[10] In fact, several of the definitions of ecopreneurship explicitly incorporate a social dimension.[11] However, as opposed to the ecological and environmental issues and problems that ecopreneurs were focusing on, social entrepreneurship gathered

---

[8] van Eijck, P. January 2012. *Sustainable Entrepreneurship: Institutional profile and Cross-Country Comparison Denmark & US and its Viability*, 7–8. Rotterdam: Bachelor Thesis in Entrepreneurship, Strategy and Organizations Economics from Erasmus School of Economics.

[9] Crals, E., and L. Vereeck. 2005. "The Affordability of Sustainable Entrepreneurship Certification for SMEs." *International Journal of Sustainable Development & World Ecology* 12, no. 2, p. 173.

[10] Bell, J., and J. Stellingwerf. 2012. *Sustainable Entrepreneurship: The Motivations & Challenges of Sustainable Entrepreneurs in the Renewable Energy Industry*, 9. Jonkoping, Sweden: Jonkoping International Business School Master Thesis in Business Administration.

[11] Dixon, S., and A. Clifford. 2007. "Managing Ecopreneurship—A New Approach the Triple Bottom Line." *Journal of Organisational Change Management* 20, no. 3, p. 326. See "Ecopreneurship" in "Entrepreneurship: A Library of Resources for Sustainable Entrepreneurs" prepared and distributed by the Sustainable Entrepreneurship Project (www.seproject.org).

speed on the heels of four trends: global wealth disparity; the growth of the corporate social responsibility movement; market, institutional, and state failures; technological advances and shared responsibility.[12]

Lumpkin et al. suggested that both "traditional" and social entrepreneurs have a lot in common and that many entrepreneurial processes used by the two groups remained the same or are affected only slightly.[13] However, while a traditional entrepreneur measures his or her performance primarily through profits and return on investment, social entrepreneurs generally measure success by creating social capital, social change and addressing social needs.[14] These distinctions are important because they influence the opportunities that social entrepreneurs pursue and their behaviors while operating their businesses (i.e., as opposed to traditional entrepreneurs who are comfortable with and must engage in high risk/high reward behaviors, social entrepreneurs, who are not focused on quick economic profits, are more risk averse but no less committed to their goals of social improvement). As is the case with ecopreneurs, social entrepreneurs are not totally indifferent to profits, or at least "breaking even," since capital is necessary in order for their businesses to survive over the often lengthy journeys to the desired social impact. This is no small challenge for social entrepreneurs since they often are involved in activities that address a social-market failure caused by a lack of interest of traditional entrepreneurs due to the belief that there is no viable commercial market that will generate an acceptable level of revenues to justify the investment of capital.[15]

_____

[12] Zahra, S., H. Rawhouser, N. Bhaw, D. Neubaum, and J. Hayton. 2008. "Globalisation of Social Entrepreneurship Opportunities." *Strategic Entrepreneurship Journal* 2, no. 2, p. 117.

[13] Lumpkin, G., T. Moss, D. Gras, S. Kato, and A. Amezua. 2011. "Entrepreneurial Processes in Social Contexts: How are they Different, If at All?" *Small Business Economics* 1.

[14] Bornstein, D. 2004. *How to Change the World: Social Entrepreneurs and the Power of New Ideas*, 15. New York, NY: Oxford University Press.

[15] See Austin, J., H. Stevenson, and J. Wei-Skillern. 2006. "Social and Commercial Entrepreneurship: Same, Different, or Both?" *Entrepreneurship: Theory and Practice* 30, no. 1, pp. 1–2 (stating that the existence of social-purpose organizations emerge when there is a social-market failure, that is, commercial market forces do not meet a social need).

Definitions and Conceptualizations of Social Entrepreneurship

Bell and Stellingwerf provided a variety of different definitions and conceptualizations of social entrepreneurship[16]:

- Profit making is not the primary goal of a social entrepreneur and generated profits from market activities should be used for the benefit of a specific disadvantaged group.[17]
- Profit is less important, and the social aspect should be balanced at least equally to profit, a challenge that has been conceptualized as the "double bottom line" that balances both social (people) and economic (profit) returns on investment.[18]
- Social entrepreneurs "play the role of change agents in the social sector, by adopting a mission to create and sustain social value (not just private value), recognizing and relentlessly pursuing new opportunities to serve that mission, engaging in a process of continuous innovation, adaptation, and learning, acting boldly without being limited by resources currently in hand, and exhibiting heightened accountability to the constituencies served and for the outcomes created."[19]
- Social entrepreneurship "emphasizes innovation and impact, not income, in dealing with social problems" and social entrepreneurs are focused on introducing a novel, innovative technology or approach aimed at creating social impact.[20]

---

[16] Bell, J., and J. Stellingwerf. 2012. *Sustainable Entrepreneurship: The Motivations & Challenges of Sustainable Entrepreneurs in the Renewable Energy Industry*, 10. Jonkoping, Sweden: Jonkoping International Business School Master Thesis in Business Administration.

[17] Leadbeater, C. 1997. *The Rise of the Social Entrepreneur*. London: Demos.

[18] Zahra, S., H. Rawhouser, N. Bhaw, D. Neubaum, and J. Hayton. 2008. "Globalisation of Social Entrepreneurship Opportunities." *Strategic Entrepreneurship Journal* 2, p. 117.

[19] Dees, G. 1998. *The Meaning of Social Entrepreneurship*.

[20] Dees, G. 2003. *New Definitions of Social Entrepreneurship: Free Eye Exams and Wheelchair Drivers*.

- Social Entrepreneurship is "the innovative use and combination of resources to pursue opportunities to catalyze social change and/or address social needs."[21]
- "Social Entrepreneurship encompasses the activities and processes undertaken to discover, define, and exploit opportunities in order to enhance social wealth by creating new ventures or managing existing organizations in an innovative manner."[22]

Like traditional entrepreneurs, social entrepreneurs need to identify and exploit opportunities, create and manage their organizations in innovative ways and, as emphasized by Bell and Stellingwerf, "acquire substantial resources including, human, social, and financial capital to not only accomplish their mission, but also to ensure such resources are sustaining the organization's longevity."[23] This is often quite challenging to social entrepreneurs who often are surprised to find competition that is intense as what is commonplace in the commercial sector. For example, social entrepreneurs must be able to differentiate themselves from other worthy causes and forge and maintain relationships with a number of stakeholder groups including donors, professional employees, volunteers, and the intended beneficiaries of the entrepreneurial initiatives.[24]

Bell and Stellingwerf observed that the obvious similarity between ecopreneurship and social entrepreneurship is that they both incorporate a "double bottom line" within the company's mission: balancing

---

[21] Mair, J., and I. Marti. 2006. "Social Entrepreneurship Research: A Source of Explanation, Prediction, and Delight." *Journal of World Business* 41, no. 1, p. 36.
[22] Zahra, S., E. Gedajlovic, D. Neubaum, and J. Shulman. 2009. "A Typology of Social Entrepreneurs: Motives, Search Processes and Ethical Challenges." *Journal of Business Venturing* 24, no. 5, p. 519.
[23] Bell, J., and J. Stellingwerf. 2012. *Sustainable Entrepreneurship: The Motivations & Challenges of Sustainable Entrepreneurs in the Renewable Energy Industry*, 11. Jonkoping, Sweden: Jonkoping International Business School Master Thesis in Business Administration.
[24] Zahra, S., E. Gedajlovic, D, Neubaum, and J. Shulman. 2009. "A Typology of Social Entrepreneurs: Motives, Search Processes and Ethical Challenges." *Journal of Business Venturing* 24, no. 5, p. 526.

economic returns with other considerations (i.e., environmental or social impact).[25] This observation is consistent with the views of Schaltegger and Wagner, who wrote: "Even though the historic trajectories of these types (Eco—and Social Entrepreneurship) differ, it seems that the underlying motivations for the activities are very similar and this seems to make likely a convergence of these currently rather independent literatures."[26] As discussed in the following texts, the anticipated convergence is often defined and described as "sustainable entrepreneurship" or "sustainability entrepreneurship" and is based on the conceptualization the deployment of entrepreneurial tools and practices to solve either an environmental or societal problem (i.e., recognize market imperfections and/or unmet needs in the realms of ecology or society and address them through the introduction of innovative products, services, and processes) while maintaining a focus on creating economic value—in other words, businesses that use the "triple bottom line" as their guide.[27]

Differentiating Between Commercial and Social Entrepreneurship

Austin et al. surveyed various definitions of social entrepreneurship and observed that they ranged from broad to narrow.[28] Among the broader definitions are those see social entrepreneurship as an

[25] Bell, J., and J. Stellingwerf. 2012. *Sustainable Entrepreneurship: The Motivations & Challenges of Sustainable Entrepreneurs in the Renewable Energy Industry*, 12. Jonkoping, Sweden: Jonkoping International Business School Master Thesis in Business Administration.
[26] Schaltegger, S., and M. Wagner. 2011. "Sustainable Entrepreneurship and Sustainability Innovation: Categories and Interactions." *Business Strategy and the Environment* 20, pp. 222–26.
[27] See Cohen, B., B. Smith, and R. Mitchell. 2008. "Toward a Sustainable Conceptualisation of Dependent Variables in Entrepreneurship Research." *Business Strategy and the Environment* 17, no. 2, p. 107; and Cohen, B., and M. Winn. 2007. "Market Imperfections, Opportunity and Sustainable Entrepreneurship." *Journal of Business Venturing* 22, no. 1, p. 29.
[28] Austin, J., H. Stevenson, and J. Wei-Skillern. 2006. "Social and Commercial Entrepreneurship: Same, Different, or Both?" *Entrepreneurship Theory and Practice* 30, no. 1, p. 1.

innovative activity with a social objective in either the for-profit sector, such as in social-purpose commercial ventures[29] or in corporate social entrepreneurship[30]; or in the nonprofit sector, or across sectors, such as hybrid structural forms which mix for-profit and nonprofit approaches.[31]

A much narrower definition focuses on "applying business expertise and market-based skills in the nonprofit sector such as when nonprofit organizations develop innovative approaches to earn income."[32] Austin et al. noted that the common factor across all the definitions of social entrepreneurship appears to an underlying drive "to create social value, rather than personal and shareholder wealth,"[33] and that the activities of the social entrepreneur could be characterized as innovative (i.e., the creation of something new rather than simply the replication of existing enterprises or practices). For themselves, Austin et al. defined social entrepreneurship as "innovative, social value creating activity that can occur within or across the nonprofit, business, or government sectors."[34]

---

[29] Dees, J., and B. Anderson. 2003. "For-Profit Social Ventures." *International Journal of Entrepreneurship Education Special Issue on Social Entrepreneurship* 2, no. 1, pp. 1–26; and Emerson, J., and F. Twersky, eds. 1996. *New Social Entrepreneurs: The Success, Challenge and Lessons of Non-Profit Enterprise Creation.* San Francisco: Roberts Foundation, Homeless Economic Development Fund.

[30] Austin, J., H. Leonard, E. Reficco, and J. Wei-Skillern. 2004. "Corporate Social Entrepreneurship: A New Vision of CSR." *Harvard Business School.* Working Paper No. 05-021, Boston: Harvard Business School.

[31] Dees, J. 1998. *The Meaning of "Social Entrepreneurship," Comments and Suggestions Contributed from the Social Entrepreneurship Founders Working Group.* Durham, NC: Center for the Advancement of Social Entrepreneurship. Fuqua School of Business, Duke University.

[32] Reis, T. 1999. *Unleashing the New Resources and Entrepreneurship for the Common Good: A Scan, Synthesis and Scenario for Action.* Battle Creek, MI: W.K. Kellogg Foundation; and Thompson, J. 2002. "The World of the Social Entrepreneur." *International Journal of Public Sector Management* 15, no. 5, p. 412.

[33] Zadek, S., and S. Thake. 1997. "Send in the Social Entrepreneurs." *New Statesman* 26, p. 31.

[34] Austin, J., H. Stevenson, and J. Wei-Skillern. 2006. "Social and Commercial Entrepreneurship: Same, Different, or Both?" *Entrepreneurship Theory and Practice* 30, no. 1, p. 1.

As noted earlier, Austin et al., as well as others, acknowledge that social entrepreneurship can be practiced in multiple sectors using different organizational forms and the decision as to form depends, among other things, on the objective of the activity and the optimal strategy for mobilizing the required resources. Austin et al. focused their interest on the nonprofit and business sectors and on differentiating between "commercial entrepreneurs" and "social entrepreneurs" through the examination of four fundamental theoretical propositions:

- *Market failure*: Market failure creates different opportunities for commercial and social entrepreneurs. For example, commercial entrepreneurship may not be a viable option when commercial market forces do not meet a social need (e.g., public goods or situations where the customers needing a product or service are not able to pay). In these situations, social entrepreneurs may see an opportunity where commercial entrepreneurs only see problems in achieving their economic objectives.
- *Mission*: Differences in mission are a fundamental distinguishing factor: "the fundamental purpose of social entrepreneurship is creating social value for the public good, whereas commercial entrepreneurship aims at creating profitable operations resulting in private gain." This is not to say that social entrepreneurs do not seek, or cannot obtain, profits, nor does it mean that products and services created by commercial entrepreneurs do not have some social value. The key point is that differences in mission will likely manifest itself in multiple areas of enterprise management and personnel motivation.
- *Resource mobilization*: Commercial and social entrepreneurs face different challenges with respect to financial and human resource mobilization that causes them to take fundamentally different approaches to managing their financial and human resources. For example, social entrepreneurs are largely restricted in their ability to tap into the same capital markets as commercial entrepreneurs due to the non-distributive

restriction on surpluses generated by nonprofit organizations and the social purposes that are deeply embedded in social enterprises. Social entrepreneurs may also find that their inability to compensate staff as competitively as in commercial markets makes it more difficult to recruit the talent needed in order for the venture to be successful and they must often rely on nonpecuniary compensation that is valued by people interested in working on social causes.

- *Performance measurement*: Difficulties in measuring a social entrepreneur's performance with respect to social impact are a distinguishing factor from commercial entrepreneurship and create complications for social entrepreneurs with respect to accountability and relations with stakeholders. Commercial entrepreneurs, and the stakeholders of such entrepreneurs interested in measuring their performance, have been able to rely on relatively tangible and quantifiable measures of performance such as financial indicators, market share, customer satisfaction, and quality. However, there is far from any consensus on measuring social change due to non-quantifiability, multicausality, temporal dimensions, and perceptive differences of the social impact created. Moreover, social entrepreneurs have a higher number and wider range of stakeholder relationships, thus increasing the time and effort that must be invested in managing those relationships.[35]

Austin et al. cautioned that the propositions were presently primarily to facilitate comparisons and that in reality one can find many social purpose enterprises that are quite similar to their commercial counterparts, particularly when the social purpose enterprise is engaged in operational activities that include development and sale of products and services that both meet a social need and generate revenues needed in order for

---

[35] See also Kanter, R., and D. Summers. 1997. "Doing Well While Doing Good: Dilemmas of Performance Measurement in Nonprofit Organizations and the Need for a Multiple-Constituency Approach." In *The Nonprofit Sector: A Research Handbook*. ed. W. Powell, 154. New Haven: Yale University Press.

the enterprise to remain viable and sustainable and attract financial and human resources. In turn, many commercial enterprises have recognized that there are opportunities for enhancing their economic value by incorporating social purpose into their products, services, and business practices, even if they have not wholly embraced "triple-bottom-line" accounting and reporting.

In order to test their propositions, Austin et al. compared commercial and social entrepreneurship using the "PCDO" analytical framework proposed by Sahlman based on four interrelated elements that are crucial for the management of entrepreneurial activity[36]:

- *People*: This element is defined as those who actively participate in the venture or who bring resources to the venture and includes both those within the organization and those outside the organization who must be involved in order for the venture to be successful.
- *Context*: This element includes relevant factors that are generally outside of the control of the entrepreneur but which be expected to have an impact on his or her activities (e.g., the general economy, taxes and other regulations, and the sociopolitical institutions in the areas in which the entrepreneur intends to operate).
- *Deal*: The term "deal" to refer to the substance of the bargaining among participants in the venture that defines who

[36] Adapted from Austin, J., H. Stevenson, and J. Wei-Skillern. 2006. "Social and Commercial Entrepreneurship: Same, Different, or Both?" *Entrepreneurship Theory and Practice* 30, no. 1, p. 1 (citing Sahlman, W. 1996. "Some Thoughts on Business Plans." In *the Entrepreneurial Venture*, eds. W. Sahlman, H. Stevenson, M. Roberts, and A. Bhide, 138. Boston: Harvard Business School Press); and van Eijck, P. January 2012. *Sustainable Entrepreneurship: Institutional Profile and Cross-Country Comparison Denmark & US and its Viability.* Rotterdam: Bachelor Thesis in Entrepreneurship, Strategy and Organizations Economics from Erasmus School of Economics. For further discussion of the "PCDO" analytical framework, see "Research on Entrepreneurship" in "Entrepreneurship: A Library of Resources for Sustainable Entrepreneurs" prepared and distributed by the Sustainable Entrepreneurship Project (www.seproject.org).

among the participants in a venture gives what, who among the participants in the venture gets what, and how and when those deliveries and receipts will take place.

- *Opportunity*: Austin et al. defined the term "opportunity" as "any activity requiring the investment of scarce resources in hopes of a future return."[37] The entrepreneur must have a vision of a future that is better for him or her and must also be able to develop and implement a credible path to change the current situation to that desired future state.

People and Financial Resources

Austin et al. observed that, in many ways, the human and financial capital inputs essential to the entrepreneurial venture are quite comparable between social and commercial entrepreneurship.[38] The "people" element of the PCDO model includes those actively participate in the venture or who bring resources to the venture and includes both those within the organization and those outside the organization who must be involved in order for the venture to be successful. This element includes not only the personal characteristics of the entrepreneur such as his or her skills, attitudes, contacts, goals, and values, but also the cumulative skills, attitudes, knowledge, contacts, goals, and values of all participants that provide the mix of resources that contribute to the success of the venture. According to Austin et al., "both commercial and social entrepreneurs must consider the managers, employees, funders, and other organizations critical to their success, and how to capture this human talent for their ventures."[39] For social ventures there will be a need for board members, managers,

---

[37] Austin, J., H. Stevenson, and J. Wei-Skillern. 2006. "Social and Commercial Entrepreneurship: Same, Different, or Both?" *Entrepreneurship Theory and Practice* 30, no. 1, pp. 1–5 (citing Sahlman, W. 1996. "Some Thoughts on Business Plans." In *the Entrepreneurial Venture*, eds. W. Sahlman, H. Stevenson, M. Roberts, and A. Bhide, 138–40. Boston: Harvard Business School Press).

[38] Adapted from Austin, J., H. Stevenson, and J. Wei-Skillern. 2006. "Social and Commercial Entrepreneurship: Same, Different, or Both?" *Entrepreneurship Theory and Practice* 30, no. 1, p. 1.

[39] Id.

and staff who believe in the mission and who have the unique skills and talents to help the entrepreneur bring the mission alive. To attract these human resources, social entrepreneurs must have a strong reputation that engenders trust among those who might be willing to work with them, a factor that is all the more important given that the social entrepreneur is asking contributors to invest their time in a cause rather than a commercial business that can be assessed using objective performance measures.

While social entrepreneurs have needs with respect to human resources that are similar to those of commercial entrepreneurs, social entrepreneurs are often unable to offer market rates to potential key hires and are generally not able to offer other incentives such as stock options unless they have elected to organize and operate their ventures using a for-profit organizational form.[40] Because of these limitations, social entrepreneurs must develop different tools for motivating potential participants in the venture. Social entrepreneurs also rely heavily on volunteers to serve in key positions, such as serving on the board of directors, and to carry out important activities such as fundraising, and working with volunteers creates special management issues that need to be understood and addressed by social entrepreneurs. Issues relating to limited financial resources extend outside the organization also and many social entrepreneurs depend on the willingness of professional service providers such as lawyers and accountants to provide their service for free or at heavily reduced rates.

Austin et al. noted that while commercial entrepreneurs, once they have achieved a minimum level of economic success, will generally have access to capital from a range of investors and financial institutions offering a wide array of financing instruments and terms, social entrepreneurs have fewer channels for accessing unrestricted sources of capital and must also rely heavily on a range of funding sources such as individual contributions, foundation grants, member dues, user fees, and government payments. Other unique issues that social entrepreneurs must confront is the need to be continuously engaged in some sort of fundraising activity given that revenues from operations rarely cover all of the costs associated

---

[40] Oster, S. 1995. *Strategic Management for Nonprofit Organizations: Theory and Cases.* New York, NY: Oxford University Press.

with carrying out the organization mission and the lack of flexibility to shift the organization's products or services quickly, as commercial entrepreneurs often do, to take advantage of new funding opportunities since such a transition will typically face opposition from participants who have become emotionally and psychologically invested in focusing on the current need or problem using the existing products and services.

Austin et al. concluded that while commercial and social entrepreneurs have similar needs with respect to human and financial resources,

> social entrepreneurs are often faced with more constraints: limited access to the best talent; fewer financial institutions, instruments, and resources; and scarce unrestricted funding and inherent strategic rigidities, which hinder their ability to mobilize and deploy resources to achieve the organization's ambitious goals.[41]

While social entrepreneurship can be pursued using for-profit organizational forms, such a path creates challenges for social entrepreneurs with respect to maintaining a focus on the social mission while meeting the expectations of investors for economic returns. Austin et al. advised that the constraints on their actions made it imperative for social entrepreneurs "to develop a large network of strong supporters, and an ability to communicate the impact of the venture's work to leverage resources outside organizational boundaries that can enable them to achieve their goals."[42]

Austin et al. also highlighted a specific managerial challenge for social entrepreneurs, namely the need to be able to manage

> a wider diversity of relationships with funders, managers, and staff from a range of backgrounds, volunteers, board members, and other partners, with fewer management levers, as financial

---

[41] Austin, J., H. Stevenson, and J. Wei-Skillern. 2006. "Social and Commercial Entrepreneurship: Same, Different, or Both?" *Entrepreneurship Theory and Practice* 30, no. 1, p. 1.

[42] Id.

incentives are less readily available, and management authority over supporters, volunteer staff, and trustees is rather limited.[43]

In addition, social entrepreneurs must become adept at working collaboratively with other social entrepreneurs, for-profit businesses and governmental units to gain access to critical resources that the social entrepreneur cannot build and maintain on his or her own. For example, social entrepreneurs will need to be able to work with outside for-profit vendors to develop information systems for communicating with members, volunteers, and funders, and will need to have skills required to forge and maintain successful strategic alliances with corporate and governmental partners.[44] Finally, Austin et al. suggested that it was important for social entrepreneurs to proactively participate in professional and sector-wide knowledge sharing networks in order to broaden their own skills and remained connected to ideas and talent available through other sector participants.

Austin et al. argued that social entrepreneurs needed to develop and remain intensely focused on their specific social value principal derived from scanning the context for opportunities and the availability of the human and financial resources necessary to achieve the greatest social impact.[45] They cautioned social entrepreneurs about the dangers of becoming too obsessed on organizational aspects of their mission. Austin et al. noted that if social entrepreneurs will naturally assume that the bigger the organization becomes, and the more resources it has at its disposal, the more effective it will be at creating social impact; however, many social entrepreneurs veer off track when furthering the organization becomes an end in and of itself. Similar problems arise when social entrepreneurs are tempted to expand their mission beyond available resources. Austin et al. pointed out that societal demand for social-value creation is enormous and social entrepreneurs will have more opportunities than they can possible handle. As such, they need to pay careful attention to

---

[43] Id.

[44] Austin, J. 2000. *The Collaboration Challenge: How Nonprofits and Business Succeed Through Strategic Alliances.* San Francisco: Jossey-Bass Publishers.

[45] Id.

the scope of the opportunity that they can pursue effectively given the constraints on human and financial resources applicable to them. Austin et al. also admonished social entrepreneurs to be open to working with complementary organizations outside of their own venture's organizational boundaries to create social value and engage in networking activities with stakeholders in the relevant context to identify methods for collaborating with others in order to leverage resources that are outside of the social entrepreneur's own organizational boundaries.

Context

The external context for entrepreneurship includes factors that are relevant to the conduct and outcome of the entrepreneurial activities but which are generally outside of the control of the entrepreneur. Examples include the general economy, taxes and other regulations, and the sociopolitical institutions in the areas in which the entrepreneur intends to operate. Specific contextual factors identified by Austin et al. included economic environment, tax policies, employment levels, technological advances, and social movements such as those involving labor, religion, and politics. All of these factors are important to both commercial and social entrepreneurs and all of them need to understand that context frames the opportunities and risks for every new venture and that they need to determine which factors must be consciously addressed from a strategic perspective and which are best left to play out as they will since the entrepreneur has limited time and ability to attend to everything that might have an impact on the venture.

A substantial amount of research has been conducted on the relationship between context and entrepreneurship generally and context and social entrepreneurship specifically. For example, Meek et al. and Kerlin have argued that the incidence of environmental and social entrepreneurship in a given region or country is influenced by the broader institutional context (i.e., social norms and government incentives) and dominant socioeconomic factors.[46] Schick et al. contend that the most

---

[46] Meek, W., D. Pacheco, and J. York. 2010. "The Impact of Social Norms on Entrepreneurial Action: Evidence from the Environmental Entrepreneurship

crucial factors relating to the success of ecopreneurial start-ups are the entrepreneur and the local culture.[47] In their model for sustainability entrepreneurship, O'Neill et al. argued that various contextual factors materially influence the sustainability entrepreneurship process including regulatory, sociocultural, place, macroeconomic, political, demographics, tax, and environment.[48]

Austin et al. explained the particular influence of various contextual factors on social entrepreneurs.[49] For example, the philanthropic market that provides capital to social entrepreneurs is highly affected by economic activity: the philanthropic activities of for-profit organizations depend on the commercial success of their products and services, many nonprofit endowment funds are invested in stock markets and the peaks and valleys of those market impact the amounts that funds are comfortable donating to social entrepreneurs and charitable contributions by individuals depend on their feelings about their level of discretionary income. As for laws and regulations, Austin et al. stressed that social entrepreneurship will be impacted by laws regulating the tax-exempt status or operations of nonprofits, tax policies that influence the amount of giving to the sector in which the social entrepreneur is operating, and specific political and social policies that affect the needs or resources available for certain types of issues most commonly addressed by social entrepreneurs (i.e., education, environment, health, and housing). In addition, social entrepreneurs must be able to compete with other organizations in their own "industry" contexts for scarce resources needed in order to their ventures

---

Context." *Journal of Business Venturing [e-journal]* 25, no. 5, p. 493; and Kerlin, J. 2010. "A Comparative Analysis of the Global Emergence of Social Enterprise." *VOLUNTAS: International Journal of Voluntary and Nonprofit Organizations [e-journal]* 21, no. 2, p. 162.

[47] Schick, H., S. Marxen, and J. Freimann. 2002. "Sustainability Issues for Start-Up Entrepreneurs." *Greener Management International [e-journal]* 38, p. 56.

[48] O'Neill, G., J. Hershauer, and J. Golden. 2009. "The Cultural Context of Sustainability Entrepreneurship." *Greener Management International [e-journal]* 55, p. 33.

[49] Adapted from Austin, J., H. Stevenson, and J. Wei-Skillern. 2006. "Social and Commercial Entrepreneurship: Same, Different, or Both?" *Entrepreneurship Theory and Practice* 30, no. 1, p. 1.

to be viable (e.g., philanthropic dollars, government grants and contracts, managerial talent, volunteers, community mindshare, political attention, and clients or customers).

Austin et al. argued that while the critical contextual factors are analogous in many ways, the impact of the context on a social entrepreneur differs from that of a commercial entrepreneur because of the way the interaction of a social venture's mission and performance measurement systems influences entrepreneurial behavior. One difference cited by Austin et al. was the social entrepreneurs can, in many instances, achieve some degree of success with respect to their primary goal of social impact even in circumstances where the context would otherwise be inhospitable for commercial entrepreneurs. For example, an economic downturn will generally make it difficult for commercial entrepreneurs to accumulate resources and identify viable economic markets; however, tough economic times intensify social needs and create opportunities for social entrepreneurs to take steps to meet those needs. Social entrepreneurs can also make an impact with relatively small constituencies initially and then build on those successes to change the overall context by raising awareness and attention to a social issue and messaging about how they have been able to develop solutions that can be scaled with greater participation from others willing to join the movement. Another factor mentioned by Austin et al. was that while the social marketplace does not reward entrepreneurs for superior performance as readily as commercial entrepreneurs are recognized in their marketplace, the marketplace for social entrepreneurship is more patient and is slow to punish inferior performance, perhaps because supporters of social entrepreneurs are most focused on their social mission and not as interested in emphasizing the same level of accountability and performance that is rigorously measured for commercial ventures.[50]

Austin et al. cautioned, however, that while the impact of contextual factors on social entrepreneurship is often ambiguous, perhaps causing social entrepreneurs to pay less attention to their operating context, they nonetheless should be doing appropriate monitoring of their context for opportunities and threats in order to develop an adaptive strategy that

---

[50] Letts, C., A. Grossman, and W. Ryan. 1999. *High Performance Nonprofit Organizations: Managing Upstream for Greater Impact.* New York, NY: Wiley.

takes into account various contingencies.[51] One obvious illustration of how monitoring can be important to a social entrepreneur is when it provides information about changes in direction and focus of philanthropic capital markets that can be used to identify useful new programs, fundraising strategies, and potential alliances.

"Deal"

Austin et al. used the term "deal" to refer to the substance of the bargain that defines who among the participants in a venture gives what, who among the participants in the venture gets what, and how and when those deliveries and receipts will take place.[52] The deal emerges from a bargaining process that normally addresses topics such as economic benefits, social recognition, autonomy and decisions rights, satisfaction of deep personal needs, social interactions, fulfillment of generative and legacy desires, and delivery on altruistic goals.[53] Both commercial and social entrepreneurs need to engage in negotiations to create mutually beneficial contractual relationships (i.e., "deals") with investors to gain access to financial resources and with potential participants with the skills and talent required in order for the venture to achieve its goals, whether economic or social. However, according to Austin et al. the terms of these deals are fundamentally different for commercial and social entrepreneurs due to the way in which resources must be mobilized and because of the ambiguities associated with performance measurement. Austin et al. explained specific differences with respect to so-called "value transactions" in the following areas[54]:

---

[51] Austin, J., H. Stevenson, and J. Wei-Skillern. 2006. "Social and Commercial Entrepreneurship: Same, Different, or Both?" *Entrepreneurship Theory and Practice* 30, no. 1, p. 1.

[52] Adapted from Austin, J., H. Stevenson, and J. Wei-Skillern. 2006. "*Social and Commercial Entrepreneurship: Same, Different, or Both?*" *Entrepreneurship Theory and Practice*, 30. no. 1, p. 1.

[53] Martin, R., and S. Osberg. Spring 2007. "Social Entrepreneurship: The Case for Definition." *Stanford Social Innovation Review* 28.

[54] Adapted from Austin, J., H. Stevenson, and J. Wei-Skillern. 2006. "Social and Commercial Entrepreneurship: Same, Different, or Both?" *Entrepreneurship Theory and Practice* 30, no. 1, p. 1.

- Given the relative dearth of financial awards and incentives available to social entrepreneurs, they must rely more heavily on creative strategies that emphasize nonfinancial incentives in order to recruit, retain, and motivate staff, volunteers, members, and funders.
- While commercial entrepreneurs are used to dealing with consumers with bargaining power, including the ability to switch their buying activities to competitors of the entrepreneur, social entrepreneurs are generally working with consumer with little or no economic capability and few alternatives for obtaining and consuming the products and services available from the social entrepreneur. While this certainly impacts the nature of the "deal" with consumers for social entrepreneurs, it does not mean that they operate without a market since they often must bargain with third-party payers and other sources of subsidy working on behalf of the ultimate consumers.
- While commercial entrepreneurs have a wider range of financial deals to consider and generally can strike bargains with investors and other sources of financing that provide them with more flexibility and time to put the funds to good use, social entrepreneurs work with investors that provide capital that covers only a small portion of the needs of the venture and which will typically be exhausted with a short period of time.[55] As a result, according to Austin et al., "social entrepreneurs are thus required to spend a significant portion of their time, on an ongoing basis, cobbling together numerous grants, many of which come with spending restrictions and varied expectations of accountability, just to meet day-to-day operating costs."
- Striking a bargain with investors is complicated by the absence of an objective measure of performance similar to the economic returns and valuation metrics used in structuring

---

[55] Letts, C., A. Grossman, and W. Ryan. 1999. *High Performance Nonprofit Organizations: Managing Upstream for Greater Impact.* New York, NY: Wiley.

deals for commercial ventures. Since the goal of social entrepreneurship is to have social impact, and the quantification or
precise measurement of social impact is complicated, Austin
et al. counseled social entrepreneurs to focus on, and be able
to explain, their mission, theory of change and the process
by which their social innovations will eventually have a social
impact and generate superior social returns.

Austin et al. commented that social entrepreneurs face different challenge from their counterparts in the commercial sector when negotiating
the terms of the deal with social investors and other looking to participate in the mission of the social entrepreneur. Philanthropic funders
and volunteers are less interested in the economic returns and incentives
offered by commercial entrepreneurs and instead bring a different set of
personal motivations and requirements that must be acknowledged and
satisfied by social entrepreneurs. For example, a donor may want a position on the board of directors, impose restriction on the use of the funds
provided by the donor and/or require that the social entrepreneur provide reports on the use of the funds and the progress of the organization
toward achieving the projected social impact. The goals and requirements
of various donors may sometimes be conflicting, add obligations to an
already full agenda for the social entrepreneur and limit the social entrepreneur's flexibility in allocating resources to reach organizational goals.
All this led Austin et al. to observe that "negotiating deals between the
social entrepreneur and various resource providers that create alignment
between goals and incentives is considerably more complex and challenging in social than in commercial entrepreneurship."[56]

Opportunity

An entrepreneur sees an opportunity as a desired future state that is different from the present and which he or she believes is possible to achieve.

---

[56] Austin, J., H. Stevenson, and J. Wei-Skillern. 2006, "Social and Commercial Entrepreneurship: Same, Different, or Both?" *Entrepreneurship Theory and
Practice* 30, no. 1, p. 1.

In order to exploit an opportunity in either the commercial or social sector, there must be an investment of scarce resources in hopes of a future return. In general, both commercial and social entrepreneurs are concerned about customers, suppliers, entry barriers, substitutes, rivalry, and the economics of the venture; however, Austin et al. emphasized that a key difference between them is that commercial entrepreneurship focuses on economic returns while social entrepreneurship focuses on social returns.[57] Austin et al. observed that "change" is generally difficult and it is challenging for both commercial and social entrepreneurs to bring followers together to agree on a common definition of opportunity and change that can be shared and used as motivation for joint action by the multiple constituencies that must work together in order to create change. For example, change usually impacts power relationships, economic interests, personal networks, and even the self-image of participants.

In addition, the opportunities pursued by the two types of entrepreneurs vary due to fundamental difference in missions and response to market failure. According to Austin et al., commercial entrepreneurship tends to focus on breakthroughs and new needs, whereas social entrepreneurship often focuses on serving basic, long-standing needs more effectively through innovative approaches, often when there has been some type of market failure that has caused commercial entrepreneurs to abandon attempts to service the need. Austin et al. explained that commercial entrepreneurs are only interested in opportunities that involve a large, or growing total market size and the industry must be structurally attractive; however, social entrepreneurs are less concerned about market size so long as there is a recognized social need, demand, or market failure.

Austin et al. observed that while commercial entrepreneurs often find it challenging to identify and capture opportunities that are unexploited, profitable, and high-growth, social entrepreneurs usually have little problem finding unmet social needs or demands, particularly since they can either finance their activities through revenues generated from operations or, if necessary, turn to donors to provide capital in the event that the

---

[57] Adapted from Austin, J., H. Stevenson, and J. Wei-Skillern. 2006. "Social and Commercial Entrepreneurship: Same, Different, or Both?" *Entrepreneurship Theory and Practice* 30, no. 1, p. 1.

activity is not financial sustainable on its own (e.g., if the ultimate consumers are not able to cover enough of the costs of the goods or services for the social entrepreneur to "break even"). While having so many opportunities would seem to be an advantage for a social entrepreneur, Austin et al. cautioned that the breadth and intensity of the needs among the consumers often propels social entrepreneurs into unexpected and rapid growth caused by pressures from funders, demand for their products or services, and the social entrepreneur's own conviction that growth is necessary in order for the organization to achieve the desired social impact.[58]

While growth due to acceptance in the marketplace fulfills the personal needs of social entrepreneurs and builds upon their values, such situations may lead to a crisis for the social entrepreneur if expansion comes before he or she has had a change to make plans on how to manage the pace of growth. Austin et al. advised that social entrepreneurs need to realize that they have great latitude in the paths that they can choose to pursue their chosen opportunities and that there may be times when growth is not the best approach to take in order to achieve the goals of the organization or have greatest social impact. Lack of financial resources is obviously one reason for not pursuing rapid growth; however, social entrepreneurs must also make a candid assessment of their organizational capacities with respect to human resources and the impact that growth might have on the quality of products and services the organization offers.

If growth is the preferred approach, the social entrepreneur must plan for a long-term growth strategy and avoid actions that needlessly squander the limited resources of the organization. Social entrepreneurs also need to recognize that while they might be intrigued by scaling the organization directly, the more prudent approach is often partnering with other organizations to work together to disseminate social innovation. While commercial entrepreneurs do partner with others in alliances to tap into needed resources, they are often reluctant to do so out of concern for losing control over their innovations and/or diluting their profits and

---

[58] Id. (citing Bradach, J. 2003. "Going to Scale." *Stanford Social Innovation Review* 1, p. 18; Colby, S., N. Stone, and P. Carttar. 2004. "Zeroing in on Impact." *Stanford Social Innovation Review* 2, no. 2, p. 24; and Anderson, D.B., and J. Wei-Skillern. 2004. "Scaling Social Impact." *Stanford Social Innovation Review* 1, no. 4, pp. 24–32).

market share. These concerns are not relevant to social entrepreneurs who should be primarily interested in bring their innovations to the largest consumer group possible. For example, a social entrepreneur may consciously limit the scope of products and services that his or her organization offers directly while partnering with other organizations that offer complimentary products and services and working with those partners to make it easy for the ultimate consumers to have all of their needs addressed seamlessly and efficiently.

Social Enterprises

Berge discussed the concept of a "social enterprise" including the following description: "A social enterprise's primary objective is to ameliorate social problems through a financially sustainable business model, where surpluses (if any) are principally reinvested for that purpose."[59] According to Fury, the elements of a "social enterprise" include a primary social purpose, a financially sustainable business model, and a mechanism for ensuring accountability and transparency.[60] Bergh further explained that social enterprises balance "mission" and "market" and their goals include the creation of not only economic value but also social and/or environmental value. Social enterprises are looking to perpetuate resources rather than accumulating excess profits and any profits that are derived from the activities of the enterprise are to be reinvested in the business as operational expenses or used for mission activities and/or retained for business growth and development.[61]

---

[59] Bergh, L. July 2013. *Sustainability-Driven Entrepreneurship: Perceptions of Challenges and Obstacles in a South African Context*, 6. Cambridge UK: Master Thesis for MS in Sustainability Leadership (citing Steinman, S. 2010. "An Exploratory Study into Factors Influencing an Enabling Environment for Social Enterprises in South Africa." *International Labour Organisation*).

[60] Fury, B. 2010. *Social Enterprise Development in South Africa—Creating a Virtuous Circle*. Tshikululu Social Investments.

[61] Bergh, L. July 2013. *Sustainability-Driven Entrepreneurship: Perceptions of Challenges and Obstacles in a South African Context*, 6. Cambridge UK: Master Thesis for MS in Sustainability Leadership (citing Parrish, B. 2010. "Sustainability-Driven Entrepreneurship: Principles of Organization Design." *Journal of Business Venturing [e-journal]* 25, no. 5, p. 510).

Qualities of Sustainable Enterprises

Wirtenberg et al. analyzed the sustainability initiatives at nine large, public, multinational companies that had been recognized as being among the world leaders in "sustainability," a process which included assessing how those companies handled environmental, governance, social responsibility, stakeholder management, and work environment issues. Their research allowed them to identify seven distinguishing qualities that they believed were associated with achieving "triple-bottom-line corporate sustainability" and which were also amenable to managerial intervention. These qualities included deeply ingrained values relating to sustainability, strategic positioning, senior management support, systems alignment (i.e., structures and processes around sustainability), metrics, holistic integration across functions, and stakeholder engagement. They then organized these qualities into a three level "pyramid" that they used as a representation of an organization's sustainability journey.

The bottom level of the pyramid, referred to as the "foundation," included three fundamental drivers of a successful journey to sustainable management. The first driver was corporate values consistent with sustainability which were deeply ingrained in the organizational "DNA," typically embedded by the founders. The second driver was visible support for sustainability from top management, which often took the form of members of the executive team asserting their personal and positional influence about the importance of sustainability and their personal involvement in setting the priorities as well as making important strategic decisions that affected the sustainability of the company. Top management support was important to creating an organizational culture in which extensive inquiry and self-examination was encouraged and welcome at all levels of the organizational hierarchy. Top management should evoke a long-term perspective for the company and seek to take steps that ensure the success and strength of the company for future generations. The third driver at the foundational level was placing sustainability as central to the company's business strategy, which an executive from one of the companies explained as: "For us sustainability is business. This is business stuff, it's not something that sits outside." The companies recognized that that performance was inextricably linked to caring for communities, environment, and society and developed business strategies that simultaneously took into account all stakeholders, as well as the short—and long-term view.

The second level of the pyramid, referred to as "traction," focused on executing top management decisions regarding sustainability values and strategy and included the development of sustainability metrics ("we manage what we measure") and alignment of formal and informal organization systems around sustainability. Metrics should be included in the business plans that are created during the planning stage for sustainability initiatives so that they are embedded from the very beginning, not imposed at some later date, and can be referenced when aligning the company's structures and systems to its sustainability goals. The measurement of key performance indicators relating to sustainability should be accompanied by disclosure and reporting to the company's stakeholders. Reporting obligations add rigor to the assessment and allow companies to transparently demonstrate the values and initiatives driving its sustainability program. Reporting also makes companies more accountable.

The third and top level of the pyramid, referred to as "integration," called for broad stakeholder engagement and holistic integration, which was explained as an elusive state in which all "the many facets and functional domains of sustainability were conceptualized and coordinated in an integrative fashion." Wirtenberg et al. noted that even the companies they had studied, all of which had demonstrated exemplary progress with respect to implementing sustainability strategies, "seemed to be struggling with reaching this cross-boundary, multistakeholder, integrative pinnacle." They explained that holistic integration occurs when companies are able to bring multifaceted activities under a clearly understood, unified umbrella of sustainability, which means aligning a variety of key enterprise functions around sustainability such as supply chain management, marketing and sales, accounting and finance, public relations, environment, and health and safety. An executive at one of the companies suggested that holistic integration extended beyond internal activities to include connectivity with the broader industrial ecosystem in which a firm resides.

Sources: The discussion in this section is adapted from Wirtenberg, J., J. Harmon, W. Russell, and K. Fairfield. 2007. "HR's Role in Building a Sustainable Enterprise: Insights from Some of the World's Best Companies." *Human Resource Planning* 30, no. 1, p. 10. The companies included Alcoa, Bank of America, BASF, The Coca Cola Company, Eastman Kodak, Intel, Novartis AG, Royal Philips and Unilever. For discussion of the roles of HR leaders and the contributions of the HR functions, see "Human Resources: A Library of Resources for Sustainable Entrepreneurs" prepared and distributed by the Sustainable Entrepreneurship Project (www.seproject.org). Wirtenberg et al. recommended several books on sustainability and the triple bottom line including Savitz, A., and K. Weber. 2006. *The Triple Bottom Line.* San Francisco: Jossey-Bass; Esty, D., and A. Winston. 2006. *Green to Gold.* New Haven, CT: Press by Esty Winston; and Hitchcock, D., and M. Willard. 2006. *The Business Guide to Sustainability.* London: Earthscan.

Measuring Social Impact

Several dimensions should be considered when measuring the social impact of entrepreneurial activities: the type of impact on persons and organizations, which can include outputs or outcomes (e.g., incomes, treatment of works, community, and environment); the scale of impact, which takes into account the number of people or organizations affected; and the depth of impact, which includes the amount or intensity of positive change in well-being subjectively experienced by the affected people or organizations. These dimensions can be combined to create an overall measure of social impact that incorporates the sum of the positive changes to well-being for all types of impact experienced by all affected people and organizations.[62]

LDC (http://ldc.co.uk), a private equity firm based in UK and part of the Lloyds Banking Group, suggested a technical framework for

---

[62] Adapted from McCreless, M., and B. Trelstad. Fall 2012. "A GPS for Social Impact." *Stanford Social Innovation Review* 10, no. 4, p. 21.

assessing the social value of the activities of a business that included three components:

- *Business-Level Benefits*: Business-level benefits include the social value that a business creates through its own employment, investment, and procurement activities. Direct benefits include scaling and growth of the company's business and turnover. Indirect benefits include the impact that the company's business has on other businesses through its supply chains. Finally, induced benefits include the impacts of the company's workforce spending on other local firm's goods and services (i.e., multiplier effects).
- *Wider Economic Benefits*: Wider economic benefits include the social value that a business creates through its job and business impacts on the rest of the national/regional/local economy. These include sector-specific, shared business benefits arising from spatial proximity (i.e., "cluster" growth) and shared business benefits for all sectors arising from higher critical mass of demand for infrastructure.
- *Community Benefits*: Community benefits include the shared social value that businesses contribute to by participating in partnerships working with local communities to develop solutions to their challenges and needs. Specific community projects include education, learning and skills development; employment and training; health and healthy lifestyle; personal and social well-being; arts, culture, and recreation; and climate change and environmental conservation.

Sustainability Entrepreneurship

Abrahamsson proposed the following definition of "sustainopreneurship":

To use creative business organizing to solve problems related to the sustainability agenda, to create social and environmental sustainability as a strategic objective and purpose, at the same time respecting the boundaries set in order to maintain the life support systems in the process.[63]

The definition builds on the goals of ecopreneurship and social entrepreneurship by explicitly suggesting and integrating the use of for-profit organizational practices (i.e., "creative business organizing") into activities focused on identifying and solving sustainability-related problems. Bergh described sustainability entrepreneurship as the cross-fertilization of entrepreneurship and sustainable development to create a process in which sustainable entrepreneurs act as promotors and organizers of a multistakeholder and multi-innovation process that fosters the implementation of sustainable development.[64] According to Shepherd and Patzelt, sustainability entrepreneurship is

the preservation of nature, life support, and community in the pursuit of perceived opportunities to bring into existence future products, processes, and services for gain, where gain is broadly construed to include economic and noneconomic gains to individuals, the economy, and society.[65]

O'Neill et al. defined sustainability entrepreneurship as "a process of venture creation that links the activities of entrepreneurs to the emergence

---

[63] Abrahamsson, A. June 2007. "Researching Sustainopreneurship—Conditions, Concepts, Approaches, Arenas and Questions." 10–12. Paper Presented at the 13th International Sustainable Development Research Conference, Mälardalens Högskola, Västerås, Sweden.

[64] Bergh, L. July 2013. *Sustainability-Driven Entrepreneurship: Perceptions of Challenges and Obstacles in a South African Context*, 6. Cambridge UK: Master Thesis for MS in Sustainability Leadership (citing Gerlach, A. 2003. "Sustainable Entrepreneurship and Innovation." In *Centre for Sustainability Management*. University of Lueneburg, Conference for Corporate Social Responsibility and Environmental Management, Leeds, UK).

[65] Shepherd, D., and H. Patzelt. 2011. "The New Field of Sustainable Entrepreneurship: Studying Entrepreneurial Action Linking 'What is to be Sustained' With 'What is to be Developed.'" *Entrepreneurship Theory and Practice [e-journal]* 35, no. 1, p. 137.

of value-creating enterprises that contribute to the sustainable development of the social-ecological system."[66]

Rey described a "sustainability entrepreneur" as "an entrepreneur with the mind-frame to solve an exact, particular sustainability problem."[67] It is assumed that sustainability entrepreneurs are interested in generating profits from their activities. However, while they are exploring opportunities involving sustainable products, this does not guarantee that they will do so by practicing sustainable methods throughout the organization or that they will integrate the social and environmental impact of their business practices alongside economic results when assessing the performance of their companies. For example, Rey illustrated the difference between sustainability entrepreneurship and his conceptualization of sustainable entrepreneurship by discussing a hypothetical company that was developing a solar-powered smartphone for profit. While the commercial goal of that company is to develop and commercialize a sustainable product, absent a universal commitment to sustainability throughout its business practices it is conceivable that the company might ignore abusive labor practices in its supply chain in order to reduce costs and maximize profits from sales of its sustainable product. Similarly, the company might waste limited resources when selecting the materials for its product and/or use materials that will cause ecological harm when discarded at the end of the product's lifecycle. Rey summed up the distinction as follows: "one can say that sustainable entrepreneurship sees the focus on the internal processes and everything surrounding the outputs of a business, while sustainability entrepreneurship focuses on opportunity fulfillment in the market."[68]

---

[66] O'Neill, G., J. Hershauer, and J. Golden. 2009. "The Cultural Context of Sustainability Entrepreneurship." *Greener Management International [e-journal]* 55, p. 33.

[67] Rey, L. December 2011. *Sustainable Entrepreneurship and its Viability*, 13. Rotterdam: Master Thesis for MS in Entrepreneurship, Strategy and Organizations Economics from Erasmus School of Economics.

[68] Id. at p. 14.

CHAPTER 5

Corporate Sustainability

Introduction

Dyllick and Hockerts observed that consideration and debate regarding sustainability in the 21st century has involved integrating long-standing concerns about economic growth and social equity with concern for the carrying capacity of natural systems.[1] In their words, sustainability "embodies the promise of societal evolution toward a more equitable and wealthy world in which the natural environment and our cultural achievements are preserved for generations to come." Simply put, problems relating to economic growth, social equity, and the environment must be addressed and solved simultaneously.[2] Emerging from all this has been the drive for "sustainable development" that has led to international treaties relating to the protection of bio-diversity and climate change and governmental programs focusing on national and local sustainability. In addition, sustainable development has been adopted at the firm level as companies have accepted "corporate sustainability" as a precondition for doing business, integrated sustainability into their governance structures by appointing corporate sustainability officers, published sustainability reports, and incorporated sustainability into their communication strategies.[3] However, while Dyllick and Hockerts were encouraged that companies and their managers were accepting responsibility for the environmental and social impacts of their actions, they argued that most companies had opted for "eco-efficiency" as their guiding principle for

---

[1] Dyllick, T., and K. Hockerts. March 2002. "Beyond the Business Case for Corporate Sustainability." *Business Strategy and the Environment* 11, p. 130.

[2] Keating. M. 1993. *The Earth Summit's Agenda for Change*. Geneva: Centre for Our Common Future.

[3] Dyllick. T., and K. Hockerts. March 2002. "Beyond the Business Case for Corporate Sustainability." *Business Strategy and the Environment* 11, no. 2, pp. 130–31.

sustainability and that as a sole concept this was insufficient and needed to be broadened to include other corporate sustainability criteria included in the framework described as follows.

Reasons Why Businesses Aren't More Sustainable

Laughland and Bansal described "business sustainability" as follows:

> Business sustainability is often defined as managing the triple bottom line—a process by which firms manage their financial, social, and environmental risks, obligations and opportunities. We extend this definition to capture more than just accounting for environmental and social impacts. Sustainable businesses are resilient, and they create economic value, healthy ecosystems and strong communities. These businesses survive external shocks because they are intimately connected to healthy economic, social and environmental systems.

They went on to argue that while the firms that invested in sustainability were no worse off financially than those that chose not to, many companies remained hesitant about joining the sustainability bandwagon. Building on questionnaires from, and interviews with, 15 Canadian organizations that were on the leading edge of sustainability as of 2011, Laughland and Bansal identified and explained the following 10 top reasons why Canadian firms were reluctant to take action on social and environmental issues:

- *There are too many metrics that claim to measure sustainability—and they're too confusing.* Many suites of metrics and measurement systems—such as the Global Reporting Initiative, ecological footprint, and life-cycle assessment—currently exist to help managers measure their sustainability; however, the range of options often seems to create more problems than solutions. Some metrics are relevant to particular sectors, such as manufacturing, while others focus on specific issues, products, or organizations. Businesses need more guidance on which metrics will help them benchmark, identify areas for improvement, and signal their commitment to sustainability.
- *Government policies need to incent outcomes and be more clearly connected to sustainability.* Governments have several tools at their disposal, such as taxes, regulations, and markets, to encourage businesses to steward environmental resources; however, they are often applied in piecemeal fashion, poorly measured, or used ineffectively. Businesses need to be more involved in the process so that governmental policies are effective, efficient, and consistent.
- *Consumers do not consistently factor sustainability into their purchase decisions.* Clearly many decisions that consumers make—from what food to buy to how much energy to use—involve explicit or implicit sustainability-related tradeoffs. In order for businesses to develop and implement smart strategies for sustainability while achieving their economic objectives, they need to understand how consumers value sustainability in the context of other product attributes.
- *Companies do not know how best to motivate employees to undertake sustainability initiatives.* While surveys indicate that employees prefer working for sustainable firms, even foregoing higher salaries, companies need to have a better understanding of which employee incentive plans are most valued, and so likely to be effective. Employees that buy-in to sustainability can assist companies in building the capacities necessary for pursuing sustainability goals of a long-term time horizon including recruiting other talented candidates to join the company.

- **Sustainability still does not fit neatly into the business case.** Sustainability managers are often called upon to explain and defend sustainability activities, particularly since traditional methods of financial decision-making do not fully capture the value of sustainability-related investments that are often based on long-term and intangible rewards. Sustainability managers need better tools for measuring and explaining returns on sustainability investments and demonstrating the value of sustainability within the decision-making language and framework of finance executives.

- **Companies have difficulty discriminating between the most important opportunities and threats on the horizon.** Sustainability encompasses a wide range of threats and risks for businesses—financial crises, climate change, local land issues, and health pandemics—and companies need help with deciding which risks warrant their attention and how to prioritize them for disclosure purposes and strategic planning.

- **Organizations have trouble communicating their good deeds credibly, and avoid being perceived as "greenwashing."** Claims made by some businesses and NGOs regarding sustainability are perceived to be credible, whereas others are met with skepticism or disbelief. The different reactions are likely related to attributes of the organization making the claims—its size, its structure, its actions, or its motivations—and sustainability managers need to have a better understanding of who best to communicate their message credibly and in a way in which the integrity of their efforts is clear.

- **Better guidelines are needed for engaging key stakeholders, such as aboriginal communities.** For the Canadian companies included in the survey relations with aboriginal communities are an important consideration. The experience of businesses have been both positive and negative and all businesses can benefit from developing a more robust understanding of the aboriginal perspective on sustainability in order to build a relationship between businesses and aboriginal community that is based on mutual respect and trust and leads to positive engagement.

- **There is no common set of rules for sourcing sustainably.** While businesses want to purchase products and services that are environmentally and socially responsible, the process of identifying sustainable suppliers is not always straightforward and the means for comparing products is not always obvious. Sustainable sourcing decisions may also require industry-specific knowledge and practices, or data that just may not be available. Organizations need a set of best practices for sustainable sourcing which provide organizations with targets for benchmarking as well as guidance on managing their supply chains.

- **Those companies that try leading the sustainability frontier often end up losing.** While leadership in the sustainability field can be quite rewarding for organizations—new customers and loyalty from employees and community stakeholders—taking the steps needed for sustainability leadership can also be risky. Organizations need to do their homework before introducing new sustainability targets and investing in technologies and ideas that may never yield the expected results and may be appropriated by a second-mover who builds on the leader's ideas to leapfrog into the lead. Leadership and innovation with respect to sustainability also carries the risk that early failures will cause internal stakeholders to become disenchanted and shift their priorities elsewhere.

Source: Laughland, P., and T. Bansal. January/February 2011. "The Top Ten Reasons Why Businesses Aren't More Sustainable." *Ivey Business Journal*, http://iveybusinessjournal.com/publication/the-top-ten-reasons-why-businesses-arent-more-sustainable/ [accessed July 30, 2017]. The organizations included BC Hydro, Canadian Pacific, Environment Canada, Holcim Canada Ltd., the International Institute for Sustainable Development, Industry Canada, The Pembina Institute, Research In Motion Limited, SAP Canada Inc., Suncor Energy Inc., TD Bank Group, Teck, Telus, Tembec, and Unilever Canada Inc.

Definition and Elements of Corporate Sustainability

According to Montiel, interest in corporate sustainability surged after the United Nations World Economic and Development Commission popularized the term "sustainable development" in its famous 1987 "Brundtland Report" and researchers began to adapt the concept to companies by declaring that they could pursue sustainability by meeting their present needs without compromising the ability of future generations to meet their own needs.[4] During the 1990s academics and practitioners began to argue that corporate sustainability required simultaneous attention to, and satisfaction of, environmental, social, and economic standards.[5] Dyllick and Hockerts suggested that when the fundamental principles of sustainable development are translated to the firm level, it leads to defining corporate sustainability as "meeting the needs of a firm's direct and indirect stakeholders (such as shareholders, employees, clients, pressure groups, communities, etc.), without compromising its ability to meet the needs of future stakeholders as well."[6] Dyllick and Hockerts explained that in order to achieve and maintain corporate sustainability, companies must be able to growth their economic, social, and environmental capital basis while also actively contributing to sustainability in the political domain. They went on to identify what they felt to be the three key elements of corporate sustainability[7]:

---

[4] Montiel, I. September 2008. "Corporate Social Responsibility and Corporate Sustainability: Separate Pasts, Common Features." *Organization and Environment* 21, no. 3, pp. 245–54 (citing UN World Commission on Environment and Development. 1987. *Our Common Future*, 43. Oxford, UK: Oxford University Press).

[5] Id. For further discussion, see Bansal, P. 2005. "Evolving Sustainably: A Longitudinal Study of Corporate Sustainable Development." *Strategic Management Journal* 26, no. 3, p. 197; and Gladwin, T., and J. Kennelly. 1995. "Shifting Paradigms for Sustainable Development: Implications for Management Theory and Research." *Academy of Management Review* 20, no. 4, p. 874.

[6] Dyllick, T., and K. Hockerts. March 2002. "Beyond the Business Case for Corporate Sustainability." *Business Strategy and the Environment* 11, pp. 130–31.

[7] Id. at p. 132.

- *Integrating the economic, ecological, and social aspects in a "triple-bottom line"*: Economic sustainability alone is not a sufficient condition for the overall sustainability of a company and while companies can enjoy short-term success by focusing only on economic growth they must ultimately learn how to satisfy and balance all three dimensions of the "triple-bottom-line" simultaneously, a difficult task given the complex inter-relationships among them.

- *Integrating the short-term and long-term aspects*: Many companies, large and small, have responded to the demands of their investors by over-emphasizing short-term profits, a strategy that is at odds with the spirit of sustainability and its elevation of the future needs of stakeholders to the same level as their present desires. In addition, emphasis on discounted rates of return tend to value short-term gains and minimize the costs associated with social or environmental degradation that will be incurred farther out in time as a result of the firm's current activities.

- *Consuming the income and not the capital*: Management and maintenance of economic capital has been a long-standing tenet of long-term sustainability for businesses and the fiduciary responsibility of corporate directors and managers; however, corporate sustainability requires that companies not only manage the economic capital, but also their natural and social capital stocks.

Some Sustainability Myths

New Zealand Trade and Enterprise identified and explained some of the myths about integrating sustainability with business:

Sustainability is about being an environmental activist or about philanthropy and I can't afford to give away all the profit of my business. While philanthropy can be an important and effective component of the sustainability puzzle, it is just one piece and focusing too much on philanthropy can lead to ineffective business programs that fail to achieve very dramatic benefits for the community or the company.

The sustainable option is going to be more expensive than the alternatives. It is true that certain environmental policies, such as investing in renewable energy, can be expensive, many responsible business decisions and activities actually cost little or nothing and even larger investments will ultimately pay for themselves through substantial and ongoing cost savings. Focusing on employee engagement and satisfaction, customer service and community involvement are all examples of sustainability programs that usually require surprisingly small amounts of cash and other resources. In addition, simple programs aimed at reducing overall consumption of energy and other natural resources (e.g., green commuting options and recycling) can generate savings without impairing productivity.

Sustainability is about re-cycling materials, therefore other than installing recycling bins into our offices, sustainability doesn't affect my business. Recycling is part of the sustainability puzzle; however, all companies, including those not engaged in manufacturing of products which can be recycled or which do not use recyclable materials in their operations, can find other areas to implement sustainability: employee engagement; suppliers and supply chain management; operational efficiency; resource consumption and waste; packaging and facility design; volunteerism; governance; ethics and customer service.

If we use green-colored packaging and the words "eco" or "organic" in our product, then we can sell our product as being "green." Many companies have appeared to underestimate their customer's critical thinking skills and ability to smell "Greenwash." They understand that just because products come in recycled packaging or are marketed with the latest buzzwords does not make those products, or the company itself, any more environmentally or socially responsible.

We are already doing as much as we can in our company, but it is not making a difference to sales. Customers have a limited amount of time and resources to research and understand sustainability initiatives can companies need to proactively market and thoughtfully explain their legitimate initiatives so that customers and other stakeholders understand how the business and products of the company are adding value.

Sustainability seems so complex and hard to measure, how can we hope to manage it? In order to manage anything, including sustainability, you need to measure it; however, many managers have complained that it is just too difficult and costly to measure environmental and social impact. Fortunately, a number of tools have been developed to help even the smallest businesses measure sustainability, often by applying relatively simple processes and habits. It will remain difficult to compare the value of one type of sustainability impact, such as reducing pollution, with another, such as providing educational opportunities to members of the local community; however, improvements in specifically identified dimensions can be tracked.

Source: Sustainable Business: A Handbook for Starting a Business (New Zealand Trade and Enterprise).

Table 5.1 *Corporate sustainability-related definitions*

References	Definitions
Gladwin and Kennelly (1995)	Sustainable Development. Process of achieving human development in an inclusive, connected, equitable, prudent, and secure manner. Sustainable development components are 1. Inclusiveness (environmental and human systems, near and far, present and future); 2. Connectivity (world's problems interconnected and interdependent); 3. Equity (fair distribution of resources and property rights); 4. Prudence (duties of care and prevention); 5. Security (safety from chronic threats) (p. 878).

Shrivastava (1995a)	Ecological Sustainability. It can be achieved through four different mechanisms: 1. Total quality environmental management; 2. Ecological sustainable competitive strategies; 3. Technology for nature swaps; 4. Corporate population impact control.
Starik and Rands (1995)	Ecological Sustainability. Ability of one or more entities, either individually or collectively, to exist and flourish (either unchanged or in evolved forms) for lengthy timeframes, in such a manner that the existence and flourishing of other collectivities of entities is permitted at related levels and in related systems (p. 909).
Banerjee (2003)	Sustainable Development. States that the Brundtland definition is not really a definition but a slogan. Emphasizes that sustainable development is managed through ethnocentric, capitalistic notions of managerial efficiency (sustainable capitalism).
Sharma and Henriques (2005)	Corporate Sustainability. Refers to Brundtland definition: development that meets the needs of the present without compromising the ability for future generations to meet their own needs.
Bansal (2005)	Corporate Sustainable Development (CSD). Introduces the new CSD construct based on three principles: 1. Economic integrity; 2. Social equity; 3. Environmental integrity (p. 198).

Source: Montiel, I. September 2008. "Corporate Social Responsibility and Corporate Sustainability: Separate Pasts, Common Futures." *Organization and Environment* 21, no. 3, pp. 245–56. The article reported the results of the author's extensive survey of the evolution of management literature in both general management and specialized journals with respect to CSR and corporate sustainability (CS). The article quantifies the research work and summarizes the different CSR- and CS-related definitions to identify the definitional differences between CSR and CS. This table, adapted from the article, lists different CS definitions used in the general management articles reviewed and full citations for the references can be found in the "References" section of the article.

Corporate Sustainability and Corporate Social Responsibility

Corporate sustainability and corporate social responsibility (CSR) have become popular concepts over the last two decades. Like sustainability generally, researchers and commentators have suggested a variety of definitions for CSR.[8] One of the simplest descriptions of CSR is actions taken by a company to further some social good which is outside of the company's immediate interests yet required by law. Some have focused on CSR as a strategic tool that increases the competitiveness of the company

[8] For further discussion of corporate social responsibility, see "Corporate Social Responsibility: A Library of Resources for Sustainable Entrepreneurs" prepared and distributed by the Sustainable Entrepreneurship Project (www.seproject.org).

and strengthens the company's reputation, each of which ultimately contributes to improved company performance. As noted earlier, definitions of corporate sustainability tend to incorporate the dimensions of the "triple-bottom-line" and conceptualize corporate sustainability as the long-term maintenance of responsibility from economic, environmental, and social perspectives. The consensus is that both CSR and corporate sustainability are based on attempting to operate businesses in a more humane, ethical, and transparent way[9]; however, there is an important distinction: CSR is generally seen as being a voluntary action in and of itself or as part of the company's CSR strategy while corporate sustainability is an organizational practice that is integrated into the entire business and business strategy of the company. This is important to understand because integrating sustainability into organizational practices is a time-consuming process that is heavily influenced by the organization's history, people, interests, and action. The specific organizational practices that are related to sustainability are those that are implemented in order to reduce the adverse environmental and social impacts of the company's business and operations.

Whether a company's actions can be characterized as CSR or corporate sustainability depends on the specific forces driving the company to consider and adopt sustainability practices. As mentioned earlier, companies often take their first steps with respect to CSR out of a sense that they are required to do something in order to comply with laws and regulations. In other words, the companies are "made to do it."[10] Companies may also feel "obligated" to adopt CSR if they believe that doing so would serve their long-term interests, improve their image, and fulfill the expectations of stakeholders such as employees, customers, and members of the communities in which the company operates. In contrast, corporate

---

[9] Marrewijk, M. May 2003. "Concepts and Definitions of CSR and Corporate Sustainability: Between Agency and Communion." *Journal of Business Ethics* 44, no. 2, p. 95.

[10] Marrewijk, M. May 2003. "Concepts and Definitions of CSR and Corporate Sustainability: Between Agency and Communion." *Journal of Business Ethics* 44, no. 2, p. 95 (organizations engage in corporate sustainable practices because they are "made to do it, want to do it or feel obligated to do it").

sustainability is embraced not because it is a legal duty or competitive obligation, but because the members of organization, beginning with the founders, generally "want to do it." The formal and informal institutions in the company's environment, which vary from country-to-country, provide the legal, social, and cultural context for its decisions regarding sustainability practices. Regulative institutions promulgate laws, set rules, and establish sanctions that companies must comply with in order to continue operating lawfully. However, companies must also be mindful of normative and cultural-cognitive institutions that shape the standards and values of social life and shared conceptions of how members of society should treat one another and the world in which they live.

Montiel noted that during the 1970s some CSR researchers concentrated entirely on social issues without considering environmental issues and others failed to include an economic responsibility dimension; however, beginning with Carroll's conceptualization of corporate social performance (CSP) in 1979 most scholars recognized that both CSR and CSP included economic, social, and environmental aspects.[11] With respect to corporate sustainability, Montiel found that his literature review revealed two very different constructs regarding the conceptualization of corporate sustainability. On one hand, several researchers identified sustainability with the environmental responsibility dimension of business, often using the term "ecological sustainability." At the same time, however, other scholars considered corporate sustainability from a "triple bottom line" perspective, describing the three dimensions of economic responsibility, social equity, and environmental integrity. Montiel pointed out that while the CSR and corporate sustainability constructs had similar conceptualizations of economic, social, and environmental

---

[11] Montiel, I. September 2008. "Corporate Social Responsibility and Corporate Sustainability: Separate Pasts, Common Futures." *Organization and Environment* 21, no. 3, pp. 257–63, 245 (includes detailed discussion of points of difference and overlap between CSR and corporate sustainability). In 1979, Carroll wrote: "the social responsibility of business encompasses the economic, legal, ethical, and discretionary expectations that society has of organizations at a given point in time." See Carroll, A.B. 1979. "A Three-Dimensional Conceptual Model of Corporate Performance." *Academy of Management Review* 4, no. 4, pp. 497–500.

dimensions, researchers tended to ask different questions about them. For example, corporate sustainability scholars tended to argue that the economic, social, and environmental pillars are interconnected; however, most of the empirical research on CSR and CSP treated social and economic performance as independent components. Montiel, referring to corporate sustainability as "CS," concluded:

> Current research seems to show that, because of their shared environmental and social concerns, CSR and CS are converging, despite their paradigmatic differences. In CSR, environmental issues are a subset of a broader social performance dimensions. In the CS field, the social dimension has become an increasingly important part of the sustainability paradigm. Contemporary businesses must address economic prosperity, social equity, and environmental integrity before they can lay claim to socially responsible behavior or sustainable practices. Indeed, the conceptualization of CSR that integrates economic, social, and environmental dimensions and the triple bottom line conceptualization of CS, which comprises economic, social, and environmental dimensions, are very similar. Both show that firms must balance the three elements of the triple bottom line to achieve long-term sustainability and social responsibility. Both CSR and CS aim to balance economic prosperity, social integrity, and environmental responsibility, regardless of whether they conceptualize environmental issues as a subset of social issues or as the third element of sustainability.[12]

A 2017 article in *The Economist* described "sustainability" in the corporate context as follows:

> The term "sustainability" is often used interchangeably with CSR or viewed exclusively through an environmental lens. Thought leaders, however, generally describe it as a business strategy that

---

[12] Id. at p. 260.

creates long-term stakeholder value by addressing social, economic, and environmental opportunities and risks material to a company. It is integral to a company's business and culture, rather than on the periphery. Optimizing waste reduction, or water or energy consumption, for example, can help a company reduce operational costs. Sustainability can drive innovation by reconceiving products and services for low-income consumers, opening new lines of business and boosting revenue in the process. Finally, being socially responsible can help a company earn license to operate in new markets, and attract and retain talent.[13]

Types of Capital Associated with Corporate Sustainability

As mentioned earlier, the pursuit of corporate sustainability requires companies to accept a much broader interpretation of capital than has traditionally been applied by economists. Dyllick and Hockerts explained that consideration needs to be given to three types of capital—economic, natural, and social—and that each of these types has different properties and thus require different approaches[14]:

- *Economic capital*: Companies have traditionally used fairly simply valuation and calculation methods for tracking income, fixed capital, and current operating capital; however, companies can no longer rely on those methods in a world in which they must manage several types of capital including financial capital (i.e., equity and debt), tangible capital (i.e., machinery, land, and stocks) and intangible capital (i.e., intellectual and organizational capital such as reputation, inventions and know-how and organizational routines).

---

[13] Cramer-Montes, J. March 24, 2017. "Sustainability: A New Path to Corporate and NGO Collaborations." *The Economist*, http://economist.com/node/10491124

[14] Dyllick, T., and K. Hockerts. March 2002. "Beyond the Business Case for Corporate Sustainability." *Business Strategy and the Environment* 11, pp. 132–34, 130.

Realizing that the main goal with respect to economic capital is enabling the company to pay its bills as they come due and continue to attract additional capital from investors in order to pursue the company's mission and strategic goals, Dyllick and Hockerts proposed that the definition of "corporate economic sustainability" should read as follows: "*Economically sustainable companies* guarantee at any time cash flow sufficient to ensure liquidity while producing a persistent above average return to their shareholders."[15]

- *Natural capital*: Dyllick and Hockerts noted that the concept of ecological sustainability is based on argument that the Earth has a finite amount of "natural capital" which cannot go on.[16] One type of natural capital is the natural resources that are consumed during the course of many different economic processes and which are either renewable (e.g., wood, fish, corn) or nonrenewable (e.g., fossil fuel, biodiversity, soil quality). A second type of natural capital is ecosystem services (e.g., climate stabilization, water purification, soil remediation, and reproduction of plants and animals), many of which have no known substitute or substitutes that are only available at a prohibitive price. Dyllick and Hockerts suggested the following definition for "corporate ecological sustainability":

Ecologically sustainable companies use only natural resources that are consumed at a rate below the natural reproduction, or at a rate below the development of substitutes. They do not cause emissions that accumulate in the environment at a rate beyond the capacity of the natural system to absorb and assimilate these emissions. Finally they do not engage in activity that degrades eco-system services.[17]

---

[15] Id. at p. 133.
[16] Lovins, A., L. Lovins, and P. Hawken. 1999. "A Road Map for Natural Capitalism." *Harvard Business Review* 77, no. 3, pp. 145–46.
[17] Dyllick, T., and K. Hockerts. March 2002. "Beyond the Business Case for Corporate Sustainability." *Business Strategy and the Environment* 11, pp. 130–33.

- *Social capital*: Dyllick and Hockerts identified two different types of social capital: human (i.e., the skills, motivation, and loyalty of employees and business partners) and societal (i.e., the quality of public services, such as a good educational system, infrastructure, or a culture supportive of entrepreneurship). Companies that maintain and strengthen social capital are socially sustainable enterprises, which Gladwin et al. described as firms that internalize social costs, maintain, and grow the capital stock; avoid exceeding the social carrying capacities and encourage structures for self-renewal; foster democracy; enlarge the range of people's choices and distribute resources and property rights fairly.[18] Accomplishing all of the aforementioned is often difficult given that firms cannot always meet the expectations of all stakeholder groups simultaneously and this means that firms must be able to communicate the reasons for decisions that may disappoint some stakeholders so that the firm is perceived by all stakeholders as being fair and trustworthy.[19] Dyllick and Hockerts combined the principles mentioned earlier to define "corporate social sustainability" as follows:

Socially sustainable companies add value to the communities within which they operate by increasing the human capital of individual partners as well as furthering the societal capital of these communities. They manage social capital in such a way that stakeholders can understand its motivations and can broadly agree with the company's value system.[20]

---

[18] Gladwin, T., J. Kennelly, and T. Krause. 1995. "Beyond Ecoefficiency: Towards Socially Sustainable Business." *Sustainable Development* 3, no. 1, pp. 35–42.

[19] Kaptein, M., and J. Wempe. 2001. "Sustainability Management, Balancing Conflicting Economic, Environmental, and Social Corporate Responsibilities." *Journal of Corporate Citizenship* 1, no. 2, p. 91; and Zadek, S., P. Pruzan, and R. Evans. 1997. *Building Corporate AccountAbility—Emerging Practices in Social and Ethical Accounting, Auditing and Reporting*, 13. London: Earthscan.

[20] Dyllick, T., and K. Hockerts. March 2002. "Beyond the Business Case for Corporate Sustainability." *Business Strategy and the Environment* 11, pp. 130–34.

Dyllick and Hockerts noted that natural and social capital differed from traditional notions of economic capital in several important ways. For example, they explained that while "traditional economic theory assumes that all input factors of production can be translated into monetary units, implying that they can also be substituted completely," the reality is that not all kinds of natural capital can be substituted by economic capital.[21] While technological innovations may come along that permit substitution of some natural resources, substitution of ecosystem services (e.g., the protections of the ozone layer) is unlikely. With respect to social capital, offering higher wages or more financial benefits cannot overcome stakeholder disaffection when it reaches a critical point. As for the societal capital necessary for productive economic activity, there is arguably no real substitutes for a healthy and educated workforce and an adequate infrastructure. Dyllick and Hockerts also noted that other issues such as the irreversibility and nonlinearity of natural and social capital deterioration. As illustrations they pointed to irreversible soil erosion around the world, the shocking reduction in the number of indigenous languages that are still spoken in parts of the world that have been overrun by colonial intrusions and the sudden and complete collapse of ecosystems once toxins or pollutants reach a certain level.[22]

The Three Cases For Corporate Sustainability

Dyllick and Hockerts observed that as sustainability became a more mainstream concept for businesses, the main focus of corporate leaders and academics was on the "business case" for sustainable development, which involved demonstrating how companies could further economic sustainability by increasing their ecological and social efficiency. Dyllick and Hockerts argued that the business case for corporate sustainability, while an important step forward, was not sufficient for companies to become truly sustainable and that it was necessary for companies to address two

---

[21] Id. (citing Maler, K. May 1990. "Sustainable Development." In *Sustainable Development: Science and Policy*, 8–26. Conference Report Bergen: NAVF: and Daly, H. 1991. *Steady-State Economics*, 20, 2nd ed. Washington, DC: Island).

[22] Id. at p. 135.

more cases: the "natural case," which requires companies to deal with the reality that they can never be sustainable if they are continuously operating close to (or even beyond) the environment's "carrying capacity"; and the "societal case," which is important because companies harness, manage, and preserve three types of capital that are not substitutable.[23]

Dyllick and Hockerts explained that companies typically begin their path toward corporate sustainability by looking for ways to make more efficient uses of their natural and social capital as a means for increasing their economic sustainability—in other words, a "business case" for sustainability. With respect to the use of natural capital, this generally means taking steps toward better "eco-efficiency," which

> is achieved by the delivery of competitively-priced goods and services that satisfy human needs and bring quality of life, while progressively reducing ecological impacts and resource intensity throughout the life-cycle to a level at least in line with the earth's carrying capacity.[24]

The most common indicators of eco-efficiency include energy, water and resource efficiency and waste or pollution intensity.[25] While eco-efficiency is often the guiding principle for the sustainable development contributions of companies, many also pursue socio-efficiency, which focuses on the relationship between a company's "value added" and its social impact.[26] Socio-efficiency involves both increasing positive social

---

[23] Id. at pp. 135–36.

[24] DeSimone, L., and F. Popoff. 1997. *Eco-Efficiency: the Business Link to Sustainable Development*, 47. Cambridge: MIT Press.

[25] Verfaille, H., and R. Bidwell. 2000. *Measuring Eco-Efficiency, a Guide to Reporting Company Performance*. Geneva: World Business Council for Sustainable Development; and von Weizsacker, E.U., A. Lovins, and H. Lovins. 1997. *Factor Four—Doubling Wealth, Halving Resource Use*. London: Earthscan.

[26] See, for example, Figge, F., and T. Hahn. 2001. "Sustainable Value Added—Measuring Corporate Contributions to Sustainability." In *Conference Proceedings on the 2001 Business Strategy and the Environment Conference in Leeds*, 83. Shipley: ERP Environment; Hockerts, K. 1996. *The Sustainability Radar (STAR*), A Step Towards Corporate Sustainability Accounting—A Discussion Paper*. London: New

impacts (e.g., corporate giving and creation of employment) and decreasing negative social impacts (e.g., reducing the amount of work accidents per value added and eliminating human rights abuses in the supply chain).[27]

Young and Tilley argued that socio-efficiency was analogous to corporate social responsibility (CSR), which they defined using the description offered by Holmes and Watts: "Continuing commitment by business to behave ethically and contribute to economic development while improving the quality of life of the workforce and their families as well as of the local community and society at large."[28] Young and Tilley cited with approval Michael's skepticism of the benefits of CSR:

> The adoption of social objectives by companies is not as new as the "corporate social responsibility" label suggests. Instead, it touches the 80-year debate between capitalism and socialism. The vague and all-encompassing CSR discourse serves as a forum for advocating the interests of business, government, and relatively non-accountable NGOs ... Yet, while the actors most loudly advocating CSR may benefit, society as a whole may be harmed.

Young and Tilley recommended that businesses must move beyond CSR to achieve socio-effectiveness, which is described in the following texts and can be found among organizations that have a social mission and a sustained positive impact on society.[29]

Economics Foundation; and Hockerts, K. 1999. "The Sustainability Radar–A Tool for the Innovation of Sustainable Products and Services." *Greener Management International* 25, p. 29.

[27] Dyllick, T., and K. Hockerts. March 2002. "Beyond the Business Case for Corporate Sustainability." *Business Strategy and the Environment* 11, pp. 130–36.

[28] Young, W., and F. Tilley. 2006. "Can Businesses Move Beyond Efficiency? The Shift Towards Effectiveness and Equity in the Corporate Sustainability Debate." *Business Strategy and the Environment,* 15, pp. 402–05 (citing Michael, B. 2003. "Corporate Social Responsibility in International Development: An Overview and Critique." *Corporate Social Responsibility and Environmental Management* 10, no. 3, p. 115).

[29] Id. at p. 405 (citing Michael, B. 2003. "Corporate Social Responsibility in International Development: an Overview and Critique." *Corporate Social Responsibility and Environmental Management* 10, no. 3, pp. 115–26).

The natural case for corporate sustainability is built on the premise that while eco-efficiency is valuable and important, it only leads to relative improvements (i.e., increased energy or resource efficiency per value added) and does not address the key sustainability challenge of absolute thresholds caused by the problem of nonsubstitutability. For example, it is well and good for companies to reduce their emissions of pollutants; however, if the reduced emissions are released into a system that is already close to its carrying capacity then the overall objective of sustainability is in danger regardless of how eco-efficient companies become. Dyllick and Hockerts argued that "from an environmental point of view, the main issue is therefore not eco-efficiency but eco-effectiveness."[30] Braungart and McDonough described and used the term "eco-effectiveness" as follows:

> Long-term prosperity depends not on the efficiency of a fundamentally destructive system, but on the effectiveness of processes designed to be healthy and renewable in the first place. Eco-effectiveness celebrates the abundance and fecundity of natural systems, and structures itself around goals that target 100 percent sustaining solutions.[31]

Dyllick and Hockerts explained how the pursuit of eco-efficiency is often at odds with eco-effectiveness. The cited the example of how many automobile manufacturers have deployed new technologies to develop more efficient vehicles, with the ultimate goal being to reduce the cost of driving a car to the point where more consumers can afford to purchase and use a vehicle for their individual mobility needs. While this may make life easier for large numbers of people, increasing the number of cars and miles driven each year around the globe will drive up mobility-induced

---

[30] Dyllick, T., and K. Hockerts. March 2002. "Beyond the Business Case for Corporate Sustainability." *Business Strategy and the Environment* 11, pp. 130–36.
[31] MBCD. November 2001. Eco-Effectiveness—Nature's Design Patterns. See also Braungart, M. 1994. "Ein Wirtschaftssystem f ¨ ur 'intelligente Produkte' anstatt einer High-Tech Abfallwirtschaft." In *Kreislaufwirtschaft statt Abfallwirtschaft* 45, eds. K. Hockerts et al. Kreislaufwirtschaft statt Abfallwirtschaft, 45. Ulm: Universit¨atsverlag, and Braungart, M., and W. McDonough. 1998. "The Next Industrial Revolution." *The Atlantic Monthly October* 282, no. 4, p. 82.

CO_2 emissions dramatically and exacerbate what has already been widely acknowledged as a dramatic ecological crisis. Dyllick and Hockerts suggested that the answer is to shift attention away from fossil fuel efficiency and focus on developing and implementing effective solar powered fuel cells as the means for powering vehicles.[32] Note also that the same logic applies to investments in public transit: while more efficient buses with expanded routes and underwritten by public funds arguably takes individual cars off the road, public transit solutions must also be eco-effective (i.e., buses should incorporate solar power fuel technologies).

Young and Tilley were also critical of the long-term utility of eco-efficiency and observed that "eco-efficiency is not in itself the panacea as some have presented it to business" and noted the conclusions of others that while eco-efficiency might be a valuable criterion by which to guide and measure corporate sustainability it was not on its own a sufficient guiding framework for business.[33] Concerns regarding too much emphasis on eco-efficiency included the criticism that it encouraged businesses to take advantage of eco-efficiency gains by highlighting the low hanging fruit and seeking easy gains that required limited investment.[34] Young and Tilley noted encouraging businesses to take actions that involved short payment or nonexistent reengineering simply hid the environmental problems that presented the most significant challenges. They argued that eco-efficiency simply made a "destructive system less destructive" and merely slowed what was still a seemingly inevitable destruction of ecosystems and contamination and depletion of nature. For them, and

---

[32] Dyllick, T., and K. Hockerts. March 2002. "Beyond the Business Case for Corporate Sustainability." *Business Strategy and the Environment*, 11, pp. 130–37.
[33] Young, W., and F. Tilley. 2006. "Can Businesses Move Beyond Efficiency? The Shift Towards Effectiveness and Equity in the Corporate Sustainability Debate." *Business Strategy and the Environment* 15, pp. 402–04, 403 (citing Day, R. 1998. "Beyond Eco-Efficiency: Sustainability as a Driver for Innovation, Sustainable Enterprise Perspectives." *Sustainable Enterprises Perspectives*. Washington DC: World Resources Institute); and Welford, R. 1997. *Hijacking Environmentalism: Corporate Responses to Sustainable Development*. Environmentalism: Corporate Responses to Sustainable Development London: Earthscan.
[34] Walley, N., and B. Whitehead. 1994. "It's Not Easy Being Green." *Harvard Business Review* 72, no, 3, p. 46.

others, the real answer for businesses was "eco-effectiveness": businesses needed to follow regenerative, not depletive, practices in order to remove negative impacts and develop systems to restore and enhance the natural environment. Simply put, businesses should move beyond eco-efficiency's "less bad" to embrace a new goal of "more good" by implementing new practices such as replacing the conventional cradle-to-grave approach to product design, development, and analysis with a renewing cycle of cradle-to-cradle analysis.[35]

Dyllick and Hockerts also argued that eco-effectiveness (i.e., developing and producing eco-effective products and services) is not the only criterion that needs to be considered when making the natural case for sustainability. They point out that the impact of efficiency gains depends on consumer choice and the decisions that consumers make regarding the products and services they prefer to consume. For example, even as automobile manufacturers were beginning to make progress toward developing and commercializing fuel efficient vehicles, consumers in the United States and other developed countries were demanding sport utility vehicles, or "SUVs," that were notorious "gas guzzlers." In many cases, the demand was stoked by the marketing practices of the manufacturers. Realizing that consumption preferences and patterns are important drivers of sustainability, Dyllick and Hockerts and others have included "sufficiency" as a second criterion in the natural case for corporate sustainability.[36] Hockerts explained that:

---

[35] Young, W., and F. Tilley. 2006. "Can Businesses Move Beyond Efficiency? The Shift Towards Effectiveness and Equity in the Corporate Sustainability Debate." *Business Strategy and the Environment* 15, pp. 404–05, 402. See also Ellison, H. April 12, 2001. "From Eco-Efficiency to Eco-Effectiveness." *International Herald Tribune.*

[36] Dyllick, T., and K. Hockerts. March 2002. "Beyond the Business Case for Corporate Sustainability." *Business Strategy and the Environment* 11, pp. 130–37 (citing, for example, Schumacher, E. 1974. *Small is Beautiful.* London: Abacus); Gladwin, T., J. Kennelly, and T. Krause. 1995. "Shifting Paradigms for Sustainable Development: Implications for Management Theory and Research." *Academy of Management Review* 20, no. 4, p. 874; Diekmann, J. 1999. "Ökologischer Strukturwandel also vergessene Komponente des Ressourcenverbrauchs, Zwischen Effizienz und Suffizienz." Ökologisches Wirtschaften, O. no. 3, p. 25;

... sufficiency is primarily a criterion for sustainable consumerism, the business world has at least an indirect responsibility. Marketing and corporate advertisements have an increasing influence on consumer trends and life-style developments. Rather than fueling the demand for more unsustainable products, firms might try to channel demand toward less problematic areas.[37]

However, Dyllick and Hockerts acknowledged that sufficiency is also an issue of individual choice rather than the sole responsibility of a particular firm. In other words, the case for sufficiency has to be made by members of society, perhaps by sending a strong message to businesses about the types of products and services they should be developing and promoting in order to achieve the greater environmental good.

The last of the three cases for corporate sustainability, the "social case," includes two additional criteria that go beyond the criterion of socio-efficiency associated with the business case. The first criterion is "socio-effectiveness," which is based on the premise that "business conduct should not be judged on a relative scale but rather in relation to the absolute positive social impact a firm could reasonably have achieved."[38] Dyllick and Hockerts explained this criterion by noting that while many companies pursue socio-effectiveness by working hard to serve their clients even better and at lower costs, the fact is that the customers to whom these products and services are made available are only a small part of the world population and that companies in a position to do so fail to make their products and services available to those who are truly in need (i.e., people in what Hart and Prahalad famously referred to as the "bottom of

---

and Zavestovski, S. 2001. "Environmental Concern and Anti-Consumerism in the Self-Concept: Do they Share the Same Basis?" In *Exploring Sustainable Consumption*, eds. M. Cohen and J. Murphy, 173. Exploring Sustainable Consumption Amsterdam: Pergamon.

[37] Hockerts, K. 2003. *Sustainability Innovations, Ecological and Social Entrepreneurship and the Management of Antagonistic Assets*, 30. Difo-Druck: Bamberg.

[38] Dyllick, T., and K. Hockerts. March 2002. "Beyond the Business Case for Corporate Sustainability." *Business Strategy and the Environment* 11, pp. 130–38.

the pyramid"[39]). Social effectiveness includes making basic services and products such as food, health and financial and communication services available to those who would not be able to purchase them if companies failed to consider anything other than pure economic sustainability. The second criterion embedded in the social case is "ecological equity," which means that companies must seek equitable solutions to the management and distribution of the world's natural capital between current and future generations.[40]

Dyllick and Hockerts made it clear that they believed that companies seeking to achieve corporate sustainability must satisfy all six of the criterion described earlier among the three cases for corporate sustainability (see also Table 5.2). They acknowledged that time and context will influence which of the cases command the attention of companies and their managers at a particular moment and that the business case, with its emphasis on eco-efficiency and socio-efficiency, will likely command the most attention of corporate managers unless external factors (e.g., consumers, politicians, activists) force them to consider the natural and social cases. They also noted that the natural and social cases are more difficult to administer and monitor due to the lack of the same sort of accepted measurement tools that have been created to monitor economic performance; however, they argued that "as all companies are guided to some extent by a set of political–ethical values that are entrenched in the firm's culture, business managers may promote corporate sustainability without making an explicit calculation of the economic costs and benefits."[41]

---

[39] Hart, S., and C. Prahalad. 1999. *Strategies for the Bottom of the Pyramid: Creating Sustainable Development*. Unpublished draft paper.

[40] Dyllick, T., and K. Hockerts. March 2002. "Beyond the Business Case for Corporate Sustainability." *Business Strategy and the Environment* 11, 130–38. Ecological equity is sometimes referred to as "Ecological Justice." Gray, R., and J. Bebbington. 2000. "Environmental Accounting, Managerialism and Sustainability: Is the Planet Safe in the Hands of Business and Accounting?" In *Advances in Environmental Accounting and Management*, eds. M. Freedman, and B. Jaggi, 1 vols. Advances in Environmental Accounting and Management. Amsterdam: JAI.

[41] Id. Dyllick and Hockerts argued that additional research should be conducted to fill in some of the gaps in defining their suggested criterion such as providing a systematic framework for both socio-efficiency and socio-effectiveness and developing business relevant criteria for issues such as ecological equity. Id. at p. 139.

**Table 5.2 Elements of Dyllick and Hockerts' model of corporate
sustainability**

Young and Tilley summarized the six elements of Dyllick and Hockerts' model of corporate sustainability as follows:

- *Eco-efficiency*: Refers to a firm's efficient use of natural resources and is usually calculated as the economic value added in relation to a firm's aggregate ecological impact.
- *Socio-efficiency*: Refers to the relationship between a firm's economic value added and
  its social impact and requires the minimization of negative impacts (e.g., workplace accidents) and the maximization of positive social impacts (e.g., training and
  health benefits).
- *Ecological equity*: Refers to the inter-generational inheritance of natural capital, both
  positive and negative (i.e., pollution).
- *Socio-effectiveness*: Refers to the assessment of a firm's absolute social performance
  and includes questions such as whether a company's products are accessible and thus
  benefitting all or limited in availability and just benefitting an elite few.
- *Sufficiency*: Refers to the actions of individual consumers to make responsible choices
  and the collective actions of consumers to boycott or subvert corporate branding and
  marketing strategies that are believed to lead to harm to the environment.
- *Eco-effectiveness*: Refers to either technical effectiveness or a complete alternative to
  eco-efficiency.

Source: Young, W., and F. Tilley. 2006. "Can Businesses Move Beyond Efficiency? The Shift
toward Effectiveness and Equity in the Corporate Sustainability Debate." *Business Strategy and the
Environment* 15, no. 6, pp. 402–08.

Dyllick and Hockerts were not the only ones who have suggested
a framework for corporate sustainability; however, many of the others
models include dimensions that are quite similar. For example, the
Sustainche Farm Project (http://sustainche-farm.org), focused on the
sustainable development of a smallholder family farm in Northern
Namibia, offered the following illustration of the dimensions of a sustainable development policy:

- *Economics*: Innovation; capital efficiency; risk management;
  margin improvement; growth enhancement and total
  shareholder return
- *Socio-Economics*: Jobs creation; skills enhancement; local
  economic impacts; social investments; business ethics
  and security
- *Eco-Efficiency*: Resource efficiency; product stewardship;
  life-cycle management and products to services

- *Social:* Diversity; human rights; community outreach; indigenous communities and labor relations
- *Socio-Environmental:* Global climate change; access to potable water; crisis management; environmental judgment; compliance with environmental regulations and health and safety
- *Environmental:* Clean air; reduction of water and land emissions; zero waste; elimination of releases and spills and bio-diversity

McDonough and Braungart's Model of Corporate Sustainability

McDonough and Braungart proposed a different model of corporate sustainability that was based on "triple top line" thinking and shifted the emphasis of corporate accountability to the beginning of the design process.[42] Following the "triple bottom line" framework, the McDonough and Braungart model was anchored by three value systems (economy, ecology, and equity) which were the corners of the fractal triangle they used to illustrate their model. Young and Tilley explained that "every business decision is connected to and has an impact upon all three value systems, all of which carry equal weight and require equal consideration."[43] Accordingly, it was recommended that companies should move three each zone of the triangle when designing new products to ask and answer the following questions in pursuit of identifying and acting upon opportunities to create value[44]:

- Economy-economy: Can I make my product or provide a service at a profit?

---

[42] McDonough, W., and M. Braungart. 2002. "Design for the Triple Top Line: New Tools for Sustainable Commerce." *Corporate Environmental Strategy* 9, no. 3, p. 251.
[43] Young, W., and F. Tilley. 2006. "Can Businesses move Beyond Efficiency? The Shift Towards Effectiveness and Equity in the Corporate Sustainability Debate." *Business Strategy and the Environment* 15, pp. 402–08.
[44] Id.

- Economy-ecology: Will our service or production process use resources efficiently? Will our business process reduce waste?
- Economy-equity: Are the employees producing a promising product earning a living wage?
- Equity-equity: Will the factory or office improve the quality of life of all stakeholders and restore ecosystems?
- Equity-ecology: In what ways could the product or service enhance the health of employees and customers?
- Equity-economy: Are men and women being paid the same for the same work? Are we finding new ways to honor everyone involved, regardless of race, sex, nationality, or religion?
- Ecology-ecology: Are we obeying nature's laws? Are we creating habitats?
- Ecology-equity: Will our product or service contribute to the balance of the local ecology?
- Ecology-economy: Is our ecological strategy economically viable? Will it enable us to use resources effectively?

Measuring Corporate Sustainability Performance

Montiel found substantial similarities in how CSR and corporate sustainability researchers operationalized their constructs to measure social and environmental performance, noting that both groups of scholars use similar variables to measure CSR and corporate sustainability that included economic, environmental, and social dimensions. The most common variables included ethics policy, philanthropic contributions, stakeholder interests and relationships (i.e., investors, shareholders, customers, suppliers, employees, and the community), governmental relationships, urban development, minority support programs, health and safety initiatives, community involvement and development, conserving natural resources, employee eco-initiatives, voluntary environmental restoration, eco-design practices, and systematically reducing waste and emissions from operations.[45]

---

[45] Montiel, I. September 2008. "Corporate Social Responsibility and Corporate Sustainability: Separate Pasts, Common Futures." *Organization and Environment*, 21. no. 3, pp. 245–60.

Table 5.3 Examples of performance measures for CSR, CSP, and CS

Measures	Selected studies
Corporate social responsibility	
Fortune's Corporate Reputation Survey (rates firms on financial soundness, long-term investment value, use of corporate assets, quality of management, innovativeness, quality of products and services, use of corporate talent, community and environmental responsibility)	Holmes (1977); Abbott and Monsen (1979); McGuire et al. (1988); Fryxell and Wang (1994)
11 survey items (pollution, quality of products and services, decay of cities, inflation, monopoly, quality of education, support of charities, corporate profits, human resources, minority employment, unemployment)	Grunig (1979)
Moskowitz Reputation Index (pollution control, equal employment opportunity, minority and female representation on board of directors, support of minority enterprise, responsible and irresponsible advertising, charitable contributions, community relations, product quality, plant safety, illegal politicking, disclosure of information, employee benefits, respect for privacy, support for cultural programs, responsiveness to consumer complaints, fair dealing with customers)	Cochran and Wood (1984)
Motivating principles (value, stakeholder, and performance driven), processes (programs and activities aimed at implementing CSR principles and/or addressing specific stakeholder issues, which include philanthropic, sponsorships, volunteer, code of ethics, quality, health and safety, and management of environmental impacts) and stakeholder issues (community, customer, employee, shareholder, supplier)	Maignan and Ragston (2002)
Corporate social performance	
Kinder, Lydenberg, Domini social rating service dimensions (community relations, employee relations, environmental issues, military issues, product issues, South Africa issues, nuclear power, women, or minority issues)	Graves and Waddock (1994); Turban and Greening (1996); Waddock and Graves (1997); Ruf et al. (1998); Weaver et al. (1999); Agle et al. (1999)
Corporate sustainability and sustainable development	
Pollution control, eco-efficiency, recirculation, eco-design, ecosystem stewardship, and business redefinition	Sharma and Henriques (2005)
*10 environmental integrity items (reduced product's environmental harmful impact, reduced environmentally damaging inputs, used inputs from renewable sources, reduce environmental impacts of processes, reduced operations in environmentally sensitive locations, reduced likelihood of environmental	Bansal (2005); Chan (2005)

Measures	Selected studies
accidents, reduced waste, reused waste, disposed waste responsibly, handled toxic waste responsibly);	
*6 economic prosperity items (established government relations, reduced costs of inputs, reduced cost for waste management for same level of outputs, used waste for revenue, differentiated product on environmental performance, created spin-off technologies); and	
*6 social equity items (considered stakeholder interests, communicated environmental risk, improved health and safety issues, protected local communitie's rights, improved facility's visual aspect, funded local community projects)	

Source: Montiel, I. September 2008. "Corporate Social Responsibility and Corporate Sustainability: Separate Pasts, Common Futures," *Organization and Environment* 21, no. 3, pp. 245, 261–62. The article reported the results of the author's extensive survey of the evolution of management literature in both general management and specialized journals with respect to CSR, corporate social performance (CSP), and corporate sustainability (CS). The article quantifies the research work and summarizes the different CSR-and CS-related definitions to identify the definitional differences between CSR and CS. This table, adapted from the article, lists examples of measurement instruments used by scholars to operationalize CSR, CSP, and CS in the general management articles reviewed and full citations for the references can be found in the "References" section of the article.

CHAPTER 6

Sustainable Entrepreneurship

Introduction

By the 1990s it was becoming clear that sustainability had "become a multidimensional concept that extends beyond environmental protection to economic development and social equity"—in other words, entrepreneurship guided and measured by the three pillars of the "triple bottom line."[1] Crals and Vereeck reasoned that "sustainable entrepreneurship" could be interpreted as a spin-off concept from sustainable development and that sustainable entrepreneurs were those persons and companies that contributed to sustainable development by "doing business in a sustainable way."[2] According to the Brundtland Commission, sustainable entrepreneurship is the continuing commitment by businesses to behave ethically and contribute to economic development while improving the quality of life of the workforce, their families, the local and global community as well as future generations.[3] This definition recognizes several different stakeholder groups, not just shareholders, must be taken into account when managerial decisions are made and operational activities in furtherance of the organizational purposes are carried out. Crals and Vereeck argued that in order for entrepreneurial activity to be "sustainable" it must recognize, address, and satisfy certain standards for each of

---

[1] Gladwin, T., J. Kennelly, and T. Krause. 1995. "Shifting Paradigms for Sustainable Development." *Academy of Management Review* 20, no. 4, p. 874.

[2] Crals, E., and L. Vereeck. July 18, 2016. *Sustainable Entrepreneurship in SMEs—Theory and Practice*, 2. http://inter-disciplinary.net/ptb/ejgc/ejgc3/cralsvereeck%20paper.pdf (accessed July 18, 2016).

[3] Id.

the three P's of the triple bottom-line described earlier.[4] Crals and Vereeck observed that the definition of sustainable entrepreneurship was not static given the dynamism of new ideas and standards with respect to the social and natural environment.

Definitions and Conceptualizations of Sustainable Entrepreneurship

Bell and Stellingwerf compiled what they considered to be a representative list of definitions of "sustainable entrepreneurship" that were suggested from 2003 through 2011, all of which are presented as follows, in chronological order[5]:

- "Innovative behavior of single or organizations operating in the private business sector who are seeing environmental or social issues as a core objective and competitive advantage."[6]
- "The continuing commitment by business to behave ethically and contribute to economic development, while improving the quality of life of the workforce, their families, local communities, the society, and the world at large, as well as future generations. Sustainable Entrepreneurs are for-profit entrepreneurs that commit business operations toward the objective goal of achieving sustainability."[7]

---

[4] Id. at pp. 3–4.

[5] Bell, J., and J. Stellingwerf. 2012. *Sustainable Entrepreneurship: The Motivations & Challenges of Sustainable Entrepreneurs in the Renewable Energy Industry*, 13–14. Jonkoping, Sweden: Jonkoping International Business School Master Thesis in Business Administration.

[6] Gerlach. A. 2003. "Sustainable Entrepreneurship and Innovation." In *University of Leeds: The 2003 Corporate Social Responsibility and Environmental Management Conference*, 101–103. Leeds, UK: University of Leeds.

[7] Crals, E., and L. Vereeck. 2005. "The Affordability of Sustainable Entrepreneurship Certification for SMEs." *International Journal of Sustainable Development and World Ecology* 12, p. 173.

- "The process of discovering, evaluating, and exploiting economic opportunities that are present in market failures which detract from sustainability, including those that are environmentally relevant."[8]
- "The examination of how opportunities to bring into existence future goods and services are discovered, created, and exploited, by whom, and with what economic, psychological, social, and environmental consequences."[9]
- "Create profitable enterprises and achieve certain environmental and/or social objectives, pursue and achieve what is often referred to as the double bottom-line or triple bottom line"[10]
- "The discovery and exploitation of economic opportunities through the generation of market disequilibria that initiate the transformation of a sector toward an environmentally and socially more sustainable state."[11]
- "An innovative, market-oriented and personality driven form of creating economic and societal value by means of breakthrough environmentally or socially beneficial market or institutional innovations."[12]
- "Sustainable Entrepreneurship is focused on the preservation of nature, life support, and community in the pursuit of perceived opportunities to bring into existence future

---

[8] Dean, T., and J. McMullen. 2007. "Towards a Theory of Sustainable Entrepreneurship: Reducing Environmental Degradation through Entrepreneurial Action." *Journal of Business Venturing* 22, pp. 50–58.

[9] Cohen, B., and M. Winn. 2007. "Market Imperfections, Opportunity and Sustainable Entrepreneurship." *Journal of Business Venturing* 22, no. 1, pp. 29–35.

[10] Choi, D., and E. Gray. 2008. "The Venture Development Process of 'Sustainable' Entrepreneurs." *Management Research News* 31, no. 8, pp. 558–59.

[11] Hockerts, K., and R. Wüstenhagen. 2010. "Greening Goliaths Versus Emerging Davids—Theorizing about the Role of Incumbents and New Entrants in Sustainable Entrepreneurship." *Journal of Business Venturing* 25, pp. 481–82.

[12] Schaltegger, S., and M. Wagner. 2011. "Sustainable Entrepreneurship and Sustainability Innovation: Categories and Interactions." *Business Strategy and the Environment* 20, pp. 222–24.

products, processes, and services for gain, where gain is broadly construed to include economic and noneconomic gains to individuals, the economy, and society."[13]

From their perspective, Bell and Stellingwerf believed that the definitions collectively identified four defining attributes of sustainable entrepreneurship[14]:

- *Balancing environmental and social concerns*: Bell and Stellingwerf observed that sustainable entrepreneurship was "a balancing act of strategically managing and orienting environmental and social objectives and considerations, with entity specific financial goals steering the business objective" and that sustainable entrepreneurship required finding the right balance with the disparate economic, social, cultural, and ecological environments in which businesses must operate. They also noted that in the course of their efforts to limit and minimize the environmental and social impact of their activities sustainable entrepreneurs focused on improving the quality of their processes.[15]
- *Economic gains*: Entrepreneurship, sustainable or otherwise, has making a profit as an essential characteristic and objective and the concept of "gain" can be found throughout the definitions reproduced earlier. However, sustainable entrepreneurship is a based on a broad construction of gain that includes economic and noneconomic gains to individuals,

[13] Shepherd, D., and H. Patzelt. 2011. "The New Field of Sustainable Entrepreneurship: Studying Entrepreneurial Action Linking 'What is to be Sustained' with 'What is to be Developed.'" *Entrepreneurship Theory and Practice* 35, no. 1, pp. 137–42.

[14] Bell, J., and J. Stellingwerf. 2012. *Sustainable Entrepreneurship: The Motivations & Challenges of Sustainable Entrepreneurs in the Renewable Energy Industry*, 14–17. Jonkoping, Sweden: Jonkoping International Business School Master Thesis in Business Administration.

[15] Choi, D., and E. Gray. 2008. "The Venture Development Process of 'Sustainable' Entrepreneurs." *Management Research News* 31, no. 80, p. 558.

the economy, and society. Profits are recognized as being essential to sustaining the livelihood of businesses and providing entrepreneurs with the resources that are needed for reinvestment in the sustainable goals of their companies. Bell and Stellingwerf argued that entrepreneurial activities can only be labelled sustainable, and therefore satisfy sustainable development, if there is an equal blending of, and equal consideration for, each of the three P's of the triple bottom line described earlier.[16]

- *Market failures and disequilibria*: Half of the definitions reproduced earlier explicitly mentioned recognition and exploitation of opportunities caused by environmental and/or social imperfections and identification of opportunities has been a long-standing tenant of disruptive entrepreneurship. Cohen and Winn argued that there are four types of market imperfections (i.e., inefficient firms, externalities, flawed pricing mechanisms, and information asymmetries) that contribute to environmental degradation and provide opportunities for sustainable entrepreneurs to create radical technologies and innovative business models that can achieve profitability while simultaneously improving local and global social and environmental conditions.[17]

- *Transforming sectors toward sustainability*: A number of theorists have argued that start-ups launched by sustainable entrepreneurs can solve sustainability-related problems

---

[16] Bell, J., and J. Stellingwerf. 2012. *Sustainable Entrepreneurship: The Motivations & Challenges of Sustainable Entrepreneurs in the Renewable Energy Industry*, 15. Jonkoping, Sweden: Jonkoping International Business School Master Thesis in Business Administration.

[17] Cohen, B., and M. Winn. 2007. "Market Imperfections, Opportunity and Sustainable Entrepreneurship." *Journal of Business Venturing* 22, no. 1, p. 29. See also Dean, T., and J. McMullen. 2007. "Towards a Theory of Sustainable Entrepreneurship: Reducing Environmental Degradation through Entrepreneurial Action." *Journal of Business Venturing* 22, pp. 50–58. ("Environmentally relevant market failures represent opportunities for simultaneously achieving profitability while reducing environmentally degrading economic behaviors.")

through the introduction of innovative products, process, and services and that the commercial success of these solutions, and accompanying support of professional investors and other influential stakeholders, can and will eventually influence incumbents to adopt similar solutions and otherwise take steps that will lead to the transformation of the entire industry toward sustainability.[18] Under these theories, sustainable entrepreneurs make their impact by targeting market niches defined by a particular sustainability-related problem, generally introducing the radical changes that are outside the comfort zone of incumbents that prefer change to be incremental; however, Bell and Stellingwerf cautioned that research "in the field" lacked support.[19]

From all of this, Bell and Stellingwerf proposed their own definition of sustainable entrepreneurship as "startups that introduce an innovation, with the aim to solve a sustainability-related market failure, which initiates the transformation of an industry toward sustainability."[20] The "innovation" could take the form of a product, process, or service and the sustainability objectives behind these innovations were equally important as the economic objectives associated with them. The use of the term "startups" is intentional and significant as it explicitly differentiates sustainable entrepreneurship from the activities of established organizations, such as corporations, to address sustainable development issues in their environment (i.e., corporate-sustainability/CSR initiatives).

Rey synthesized the results of his review of various definitions of sustainable entrepreneurship as follows: "conducting business which commits

[18] See, for example, Hockerts, K., and R. Wüstenhagen. 2010. "Greening Goliaths Versus Emerging Davids—Theorizing about the Role of Incumbents and New Entrants in Sustainable Entrepreneurship." *Journal of Business Venturing* 25, pp. 481–82.
[19] Bell, J., and J. Stellingwerf. 2012. *Sustainable Entrepreneurship: The Motivations & Challenges of Sustainable Entrepreneurs in the Renewable Energy Industry*, 17. Jonkoping, Sweden: Jonkoping International Business School Master Thesis in Business Administration.
[20] Id.

to ethical standards and behavior, contributing to economic development, all the while maintaining a progressive upkeep of the well-being of society—including the labor-force and their families, their communities and the world on a whole, for the present and future inhabitants."[21] According to Rey, a sustainable company is one that operates in accord with the philosophy of the Brundtland Report while recognizing and balancing the economic, social, and environmental aspects and impacts of their businesses.[22] Rey noted that "sustainable entrepreneurship may seem odd as entrepreneurship is principally associated with accomplishing certain goals while maximizing profits in the most efficient way possible" and entrepreneurs who are focused on projecting a sustainable outlook for their business will likely stray from profit maximization due to the added costs of sustainable goods and practices that traditional entrepreneurs are able to avoid by simply going for the cheapest alternative.[23]

Rey noted that while CSR is often compared to sustainable entrepreneurship, he believed that there are significant differences between the two concepts. Most importantly, according to Rey, CSR is primarily concerned with the actions of corporations that have been operating for a significant period of time and which have reached a certain size and determined that they have a responsibility, beyond the traditional profit-making objectives, to be more aware of their *external* environment and stakeholders and find ways to give back to their local communities beyond their mandatory legal obligations. While these initiatives are generally welcomed, they typically lack certain core characteristics of sustainable entrepreneurship such as offering environmentally-friendly products and services and making changes to *internal* operations of the company to bring sustainability practices to personnel matters and production processes.[24]

---

[21] Rey, L. December 2011. Sustainable Entrepreneurship and its Viability, 12. Rotterdam: Master Thesis for MS in Entrepreneurship, Strategy and Organizations Economics from Erasmus School of Economics.

[22] Id.

[23] Id. at p. 9.

[24] Id.

Muñoz observed that the specific form of entrepreneurship engaged in by sustainability-driven enterprises is about simultaneously achieving three objectives (i.e., social, environmental, and economic), while committing to securing the economic welfare and social well-being of future generations and ensuring a long-term sustainability of the environment.[25] He then went on to propose that sustainable entrepreneurship should be defined and conceptualized as being "focused on pursuing business opportunities to bring into existence future products, processes and services, while contributing to sustain the development of society, the economy and the environment and consequently to enhance the well-being of future generations."[26] From this definition it is possible to identify certain central factors that sustainable entrepreneurs need to consider in developing and executing their business models: integrating environmental best practices and protection into all business activities; social justice; economic prosperity for investors, entrepreneurs, and economies; improving the well-being of communities; and intra and intergenerational equity.[27] Muñoz pointed out that his definition acknowledged and integrated constructs from both sustainable development and entrepreneurship literature, a path also taken by Shepherd and Patzelt's opinion that the practice of sustainable entrepreneurship called for sustaining and developing three constructs informed by sustainable development literature (i.e., sustain nature, life support systems, and communities) and three constructs informed by entrepreneurship literature (i.e., develop economic gains, noneconomic gains to individuals, and noneconomic gains to society).[28]

---

[25] Muñoz, P. November 2013. "The Distinctive Importance of Sustainable Entrepreneurship." *Creativity, Innovation and Entrepreneurship* 2, no. 1 (citing Young, W., and F. Tilley. 2006. "Can Businesses Move beyond Efficiency? The Shift Towards Effectiveness and Equity in the Corporate Sustainability Debate." *Business Strategy and the Environment* 15, no. 6, p. 402).

[26] Id.

[27] Id. (citing Dresner, S. 2008. *The Principles of Sustainability*, 2nd ed. London: Earthscan; and Beckerman, W. 1999. "Sustainable Development and Our Obligations to Future Generations." In *Fairness and Futurity: Essays on Environmental Sustainability and Social Justice*, ed. A. Dobson, 71. Oxford: Oxford University Press).

[28] Shepherd, D., and H. Patzelt. 2011. "The New Field of Sustainable Entrepreneurship: Studying Entrepreneurial Action Linking 'What is to be Sustained' with 'What is to be Developed.'" *Entrepreneurship Theory and Practice* 3, pp. 51–137.

Racelis used the term "authentic sustainable entrepreneurship" to describe the situation "when the economic, environmental, and social motives come together in the business action of the entrepreneur, along with the internalization of the fiduciary, stewardship, and moral responsibilities to future generations."[29] Racelis went on to suggest that the specific normative elements that should be found in the activities of the authentic sustainable entrepreneur should include "production of socially desirable products in a socially desirable manner, and advancement of the health and well-being of those affected by such, all within a values-driven framework."[30] Racelis pointed out that sustainable entrepreneurship is a model of entrepreneurship that enables founders to seize opportunities relating to environmental and social degradation which are created by market imperfections (e.g., inefficient firms, externalities, flawed pricing mechanisms, and information asymmetries) to obtain entrepreneurial rents while simultaneously improving social and environmental conditions both locally and globally.[31] Racelis argued that the core motivation for sustainable entrepreneurs is to "contribute to solving societal and environmental problems through the realization of a successful business," while their main goal "is to create sustainable development through entrepreneurial corporate activities."[32]

Another important implicit condition for sustainable entrepreneurship is the capacity of the venture to survive, develop, and grow. Rey referred to this condition as "viability" and emphasized that a sustainable entrepreneurial company must, at a minimum, cover all costs, enjoy continuous growth in size and output, make a positive return on

---

[29] Racelis, A. 2014. "Sustainable Entrepreneurship in Asia: A Proposed Theoretical Framework Based on Literature Review." *Journal of Management for Global Sustainability* 2, no. 4.

[30] Id. (citing Hodgkin, S. 2002. *Business Social Entrepreneurs: Working Towards Sustainable Communities Through Socially Responsible Business Practices*. Master's thesis, University of Calgary, Calgary, Alberta, Canada).

[31] Id. (citing Dean, T., and J. McMullen. 2007. "Toward a Theory of Sustainable Entrepreneurship: Reducing Environmental Degradation through Entrepreneurial Action." *Journal of Business Venturing* 22, p. 50).

[32] Id.

turnover and, fundamentally, "remain out of financial danger for years."[33] In other words, the company must seek and achieve long-term sustainability in order to successfully pursue and achieve its goals and purposes and provide prospective stakeholders, including employees, with security that their contributions to the enterprise will be product value over an extended period.

Build Lasting Visionary Companies—Habits of Sustainable Entrepreneurs

Writing in the early 1990s, a time when management books had become somewhat of a fad, Collins and Porras claimed that they were doing something different in their best-selling book *Built to Last: Successful Habits of Visionary Companies*. They weren't writing about charismatic visionary leaders, visionary product concepts, or visionary market insights, and reminded readers that all leaders eventually die, all products become obsolete, and all markets mature. Instead, they believed that one of the most important economic challenges and issues was figuring out how to build enduring "visionary companies" that met the following criteria: a premier institution in their industry that was widely admired by knowledgeable businesspeople; a company that had made an indelible imprint on the world; and a company that had been in business for at least 50 years and gone through multiple generations of chief executives and multiple product (or service) life cycles. Collins and Porras tackled two fundamental and difficult questions: "What makes the truly exceptional companies different from the other companies?" and "Is it possible to discover the timeless management principles that have consistently distinguished outstanding companies and which apply over long stretches of time and across a wide range of industries?" Based on their extensive research, Collins and Porras argued that such timeless management principles did exist and can and should be applied by managers, CEOs, and entrepreneurs all over the world to create their own visionary companies and effectively practice sustainability leadership.

In *Built to Last* and other articles regarding their research, Collins and Porras listed and described at least ten management principles they had identified from looking at both companies that they believed had achieved visionary status and at comparison companies which, while "born in the same era, with the same market opportunities, facing the same demographics, technology shifts, and socioeconomic trends," had been less successful. Of those principles the authors felt that four of them stood out—"be a clock builder—an architect—not a time teller; embrace the "Genius of the AND"; preserve the core/stimulate progress; and seek consistent alignment"—and most of the book was about explaining and illustrating each of these concepts.

For example, the authors explained that "[h]aving a great idea or being a charismatic visionary leader is 'time telling'; building a company that can prosper far beyond the presence of any single leader and through multiple product life cycles is 'clock building.'" Embrace the "Genius of the And" meant that visionary companies had "the ability to embrace both

---

[33] Rey, L. December 2011. *Sustainable Entrepreneurship and its Viability*, 14. Rotterdam: Master Thesis for MS in Entrepreneurship, Strategy and Organizations Economics from Erasmus School of Economics.

extremes of a number of dimensions at the same time" such as having a purpose beyond profit while engaging in the pragmatic pursuit of profit. Preserve the Core and Stimulate Progress meant that "[a] visionary company carefully preserves and protects its core ideology, yet all the specific manifestations of its core ideology must be open for change and evolution." Finally, visionary companies achieved alignment by making sure "that all the elements of a company work together in concert within the context of the company's core ideology and the type of progress it aims to achieve." On a day-to-day basis, alignment met making sure companies didn't adopt incentive systems that rewarded behaviors that were inconsistent with the company's core values or policies and procedures that inhibited change and improvement.

As mentioned earlier, Collins and Porras identified and followed pairs of companies, 18 in all, over a long period of time in order to identify those capable of achieving enduring success and not get caught up celebrating a company that may have had just one or two moments of good fortune. It was interesting that more often than not the comparison company had greater initial success during the entrepreneurial phase than the visionary company. While all of the pairs were used to illustrate the four key concepts mentioned earlier, let's look at just three examples starting with Hewlett-Packard (a visionary company founded in 1937) and Texas Instruments (the comparison company founded in 1930). HP was consistently applauded by the researchers as an example of the clock-building orientation and the researchers noted that it was telling that when Dave Packard, one of the HP founders, was asked about which product decisions were most important to the growth of the company his response completely ignored specific products and focused on organizational decisions that are so much a part of clock-building: "developing an engineering team, a pay-as-you-go policy to impose fiscal discipline, a profit-sharing program, personnel and management policies [and] the 'HP Way' philosophy of management." The researchers also praised Packard as a strong example of understanding "Genius of the AND" in the way that he and his company simultaneously pursued "profit and purpose beyond profit." In order to illustrate their point the researchers provided a quote from a presentation that Packard made to HP personnel who would be responsible for management development training which included the following: "I want to discuss why a company exists in the first place. In other words, why are we here? I think many people assume, wrongly, that a company exists simply to make money. While this is an important result of a company's existence, we have to go deeper and find the real reasons for our being … The real reason for our existence is that we provide something which is unique [that makes a contribution]." In contrast, the researchers "could find not one single statement that TI exists for reasons beyond making money." HP also received high marks with respect to the way it aligned its practices and policies with its "lofty values and aspirations" by finding ways to show respect for its employees, reinforce the importance of technological contribution, promote an entrepreneurial environment, and "immerse employees in the tenets of what became known as the 'HP Way.'"

A second pair of twins was Wal-Mart (a visionary company founded in 1945) and Ames (the comparison company founded in 1958). The researchers complimented legendary Wal-Mart founder Sam Walton for implementing "concrete organizational mechanisms to stimulate change and improvement" and noted that he "concentrated on creating an organization that would evolve and change on its own," each of which were consistent with clock building. Walton also knew the importance of succession planning to make sure that the company philosophies survived. In contrast, "Ames leaders dictated all change from aforementioned and detailed in a book the precise steps a store manager should take, leaving no room for initiative" and the researchers noted that Ames had no succession plan in place and eventually management control fell into the hands of outsiders with no ideas about the philosophies of the founders.

A third pair of twins was Walt Disney (a visionary company founded in 1923) and Columbia Pictures (the comparison company founded in 1920). With respect to clock building the researchers judged Harry Cohn, one of the founders of Columbia to be a complete failure who "cared first and foremost about becoming a movie mogul and wielding immense personal power in Hollywood and cared little or not at all about the qualities and identify of the Columbia Pictures Company that might endure beyond his lifetime." On the other hand Walt Disney spent every moment from the day that he founded the company to the day that he died thinking about future ways that the company could make people happy. Disney was also praised for its efforts to institutionalize its core technologies while simultaneously maintaining ongoing efforts to stimulate progress and the researchers took particular note of how Disney developed a cult-like culture through "intensive screening and indoctrination of employees." For its part, Columbia, like Ames, was criticized for its neglect of investments for long-term growth and failure to invest in employee recruiting, training, and professional development. Today Disney remains an important force in entertaining children and adults all around the world while Columbia, lacking a strong heritage or reasons to exist beyond its cash and assets, ceased to exist as an independent company.

As to how the research they conducted 20 years ago might relate to the future, such as today, Collins and Porras predicted that clock building would become even more important as ideas, products, and markets became obsolete more quickly due to "accelerating rate of technological change, increasing global competition and dramatically shorter product life cycles." They also thought that preserving the core/stimulating progress would become more important as companies became "flatter, more decentralized, more geographically dispersed" and workers became more knowledgeable and seek more and more individual autonomy. In other articles Collins talked about how the work done to write *Built to Last* might be helpful in understanding dramatic and seemingly sudden failures of high flying companies like we seen so often recently and mentioned the dangers of "hubris born of success" and undisciplined and reckless pursuit of more success—more money, larger size, more celebrity. The stories collected, and lessons learning, in creating *Built to Last* should be useful for the current crop of celebrity companies such as Facebook, Google, Amazon, and Apple that have been so successful in their start-up phase, but must now settle in for the long haul of decades of ups and downs before they are eligible for entering the visionary class. The founders and other leaders of these companies have often spoken of their intent to achieve and sustain long-term greatness and impact. Perhaps the trials and triumphs of the legendary sustainable entrepreneurs from the past, such as Packard, Walton, and Disney, can be valuable teaching tools.

Sources: Collins, J., and J. Porras. 1994. *Built to Last: Successful Habits of Visionary Companies.* New York, NY: HarperBusiness; Collins, J. 1995. "Building Companies to Last." INC. Special Issue— The State of Small Business; and Collins, J. May 2009. "How the Mighty Fall: A Primer on the Warning Signs." *Businessweek.*

Determinants of Sustainable Entrepreneurship

Lawai et al. provided a summary of research that was relevant to identifying the key determinants of successful sustainable entrepreneurship[34]:

---

[34] Lawai, F., R. Worlu, and O. Ayoade. May 2016. "Critical Success Factors for Sustainable Entrepreneurship in SMEs: Nigerian Perspective." *Mediterranean Journal of Social Sciences* 7, no. 3, pp. 342–43, 338.

- According to Koe et al., attitudinal factors (i.e., sustainable attitude) and perceptual factors (i.e., perceived desirability and perceived feasibility) were important in influencing a person's level of propensity to sustainable entrepreneurship.[35]
- Cambra-Fierro et al. argued that variables relevant to sustainable entrepreneurship included legal context, management's personal values, socio-cultural context, market forces, ownership management structure, and industry-sector characteristics.[36]
- Uhlaner et al. found evidence that indicated that larger firms, firms from more tangible products, family owned firms, and firms with a more innovative orientation have more inclination toward manifesting sustainable entrepreneurship behaviors.[37] Larger firms are able to bring more resources (financial and human) to bear on sustainability initiatives and have more to lose in terms of reputational damage due to irresponsible behavior. The responsiveness of family firms is consistent with their stronger ties to the local communities in which they operate.[38]

---

[35] Koe, W., R. Omar, and J. Sa'ari. 2015. "Factors Influencing Propensity to Sustainable Entrepreneurship of SMEs in Malaysia." *Procedia Social and Behavioral Sciences*, p. 172.

[36] Cambra-Fierro, J., S. Hart, and Y. Polo-Redondo. 2008. "Environmental Respect: Ethics or Simply Business? A Study in the Small and Medium (SME) Context." *Journal of Business Ethics* 82, p. 645. For discussion of sustainable entrepreneurship in Asia, see Racelis, A. 2014. "Sustainable Entrepreneurship in Asia: A Proposed Theoretical Framework Based on Literature Review." *Journal of Management for Global Sustainability* 2, pp. 8–10.

[37] Uhlanar, L., M. Berent, and R. Jeurissen. 2010. "Family Ownership." *Innovation and Other Context Variables as Determinants of Sustainable Entrepreneurship in SMEs: An Empirical Research Study.*

[38] Uhlaner, L., H. Goor-Balk, and E. Masurel. 2004. "Family Business and Corporate Social Responsibility in a Sample of Dutch Firms." *Journal of Small Business and Enterprise Development* 11, p. 186; and Dyer, W., and D. Whetten. 2006. "Family Firms and Social Responsibility: Preliminary Evidence from the S&P 500." *Entrepreneurship: Theory & Practice* 30, p. 785.

- Fedderke and Garlic opined that sustainable entrepreneurship was dependent on the adequacy and sufficiency of both the economic infrastructure (i.e., transport, communications, power generation, water supply, and sanitation facilities) and the social infrastructure (i.e., educational and health-care facilities). They observed that improvements to infrastructure can contribute to reduction of income inequality, alleviation of poverty, and improved economic growth.[39]

Lawai et al. noted that sustainable entrepreneurs are also subject to many of the same factors that influence commercial entrepreneurs and that the success of both types of entrepreneurs will be influenced by motivating factors, personality characteristics, family support, friend circle/peer group support, management skills and abilities, level of education, and environmental forces.[40] Market conditions are also obviously very important and Rahman and Singh observed that the chances of entrepreneurial success increase substantially with competitive pricing, power supply, access to latest technology, access to market channels, and access to business associations.[41] Researchers also frequently mentioned government support which can come in many forms: financing, infrastructure development, subsidies for accessing raw materials, and assistance with research and development and access to technology. The government can also serve a valuable role as a customer, not only as a source of revenues for the venture but also as a means for the new venture to test and improve the quality of its products before broader commercial launch.

---

[39] Fedderke, J., and R. Garlic. 2008. *Infrastructural Development and Economic Growth in South Africa: A Review of Accumulated Evidences.*

[40] Dionco-Adetayo, E. 2004. *Determinants of Small Firm's Entrepreneurial Success in a Developing Economy*; and Rahman, H., and H. Singh. 2014. "Entrepreneurial Support and its Levels of Success." *Global Journal for Research Analysis* 3, p. 11.

[41] Rahman, H., and H. Singh. 2014. "Economic and Environmental Factors Leading to Entrepreneurial Success." *Indian Journal of Applied Research* 4, p. 12.

Ground Rules for Becoming a Sustainable Entrepreneur

In order to effectively pursue sustainable entrepreneurship and achieve some of the benefits associated with sustainable entrepreneurship policies and practices companies must continuously engage in dialogues with all interested stakeholders. Shareholders must be educated on, and convinced of, the benefits of aspiring for social and environmental responsibility, even though pursuit and achievement of goals in those areas may have an impact on the financial bottom line. For their part, stakeholders that are more focused on social and environmental performance must also acknowledge that the company needs to be financially sustainable in order to survive and thrive.

Groesbeek and Bos collectively offered the following list of ground rules for becoming a sustainable entrepreneur:

1. The corporation should start reducing the environmental damage, respecting human rights and treating its employees with great care;
2. Sustainable entrepreneurship has to be a self-initiated process and should not simply be a response to external pressure;
3. If a corporation wants to practice sustainable entrepreneurship, it should identify clear aims and targets;
4. The aims should be closely related to the corporation's practice and should match the corporate values and its primary activities;
5. The aims have to be closely related to the consumer's needs;
6. The corporation has to be capable of explaining the relationship between sustainability and its activities and production process;
7. The corporation should adhere to these aims on a long term basis;
8. Consumers and pressure groups should have a transparent overview of investments made by the corporation related to sustainable entrepreneurship;
9. Sustainable entrepreneurship practiced by the corporation should not be shifted to the consumers via a price increase;
10. A corporation should not attempt to overemphasize its efforts; and
11. A corporation should make sure that its practices are shared by the corporation as a whole, and that they are not solely efforts of the management.

Sources: The first ten rules on the list were offered by Janssen Groesbeek in 2001 and the final rule was added by Bos a year later in another publication. See Janssen Groesbeek, M. 2001. *Sustainable Entrepreneurship–Theory, Practice, Instruments*. Amsterdam: Business Contact); and Bos, A. 2002. "Sustainable Entrepreneurship in a Changing Europe: Pedagogy of Ethics for Corporate Organizations in Transformation," In *EuroDiversity: A Business Guide to Managing Differences*, 16. eds. G.F. Simons, D. Min et al. Oxford, UK and Woburn, USA: Butterworth-Heinemann).

Young and Tilley's Sustainable Entrepreneurship Model

Young and Tilley noted that Crals and Vereeck had defined sustainable entrepreneurship as the "continuing commitment by businesses to behave ethically and contribute to economic development while improving the quality of life for the workforce, their families, the local and global community as well as future generations" and then went on to take the position that the definition applied to "existing businesses" and not to entrepreneurs who set out to start up and grow a sustainable enterprise from the very beginning.[42] Young and Tilley believed that mainstream businesses interested in pursuing social, environmental, or sustainable actions encountered difficulties in reconciling economic value, which is relatively easy to measure objectively, and the form of moral value, which is subjective, associated with such actions.[43] Because of these difficulties, entrepreneurship, specifically sustainable entrepreneurship, may arguably be the preferred form for the pursuit of sustainability because it is unique and allows for incorporation and consolidation of the value perceptions of the individual entrepreneur in ways that reconcile differences between society and mainstream businesses.

Young and Tilley described sustainable entrepreneurs as entrepreneurs who apply their values to generate a sustainable form of wealth, which means contributing a holistic net benefit to the economy, community, and the natural environment.[44] They proposed a model for understanding the concept of "sustainable entrepreneurship," which they described as an "organization that has sustainability at the center of its structure, operations and management."[45] Young and Tilley explained that their goal was to put forward a model for sustainable entrepreneurship that distinguished it from the conventions of economic, social, and environmental entrepreneurship.[46] They were very clear that while it was true that

---

[42] Tilley, F., and W. Young. 2009. "Sustainability Entrepreneurs—Could they be the True Wealth Generators of the Future?" *Greener Management International* 55, p. 79 (citing Crals, E., and L. Vereeck. February 2004. "Sustainable Entrepreneurship in SMEs." *Theory and Practice*, 2. Copenhagen: 3rd Global Conference in Environmental Justice and Global Citizenship).

[43] Id. (citing Seiler-Hausmann, J., C. Liedtke, and E. von Weizsacker. 2004. "Introduction." In *Eco-efficiency and Beyond: Towards the Sustainable Enterprise*, eds. J. Seiler-Hausmann, C. Liedtke, and E. von Weizsacker, Sheffield, UK: Greenleaf Publishing).

[44] Id.

[45] Young, W., and F. Tilley. 2006. "Can Businesses Move Beyond Efficiency? The Shift towards Effectiveness and Equity in the Corporate Sustainability Debate." *Business Strategy and the Environment* 15, p. 402.

[46] Tilley, F., and W. Young. 2009. "Sustainability Entrepreneurs Could They be the True Wealth Generators of the Future?" *Greener Management International* 55, p. 79.

economic, social, and environmental entrepreneurs could contribute to sustainable development, they were not going be fully sustainable so long as they maintained a single primacy.[47]

Young and Tilley emphasized that sustainable entrepreneurship is based on moving beyond "efficiency" to seeking and achieving "sustainability," a path that was consistent with the evolution in the way in which businesses have encompassed changing attitudes toward environmental and social issues. They explained that when businesses first started considering environmental issues during the early 1960s their primary concern was controlling pollution and their responses tended to be bolt-on solutions to manage compliance with emerging regulations. Two decades later, beginning in the mid-1980s and extending through the 1990s, businesses identified opportunities to reduce costs through the implementation of environmental management practices: the so-called "eco-efficiency" strategy that was touted as a "win-win" solution that minimized resource consumption and waste while affording companies a competitive advantage.[48] By the beginning of the 21st century, however, environmental management theorists and activists had pivoted toward a new approach: businesses should seek "eco-effectiveness" by adopting business practices that went beyond pollution control and eco-efficiency to operating in a manner that restored and enhanced the environment.[49]

The expansive approach to sustainability advocated by Young and Tilley fits within the debate and contrast between "weak," sometimes referred to as "incremental," and "strong" sustainability.[50] Weak sustainability has been described as the expansion of the breadth of what a business considers to be important beyond the traditional financial bottom line focus to include ethical, environmental, and community

---

[47] Id.

[48] Holliday, C., S. Schmidheiny, and P. Watts. 2002. *Walking the Talk—the Business Case for Sustainable Development.* Sheffield: Greenleaf.

[49] Young, W., and F. Tilley. 2006. "Can Businesses move Beyond Efficiency? The Shift towards Effectiveness and Equity in the Corporate Sustainability Debate." *Business Strategy and the Environment* 15, pp. 402–03.

[50] The discussion in this paragraph has been adapted from *Sustainable Business: A Handbook for Starting a Business* (New Zealand Trade and Enterprise).

responsibility, as well as being a good employer and an advocate of ethical labor practices among its business partners. The magnitude of expansion, often referred to as the "triple bottom line," varies from case-to-case and in many businesses begin with, and limit their efforts to, environmental responsibility. In contrast, strong sustainability has been described as "a whole new approach to doing business, where every consideration is made for the business to contribute toward a sustainable society." Applicants of strong sustainability seek to build the capacity to endure within their businesses and continuously ask what they can do to add value to their business within the broader society and eco-systems.

The model suggested by Young and Tilley was based on combining the six criteria of corporate sustainability proposed by Dyllick and Hockerts with concepts that were included in the McDonough-Braungart model of corporate sustainability, all of which have already been described earlier. While Young and Tilley noted that each of the aforementioned models had value, they also had several criticisms[51]:

- While they believed that Dyllick and Hockerts provided a useful insight into new ways of advancing solutions with respect to production, their model did not properly address problems relating to consumption. Specifically, Young and Tilley cautioned that "no matter how environmentally friendly you make a product, if consumer demands are too high there is a potential for imbalance and environmental or social harm."
- Companies of all sizes, large and small, have a tendency to concentrate on just one of the business cases, rather than incorporating all elements of the model into their core missions. While the tendency among larger companies to place greater weight on the business case is well documented, smaller companies that have gone well beyond eco- and

[51] Young, W., and F. Tilley. 2006. "Can Businesses move Beyond Efficiency? The Shift towards Effectiveness and Equity in the Corporate Sustainability Debate." *Business Strategy and the Environment* 15, pp. 407–09, 402.

socio-efficiency to produce "green" products and help disadvantaged sections of society often have similar problems.
- The McDonough-Braungart model did not provide enough
  detail to translate into values and strategies for companies and
  was still concentrating on the separate elements of sustainable
  development and not the whole thing.

Young and Tilley argued that Dyllick and Hockerts and McDonough
and Braungart had focused their efforts on established businesses that
were approaching sustainable development from the eco- and socio-
efficiency end of the models and that their models failed to provide
guidance to eco-and socio-entrepreneurs in operationalizing the other
elements of the path toward sustainable development. In order to address
these shortcomings, Young and Tilley proposed several changes to the
Dyllick-Hockerts model to "focus on entrepreneurship and advance it to
sustainable entrepreneurship"[52]:

Young and Tilley began by swapping the labels "ecological
equity" and "sufficiency." They explained that ecological equity is an
environmentally-centered principle that primarily concerns with the
equal rights of all peoples and generations to environmental resources
and that sufficiency is a more social-centered principle that focuses on
individuals and companies living on needs rather than wants. They also
replaced the labels of "business cases," "natural case," and "societal case"
with "economic entrepreneurship," "environmental entrepreneurship,"
and "social entrepreneurship," respectively, and explained that the changes
were intended to develop a model for new organizations with strong economic, environmental, and social philosophies. Young and Tilley also
emphasized that an effective and comprehensive model of sustainable
entrepreneurship had to be an integrated approach that incorporated all
three components of sustainable development into the organization in
a holistic way and that no single type of entrepreneurship—economic,
environmental, or social—could have a primacy that would impede the
organization's path to sustainability.

---

[52] Id. at pp. 409–12.

Young and Tilley's main effort to advance the Dyllick-Hockerts model to a full-fledged framework for sustainable entrepreneurship involved moving the three traditional poles of entrepreneurship (i.e., economic, environmental, and social) toward a higher plane. In order to do this, Young and Tilley introduced three new two-way relationships and six new variables to be added to the six already operating in the Dyllick-Hockerts model[53]:

- A relationship between economic and sustainable entrepreneurship which involves both "economic equity," which is the distribution of economic wealth fairly between existing generations as well as future generations, and "intergenerational equity," which brings consideration of the economic welfare of future generations into the factors that companies consider when making decisions and engaging in operating activities.
- A relationship between environmental and sustainable entrepreneurship which involves both environmental stability, which is the positive forces being exerted on the environment to stabilize and where necessary restore the various ecosystem functions (e.g., climate change), and environmental sustainability, which brings consideration of the long-term sustainability into the factors that companies consider when making decisions and engaging in operating activities.
- A relationship between social and sustainable entrepreneurship which involves both social responsibility, which refers to companies and individuals taking responsibility and being accountable for direct and indirect and negative and positive impacts on existing generations, and "futurity," which brings consideration of the social well-being of future generations into the factors that companies consider when making decisions and engaging in operating activities.

---

[53] Id. at pp. 411–12.

The crux of the argument made by Young and Tilley was that "sustainable entrepreneurship is the sum of all the 12 variables of the model operating in unison" and they cautioned that sustainable entrepreneurship could not be achieved by only subscribing to social or environmental entrepreneurship.[54] They noted that while the model "does not represent a 'direct route' from any of economic, environmental or social entrepreneurship poles to sustainable entrepreneurship" it does illustrate the relationship between the three poles and sustainable entrepreneurship and thus could be used as a way for assessing whether an organization meets the criterion for one of the poles and identifying the steps that the organization should take to move from that pole toward sustainable entrepreneurship. In other words, the sustainable entrepreneurship model was developed as a framework to guide individuals seeking to start up a sustainable enterprise from the outset and Young and Tilley described the model as detailing the elements required of a sustainable entrepreneur.

According to Tilley and Young, the six initial elements of the model could be seen as the values that build an entrepreneur with social, environmental, or economic goals and the additional six elements incorporate what is needed in order for the entrepreneurial activity to be sustainable. They conceded that the additional elements would be challenging to realize in practice because many of them are at best theoretical; however, they argued that entrepreneurs are well suited to the task given their propensity for innovation, experimentation, and risk taking. Their position with regard to sustainable entrepreneurship has been succinctly explained as follows:

> The sustainable entrepreneur is the only route to fulfilling sustainable development. Firstly, an entrepreneur and their enterprise have to be financially sustainable to survive within the current economic and regulatory systems. An organization just focusing on the environment as its goal without a means of income beyond government subsidy or philanthropy cannot be an entrepreneur, for example, a change of government or change of heart by the

---

[54] Id. at p. 412.

philanthropist could remove the income for that organization and stop the environmental work. In addition, concentrating on environmental values causes social damage, that is to say, creating a nature reserve can exclude the local community from resource traditionally harvested from the land the nature reserve now occupies. Similarly, concentrating on the social values can cause financial failure and environmental damage, take a fair trade organization as an example, it can help bring disadvantaged communities out of poverty but if the organization cannot sell the fair trade products its financial failure stops its good work. In addition, the fair trade organization is damaging the environment through transporting goods across the world (contributing to climate change) and having little regard to the impacts of the production process on the environment (depletion of natural resources, pesticides, hazardous waste). Hence only those entrepreneurs that balance their efforts in contributing to the three areas of wealth generation can truly be called a sustainable entrepreneur.[55]

Assessment questions that prospective sustainable entrepreneurs can use as guides on their journey to sustainable entrepreneurship have been included in Table 6.1. Tilley and Young pointed out several challenges that sustainable entrepreneurs will need to overcome, beginning with the fundamental issue of how to measure wealth generation.[56] The traditional primacy of the business case reflects society's predisposition toward judging success in measurable quantitative, typically financial, terms alone and transition toward sustainable entrepreneurship will require the development of adequate measures of social and environmental value. Another problem is the lack of incentives and rewards to support sustainable entrepreneurs and allow them to survive in the market-based economy. Tilley and Young argued, for example, that if the sustainable entrepreneur contributes toward the economy, society and protects the environment, they

---

[55] Tilley, F., and W. Young, 2009. "Sustainability Entrepreneurs—Could they be the True Wealth Generators of the Future?" *Greener Management International* 55, p. 79.
[56] Id.

should be rewarded for taking on roles that are normally funded by the state, perhaps by being given "tax haven" status that would allow them to retain funds that would normally be paid to the state and re-invest them in the sustainable activities that have broader social value. Finally, Tilley and Young observed that sustainable entrepreneurs need more external support and that sustainable entrepreneurial networks need to be built in order to help those entrepreneurs get their businesses launched and address the challenges associated with the various elements of the sustainable entrepreneurship model.

Case Study: The Day Chocolate Company

In an effort to illustrate the application and utility of their sustainable entrepreneurship model, Young and Tilley provided a case study of the "Day Chocolate Company." They explained that the company was set up to access the chocolate market in the United Kingdom by a West African cocoa growers co-operative called Kuapa Kokoo with The Body Shop International and Christian Aid and facilitated by Twin Trading. Kuapa Kokoo, The Body Shop International, and Christian Aid each owned a third of the company, which sold two brands of Fairtrade chocolate carrying the Fairtrade Mark certified by the UK Fairtrade Foundation. Young and Tilley noted that the overall goal and purpose of the company was to improve the livelihood of smallholder cocoa producers in Ghana. They went on to first assess whether Day Chocolate Company satisfied the elements of one of the poles of their sustainable entrepreneurship model—social entrepreneurship—and then proceeded to make suggestions as to what the company would need to do in order to move from social entrepreneurship toward sustainable entrepreneurship.

As for social entrepreneurship, Young and Tilley concluded that Day Chocolate Company was a "social entrepreneur" based on its progress with respect to at least four of the elements in their sustainable entrepreneurship model:

- *Socio-efficiency*: There was evidence of a positive social impact on the cocoa growers and the local community as well as consumers; however, Young and Tilley noted that more information was needed on working conditions in the other parts of the supply chain such as chocolate production and within the company itself.
- *Socio-effectiveness*: As noted earlier, there was evidence of positive impacts on the cocoa growers and the local community.
- *Social responsibility*: The company was taking responsibility for the production of cocoa; however, further information was needed regarding the impacts on other stakeholders.
- *Economic equity*: The unique ownership structure, which included suppliers, a charity, and a for-profit company with sustainable aims, coupled with the fair trade scheme that the company was operating under allowed suppliers to receive a guaranteed price for their cocoa. However, Young and Tilley noted that more evidence needed to be collected on other economic equity issues, such as wage differentials within the company and throughout its entire supply chain.

Young and Tilley cautioned that their conclusion that the Day Chocolate Company was a social entrepreneurship did come with several caveats. First, as mentioned several times earlier, more evidence regarding certain of the elements was needed. Second, Young and Tilley wondered whether selling chocolate was at odds with the "sufficiency" element of their sustainable entrepreneurship model given the potential negative health impacts of consuming products with a high sugar content and the lack of restrictions on the amount of product that could be sold that could potentially have larger and larger environmental impacts. While it might be impossible to totally overcome these issues when the product in question is chocolate, companies can mitigate some of the potential harms by restricting/rationing sales, reducing the size of servings, educating consumers on the harm of a high sugar diet, and providing labelling that goes beyond the minimum disclosures legally required. At a more basic level, it is also fair to ask whether the sufficiency element can ever be satisfied when the product in question is a luxury item such as chocolates.

As for progress toward achieving sustainable entrepreneurship, Young and Tilley turned to examining the key elements in their model associated with the relationships between economic, environmental, and social entrepreneurs and sustainable entrepreneurship that have not already been discussed earlier and offered the following prescriptions:

- *Inter-generational equity*: The future generations in the community need to be taken into account not only by ensuring that cocoa farming is a long-term enterprise but also that the community develops a diversity of enterprise beyond cocoa farming.
- *Environmental stability*: Issues with regard to this element center around identifying and mitigating potential harmful environmental impacts of the production of the product, with ideas including shifting to organic production; changes in transport modes within the supply chain (e.g., not using air freight, shifting to rail freight, and reducing "food miles"); and addressing the impacts from the production and disposal of packaging (e.g., reducing packaging and shifting to better materials).
- *Environmental sustainability*: Starting to move to a "zero impact company" by analyzing whether the production and use of the product can be radically altered or whether another type of product with less of an impact will achieve the fair trade principles of the company.
- *Futurity*: Contributing to the well-being of future generations in the community through participation in long-term education, health, and cultural programs in collaboration with the farming community.

Young and Tilley explained that the case of Day Chocolate Company illustrates how a company can achieve social entrepreneurship status yet still remain far from what they consider to be sustainable entrepreneurship. In this instance, the company would need to evolve in several ways including changes in its overall objective and changes in many areas of its operational activities to address the other elements of the sustainable entrepreneurship model. Young and Tilley stressed that "there is nothing wrong with being a social or environmental entrepreneur if that is the aim, but all elements of the model need to be balanced, not just a few, before entrepreneurs can describe themselves as 'sustainable entrepreneurs.'"

Sources: Young, W., and F. Tilley. 2006. "Can Businesses Move Beyond Efficiency? The Shift toward Effectiveness and Equity in the Corporate Sustainability Debate," *Business Strategy and the Environment*, 15, pp. 402, 412–14; Doherty, B. 2003. "A Divine Alternative International Chocolate Business Model?" *International Sustainable Development Research Conference* ERP: Shipley.

Table 6.1 Assessment questions for sustainable entrepreneurs

The following list of assessment questions incorporate requirements for and elements of sustainable entrepreneurship proposed in several well-known models and frameworks of corporate sustainability and sustainable entrepreneurship listed as sources as follows.

Leadership and Governance Considerations

- Have we identified and integrated sustainable value propositions into our business model (e.g., climate change initiatives, "cradle-to-cradle" design, eco-premium solutions, sustainability leadership and so on)?
- Have we integrated sustainability into all aspects of our value chain (e.g., increased support for research and development and innovation, particularly eco-premium solutions; emphasis on functional excellence in sourcing arrangements and manufacturing; and emphasis on eco-premium solutions in sales and marketing)?
- Have we implemented processes and procedures necessary for compliance and ensuring a long-term license to operate (e.g., environmental management systems, product stewardship and distribution, integrity and risk management, health, safety and security management, employment practices, including people development and diversity/inclusion and community involvement)?
- Is our pursuit of sustainable entrepreneurship a self-initiated process and not simply a response to external pressures?
- Have we identified clear aims and targets with respect to sustainable entrepreneurship and are they closely related to our practices and aligned with our values and primary activities?
- Are our aims and targets with respect to sustainable entrepreneurship closely related to the actual needs and preferences of consumers?
- Are we able to explain the relationship between our activities and production processes and sustainability (e.g., are we providing consumers and pressure groups with a transparent overview of the investments we are making related to sustainable entrepreneurship)?
- Have we developed a business model and strategic plans that will enable us to adhere to our aims and targets with respect to sustainable entrepreneurship on a long-term basis?
- Have we developed and maintained an organizational culture that ensures that the preferred practices relating to sustainable entrepreneurship are shared by the organization as a whole and not just among a small group of organizational leaders (e.g., is everyone in the organization given an opportunity to participate in decision making processes and is information relating to sustainability issues widely disseminated throughout the organization)?

Economic Considerations

- Does our business model emphasize innovation, capital efficiency, risk management, margin improvement, growth enhancement and total shareholder return?
- Can we make our product or provide our service at a profit so that our business model can survive and grow to achieve economic sustainability?
- Does our business provide and ensure that the employees producing our products and providing our services will earn a living wage?
- Are men and women producing our products and providing our services being paid the same amount for the same work?

- Are we finding new ways to honor everyone involved in our business, regardless of race, sex, nationality, or religion, and respect human rights and diversity and treat our employees with great care?
- Do we acknowledge and respect the channels for fair labor relations and bargaining regarding the conditions of work?
- Have we developed and implemented a pricing structure for our products and services that does not shift the cost of our sustainable entrepreneurship practices to consumers?
- Does our business model promote the distribution of economic wealth fairly between existing generations as well as future generations?
- Do we include the economic welfare of future generations among the factors that are considered when making decisions and engaging in operating activities?

Environmental Considerations
- Is our ecological strategy economically viable and do our service or production processes use natural resources efficiently (e.g., life-cycle management) and reduce waste, air pollution, and other environmental damage (e.g., releases and spills and water and land emissions)?
- Will the operation of our factories and offices improve the quality of life of all stakeholders and restore ecosystems?
- Are we identifying ways in which our products and services could enhance the health of employees and customers?
- Do we have processes and procedures, as well an appropriate organizational culture, in place to ensure compliance with environmental and health and safety regulations and effective response to environmental crises caused by our operational activities?
- Are we obeying nature's laws and creating habitats?
- Will our product or service contribute to the balance of the local ecology?
- Are we taking steps to achieve better technical effectiveness and/or a complete alternative to eco-efficiency?
- Does our business model achieve inter-generational inheritance of natural capital, both positive and negative (i.e., pollution and so on)?
- Does our business model exert positive forces on the environment to stabilize and where necessary restore the various ecosystem functions (e.g., climate change)?
- Do we include long-term environmental stability among the factors that are considered when making decisions and engaging in operating activities?

Social Considerations
- Does our business model incorporate core socio-economics principles such as jobs creation, skills enhancement, local economic impacts, community outreach, social investments, business ethics, and security?
- How efficient is our business model with respect to the minimization of negative impacts (e.g., workplace accidents) and the maximization of positive social impacts (e.g., training and health benefits)?
- Are our products and services accessible and thus benefitting all or limited in availability and just benefitting an elite few?
- Is our business model mindful of the actions of individual consumers to make responsible choices and the collective actions of consumers to boycott or subvert corporate branding and marketing strategies that are believed to lead to harm to the environment and/or society in general?

- Are we taking responsibility and being accountable for direct and indirect and negative and positive social impacts of our activities on existing generations?
- Do we include the social well-being of future generations among the factors that are considered when making decisions and engaging in operating activities?

Sources: Young, W., and F. Tilley. 2006. "Can Businesses Move Beyond Efficiency? The Shift toward Effectiveness and Equity in the Corporate Sustainability Debate," *Business Strategy and the Environment*, 15, p. 402; Dyllick, T., and K. Hockerts. March 2002. "Beyond the Business Case for Corporate Sustainability," *Business Strategy and the Environment* 11, p. 130; McDonough, W., and M. Braungart. 2002. "Design for the Triple Top Line: New Tools for Sustainable Commerce." *Corporate Environmental Strategy* 9, no. 3, p. 251; Janssen Groesbeek, M. 2001. *Sustainable Entrepreneurship–Theory, Practice, Instruments.* Amsterdam: Business Contact; and Bos, A. 2002. "Sustainable Entrepreneurship in a Changing Europe: Pedagogy of Ethics for Corporate Organizations in Transformation," In *EuroDiversity: A Business Guide to Managing Differences,* eds. G.F. Simons, D. Min et al., 16. Oxford, UK and Woburn, USA: Butterworth-Heinemann; Sustainche Farm Project (http://sustainche-farm.org) (sustainability development policies); and AkzoNobel (https://akzonobel.com/) (sustainability framework).

Benefits of Practicing Sustainable Entrepreneurship for Companies

Bos noted two reasons for all companies, including large and established firms, to take into account the socio-and eco-ethical impact of their business activities: avoiding bad publicity and damage to their corporate reputation that can lead to losses of income, profits, and share value as consumers consciously boycott their products and services or unconsciously decide to stop doing business with the company; and a sense of idealism which leads companies to extend their goals beyond profit-making to include development of a public reputation for demonstrating respect to people and planet.[57] Sustainability has become increasingly popular with larger firms as evidence mounts that sustainable companies outperform others on indexes that measure financial results, social and environmental accountability. Among the most popular sustainable entrepreneurship policies and practices among larger companies are consultation with a broader group of stakeholders, including public opinion and environmental interest groups, and sharper focus on product-and supply chain-directed environmental care.

---

[57] Bos, A. 2002. "Sustainable Entrepreneurship in a Changing Europe: Pedagogy of Ethics for Corporate Organizations in Transformation." In *EuroDiversity: A Business Guide to Managing Differences*, eds. G.F. Simons and D. Min et al., 16. Oxford, UK and Woburn, US: Butterworth-Heinemann.

Sustainability Adoption Matrix

The Sustainable Entrepreneurship Research Platform, operating under the auspices of the Amsterdam Business School at the University of Amsterdam, used the results of a student-led study of why and how small and large fashion firms adopted sustainable practices to create a sustainability adoption matrix based on two dimensions of motivation and resource commitment.[58] The matrix categorized the following four types of sustainability adopters:

- *Catalyzing*: A catalyzing business scores high on both motivation to adopt sustainable practices and commitment of resources and, as such, can be seen as a potential catalyst for change with respect to social and ecological sustainable practices. A catalyzing business is strongly positioned as a sustainability leader in its industry because of its leverage and buying power with suppliers. Substantial resources have been invested and committed to improving sustainable practices and the company has been highly exposed to sustainability issues and responded by implementing dedicated and active monitoring and management of supplier's sustainability.

- *Compliant*: A compliant business focuses primarily on complying with the rules and regulations of sustainable practices, often committing a substantial amount of resources to the compliance function and related activities (e.g., monitoring and training employees and suppliers). While these businesses are aware and knowledgeable about sustainability requirements, their motivation to adopt sustainable practices is not driven by a desire to be a catalyst for sustainability change, perhaps because of the company's size or position in the marketplace.

---

[58] Sustainability Adoption Matrix. 2015. *Amsterdam: Sustainable Entrepreneurship Research Platform*. Amsterdam Business School at the University of Amsterdam.

- *Purposive*: A purposive business scores high on intrinsic motivation to adopt sustainable practices but has yet to make a substantial commitment of resources, perhaps because of size and/or the stage of development. These companies, through the leadership of their founders, have strong values and norms about sustainability rooted in their "organizational DNA," but need to find efficient ways to overcome their own shortage of resources in order to have greater impact as a sustainability player in their industries.
- *Hesitant*: A hesitant business is relatively new to the area of sustainability and has yet to develop motivation to adopt sustainable practices or commit substantial resources to implementing and/or improving sustainability practices. Hesitant businesses generally have some awareness of sustainability issues in their industries; however, sustainability issues have yet to become part of their strategic planning (e.g., sustainable sourcing or production) and/or employee training and resources have not been set aside yet to monitor or train suppliers. The situation can be attributed to a variety of reasons, such as low exposure to sustainability issues and/or limited available resources and the path to increasing sustainability impact is more complex for these types of businesses.

The description of the matrix and the various categories was accompanied by prescriptions for how companies can change their positions. For example, compliant businesses have already invested a substantial level of resources in complying with the rules and regulations of sustainable practices and are already aware and knowledgeable about sustainability requirements. For those businesses, the next steps are increasing intrinsic motivation within the company to be more sustainable and seeking out opportunities to collaborate with suppliers and competitors to affect more sustainable change in their industries. Purposive businesses have the requisite motivation; however, resources are a significant issue and they are advised to tap into the knowledge and resources of NGOs to help monitor and train suppliers and seek out alliances and collaborations with other similarly-minded firms in the industry value chain (e.g., producers, suppliers, and consumers) to bundle resources and generate impactful change. As for hesitant businesses, transitioning to a catalyst is probably out of reach or undesirable; however, it is feasible for them to increase their internal knowledge of sustainability in order to become more compliant without a significant investment of resources. In addition, hesitant businesses can, as their compliance practices become more mature, begin the difficult and time-consuming project of integrating sustainability into their organizational cultures and thus embedding sustainability into organizational processes, planning, and mindset (i.e., becoming more "purposive").

Instruments of Sustainable Entrepreneurship

Legal and regulatory requirements pertaining to sustainability are proliferating and consumers and other stakeholders are demanding information about sustainability-related issues and problems that go beyond that which may be required by governments. For larger companies with complex supply chains, this means that they must establish procedures with their suppliers to ensure that they receive consistent data and then integrate that data into performance measurement and reporting tools that meet the needs and expectations of all stakeholders. For smaller companies, many of which are part of the aforementioned supply chains, the pressures associated with dealing with complex social and environmental issues, including the demands of their larger customers, can create great stress given their limited financial and human resources.[59]

There is a continuously growing array of techniques and procedures that are available to promote sustainable entrepreneurship and provide companies with standards and guidelines they can follow in developing,

---

[59] Racelis, A. 2014. "Sustainable Entrepreneurship in Asia: A Proposed Theoretical Framework Based on Literature Review." *Journal of Management for Global Sustainability* 2, p. 6 (for discussion of environmental management accounting and supply chain management, see Burritt, R., S. Schaltegger, M. Bennett, T. Pohjola, and M. Csutora, eds. 2011. *Environmental Management Accounting and Supply Chain Management*. London: Springer).

implementing, and monitoring their sustainable entrepreneurship initiatives.[60] Crais and Vereeck noted that production standards focusing on measuring product quality and performance have been around for a long time and that it is relatively easy to measure whether or not a particular product complies with a standard. The more difficult task is assessing processes that are thought to be necessary in order for sustainable entrepreneurship to be successful. For example, while guidelines for human resources management, eco-design, and management systems are available they are often criticized for being either too complex or too general and thus difficult to put into practice.

Other faults with process-focused standards are that it is hard to interpret results and make comparisons among companies and that "international standards" do not take into account differences in management norms among industries. As a result, simplified and "unofficial" versions of standards have been developed to make them more accessible and/or more specialized (e.g., an unofficial version of ISO 14000 was created for auditing the "working environment") and different industries have adopted their own versions. In spite of these problems, the topics covered by standards and certification programs continue to expand and now include not only the traditional areas of product quality, environment, and management but also social accountability, information security, ethical trade, equality in the workplace, and fire prevention.[61]

---

[60] Crals, E., and L. Vereeck. July 18, 2016. "Sustainable Entrepreneurship in SMEs—Theory and Practice." 7–8. http://inter-disciplinary.net/ptb/ejgc/ejgc3/cralsvereeck%20paper.pdf (accessed July 18, 2016). For further discussion of certain of the instruments described herein, see "Governance: A Library of Resources for Sustainable Entrepreneurs" prepared and distributed by the Sustainable Entrepreneurship Project (www.seproject.org).

[61] Id. at p. 8 (citing Martensson, M. 2001. "Management Systems, Certificates, Labelling: How Many Can a Small Company Manage?" In *European Foundation for the Improvement of Living and Working Conditions, Sustainable Development, SMEs and New Enterprises*, 10–11. Conference Report Luxembourg: Office for Official Publications of the European Communities).

Sustainability Reports

The rise of interest in sustainable entrepreneurship has included sharper focus on measurement and assessment of the sustainability initiatives of companies and reporting and communication of the results of those assessments to the stakeholders of those companies. Sustainability measurement, assessment, reporting, and communication have become a well-studied phenomenon and approaches vary significantly.[62] Each company must confront and attempt to overcome several basic challenges: how to measure and assess the degree of environmental or social responsibility orientation in the company; identifying and describing the company's environmental and social goals and policies, describing how the company's environmental and social programs are organized and managed; and effectively describing and communicating the environmental and social issues the company is seeking to address.[63] In addition, measurement of results outside of the traditional economic "bottom line" (i.e., profits and losses) remains a difficult and heavily debated issue: how can companies reasonably measure how socially responsible it has been throughout its operations and how can they measure how environmentally responsible they have been in carrying out their operations?[64]

A number of larger companies have published annual sustainability reports to inform their shareholders and other stakeholders of progress that has been made with respect to pursuit of organizational goals relating to sustainability and corporate social responsibility (CSR). One basic reason for reporting is to make sure that sustainability and CSR initiatives are properly managed and that persons involved understand they will be accountable for their actions. Other good reasons for reporting include giving interested parties (i.e., stakeholders) the information they

---

[62] Godeman, J., and G. Michelsen, eds. Springer 2011. *Sustainability Communication: Interdisciplinary Perspectives and Theoretical Foundations*. London.

[63] Schaltegger, S., and M. Wagner. 2011. "Sustainable Entrepreneurship and Sustainability Innovation: Categories and Interactions." *Business Strategy and the Environment* 20, p. 222.

[64] Racelis, A. 2014. "Sustainable Entrepreneurship in Asia: A Proposed Theoretical Framework Based on Literature Review." *Journal of Management for Global Sustainability* 2, p. 3.

need in order to make decisions about purchasing the company's products and/or investing in the company (the level of funding from investors focusing their interest on ethical businesses is continuously increasing) or otherwise supporting the company's community activities; collecting information that can be used to make changes and improvements to the company's sustainability strategies and CSR commitments; improving internal operations; managing and reducing risks; and strengthening relationships with stakeholders. However, in order to achieve the greatest benefits from reporting, companies need to carry out those activities in a rigorous and professional manner using tools and standards that are widely recognized and accepted among those interested in the results.

The scope of the company's reporting efforts will depend on various factors including the size of the company, the focus of its sustainability activities, and the financial and human resources available for investment in reporting. When establishing plans for reporting it is useful to obtain and review copies of reports that have been done and published by comparable companies. Reports of larger companies are generally available on their corporate websites and extensive archives of past CSR-focused reports can be accessed through various online platforms such as CorporateRegister.com, a widely recognized global online directory of corporate responsibility reports. It is also important to have a good working understanding of well-known reporting and verification initiatives such as the Global Reporting Initiative, commonly referred to as the "GRI Guidelines"; the AccountAbility AA1000 series; the United Nations Global Compact; and the International Auditing and Assurance Standards Board ISAE 3000 standard. Country-specific information is also available through professional organizations such as the Canadian Chartered Professional Accountants, which has published an extensive report on sustainability reporting in Canada.

Smaller businesses generally do not have the resources to engage a professional auditor to collect the information normally seen in reports published by larger companies or prepare elaborate reports on their sustainability and CSR activities; however, small businesses can post information regarding their activities on their websites, communicate information to customers, suppliers and other business partners and community members by adding new sections to the company's brochures and pamphlets and posting pictures of activities that can be viewed by visitors to the company's facilities, and placing information into local newspapers.[65] In addition, staff briefings on sustainability and CSR activities should be held on a regular basis and small businesses should also invite business partners and community members to events at the company's facilities which showcase some of the things that the company is doing with respect to sustainability.

Audits

Environmental audits evaluate the organization as a whole and environmental management practices in particular. The focus of environmental audits is on the organization's environmental controls systems and includes areas such as competences, responsibilities, communication, and education. The purpose and goal of the audit process is to objectively obtain and evaluate audit evidence to determine whether the organization's environmental management system conforms to the audit criteria and then communicate the results of the audit to senior management of the organization. The International Standards Organization (ISO) first developed standards for environmental auditing (i.e., ISO 14010, ISO 14011, and ISO 14012) in 1996 and the current standards are set out in ISO 14001.

While standardization has been the trend with respect to environmental audits, there are few generally recognized and accepted standards for conducting a social audit. One notable exception is AA 1000, which is a framework for assessing, designing, implementing, and communicating stakeholder engagement. Crals and Vereeck described a social audit as the process by which an organization reflects on, measures, evaluates, and reports on its social impact and ethical behavior and adjusts them according to its goals and values and those of its stakeholders.[66] According to Borgo et al. the four key elements of an effective social audit are

---

[65] Hohnen, P., (Author), and J. Potts (Editor), ed. 2007. *Corporate Social Responsibility: An Implementation Guide for Business*, 72. Winnipeg CAN: International Institute for Sustainable Development.

[66] Id. at p. 9.

dialogue with the stakeholders; use of quantitative and qualitative performance indicators and benchmarks; external verification; and reporting of and communication about goals, efforts, and results. A social audit process requires the implantation of a social bookkeeping system that can be used to track performance indicators and benchmarks on metrics such as absenteeism, dismissals and resignations, labor accidents, and total earnings.[67]

Regardless of whether a generally-recognized audit standard is used, the recommended audit process begins with the selection of an audit team and determination of the goals and purposes of the audit by the organization. The preferred approach is for the audit team to be independent and not related to the organization or the activities that are being audited so that the audit can be conducted in an objective manner and free of conflicts of interest. Successful audits require cooperation from the organization, access to sufficient information about the activities that are being audited, and a systematic work process. The work process includes standard procedures for gathering information, questionnaires and checklists that can be used for collecting information and conducting interviews and a mutual understanding between the audit team and the organization as to schedule for the audit and content of final report. Audits can be time consuming and expensive, especially when the organization does not have a previous history of working with ISO and comparable standards.

Codes

Many large and well-known global companies have adopted corporate codes of conduct, which Crals and Vereeck described as statements of principles by which a business agrees to abide voluntarily over the course of its operation and which creates and continuously evaluates benchmarks for the senior management of the business.[68] The first codes of conduct were a reaction to criticisms and protests from activists regarding perceived

---

[67] Id. (citing Borgo, E., B. Mazijn, and S. Spillemaeckers. 2000. "Een integrale Benadering Van de Ketenanalyse Ten Behoeve Van Ketenbeheer Door Bedrijven." *Gent: Centrum Duurzame Ontwikkeling* (CDO), 46).

[68] Id. at p. 9.

problems in the way that companies related to consumers and treated the environment in which they operated. Companies implemented principles and guidelines relating to sourcing and operational practices; however, initial efforts were often vague, a problem that eventually led to creation of uniform codes.

Management Systems

Crals and Vereeck defined a management system as the organizational structure, responsibilities, procedures, processes, and operational duties necessary to carry out certain goals.[69] While well-run companies have general management systems that address overall operational, financial, and strategic management, sustainable entrepreneurship requires specialized management systems for setting and pursuing goals in areas such as environmental care, quality assurance, and safety. ISO 9001, the best-known quality management standard, have been available since the early 1990s and, as mentioned earlier, environmental audits have been facilitated by ISO 14001 and other standards relating to environment management systems. Social Accountability International has promulgated SA 8000 to assess social management systems and measure social performance against a range of indicators including the United Declaration of Human Rights, conventions of the International Labor Organization, United Nations and national laws and industry and corporate codes.

Organizations interested in improving their practices with respect to social responsibility, including engagement with their stakeholders, may also refer to International Standard 26000 (ISO 26000), which was first released by the International Organization for Standardization (ISO) in November 2010; however, ISO 26000 is not a management system standard, does not contain requirements, and thus does not facilitate certification in the manner that often occurs with other ISO standards. Instead, ISO 26000 explains the core subjects and associated issues relating to social responsibility including organizational governance, human rights, labor practices, the environment, fair operating practices, consumer issues, and community involvement and development. For each

---

[69] Id. at p. 10.

core subject, information is provided on its scope, including key issues; its relationship to social responsibility; related principles and considerations; and related actions and expectations. For example, with respect to labor practices, one of the core subjects, organizations are reminded to integrate consideration of the following issues into their policies, organizational culture, strategies, and operations: employment and employment relationships; conditions of work and social protection; social dialogue; health and safety at work; and human development and training in the workplace.

Measuring Sustainable Business Practice

Organizations must have a method for measuring the sustainability of their business practices. Companies are used to measuring financial results; however, it is only recently that focus has turned toward the development of tools for nonfinancial measurement of sustainability. Larger organizations with sufficient resources are able to apply the sophisticated and comprehensive Global Reporting Initiative (GRI) Standards for sustainability reporting developed by GRI (www.globalreporting.org); however, start-ups may find this to be too much trouble and instead may create their own systems that include the following common areas for measurement:

Environmental Results

- Energy use
- Materials use
- Energy efficiency results
- Carbon emissions
- Emissions and waste (e.g., carbon emissions, water discharged, waste by type and disposal methods)
- Water use
- Product improvements to minimize environmental impact
- Results of initiatives to mitigate negative environmental impacts

Economic Results

- Standard entry level wage compared to minimum wage
- Spending on locally based suppliers
- Financial implications for the organization's activities due to climate change

Social Results (including ethical and cultural)

- Employee time donated to voluntary causes
- Donations and in-kind support to community groups
- Breaches of ethical behavior
- Breaches of regulatory and/or legal compliance
- Customer labeling
- Customer health and safety
- Stakeholder trust

- Staff perception of the organization as a good citizen (i.e., an organization that behaves ethically and acts in an environmentally and socially responsible manner)
- Specific engagement with indigenous peoples about matters of cultural significance to them
- Results of initiatives to mitigate negative social impacts
- Partnerships within the organization's supply chain that are designed to improve industry environmental and/or social outcomes

It is important for organizations to carefully assess their operations in order to identify activities that have potential sustainability impacts. Obviously, courier drivers produce carbon emissions from their vehicles and cheap, poorly designed products are like to increase natural resource waste due to their short life cycle; however, these are rarely the only sustainability impacts for an organization. Other prompts for identifying key impacts that can and should be the targets for the organization's sustainability initiatives include the following:

- Significance to key stakeholders, including representative of future generations such as children of employees living in the community in which the company operates
- Technical information, including environmental reviews and social impact reports
- Review of current and potential sustainable development issues and trends that are of importance or potential importance to civil society, both from a risk and opportunity perspective (e.g., changing attitudes toward climate change that have created both new costs, including taxes and expenses associated with regulatory requirements, and opportunities to commercialize new product solutions)
- Review of international good practice and consideration of issues that are being addressed by industry leaders in sustainable development and the organization's peers
- Impacts and issues that are identified in standards such as the Global Reporting Initiative, SA8000, and the UN Global Compact

Source: Sustainable Business: A Handbook for Starting a Business (New Zealand Trade and Enterprise).

Sustainability Communication

Racelis explained that the chief concern of "sustainability communication" is contributing to critical awareness of, and social discourse regarding, the issues and problems that arise with respect to the relationship between humans and their environment and then relating those issues and problems to social values and norms.[70] Racelis explained that sustainability communication is a process of communication and mutual understanding that deals with both the causes of global ecological dangers

[70] Racelis, A. 2014. "Sustainable Entrepreneurship in Asia: A Proposed Theoretical Framework Based on Literature Review." *Journal of Management for Global Sustainability* 2.

that lead to severe economic, ecological, social, and cultural distortions and with the potential solutions to those problems. According to Racelis, sustainability communication is necessary in order for humans to be able to assume their responsibilities and effectively reshape their relationships with one another and with the natural world.[71] Racelis mentioned several methods and instruments for sustainability measuring, assessment and communication including environmental management accounting, social marketing, empowerment, instruments of participation and planning, and education.[72]

Labels

According to Crals and Vereeck, labeling is a means for companies to distinguish their products from others in a specific category.[73] In order for a product label to have value, however, the criteria must be well-defined and transparent and should be set by independent labeling authorities. In the environmental area, companies follow ISO-type standards in order to be able to market products that have been labeled as "environmentally friendly."

Advantages and Challenges of Sustainable Entrepreneurship for SMEs

The potential benefits available to all companies from engaging in sustainable entrepreneurship cited by Bos have already been mentioned earlier; however, he also believed that practicing sustainable entrepreneurship could provide special and badly-needed advantages for small- and medium-sized enterprises (SMEs) such as the following: kindling internal dynamics for people and production management, resulting in bolder investment engagements that could lead to superior steps in

---

[71] Id. at pp. 5–6 (citing Godeman, J., and G. Michelsen, eds. Springer 2011. *Sustainability Communication: Interdisciplinary Perspectives and Theoretical Foundations.* London: Springer).

[72] Id. at p. 7.

[73] Id. at p. 10.

technology and personnel acquirement for greater, higher-quality returns in the long run; the ability to offer their services and products to large companies who themselves turn out to be sustainability practitioners and thus require sustainable-minded suppliers, opportunities that can bring guaranteed revenues from sales that can be used to cover the increased costs of engaging in sustainable operations; and opportunities to engage with, and forge strong ties in, the local community and thus develop interpersonal relationships that sway interest in favor of that particular SME instead of the general, corporate-only, nonpersonal image of the larger companies.[74] Additional potential benefits to SMEs from choosing sustainable entrepreneurship mentioned by Bos included

> the positive image and reputation gained from these practices, lesser dependence on diminishing resources, more efficient production due to superior technologies and staff skill, higher quality of risk control to especially avoid situations like environmental debacles, labor disputes and the like, less to deal with if government makes a turn for more social and environmental requirement improvements and a greater motivational source for current employees to enjoy their work environment-plus incentive for new employees to join the company.[75]

Crals and Vereeck acknowledged that limited resources often make it difficult for SMEs to pay the same level of attention to sustainable entrepreneurship as larger companies; however, they argued that adoption of sustainable entrepreneurship policies and practices by SMEs could lead to dramatic changes in their production processes and human resource

---

[74] Bos, A. 2002. "Sustainable Entrepreneurship in a Changing Europe: Pedagogy of Ethics for Corporate Organizations in Transformation." In *EuroDiversity: A Business Guide to Managing Differences*, eds. G.F. Simons and D. Min et al., 16. Oxford, UK and Woburn, USA: Butterworth-Heinemann (as cited and described in Rey, L. December 2011. *Sustainable Entrepreneurship and its Viability*, 16. Rotterdam: Master Thesis for MS in Entrepreneurship, Strategy and Organizations Economics from Erasmus School of Economics).
[75] Id.

management practices that will trigger bolder investment in technology and human capital that will ultimately generate positive results in the long-term.[76] Other strategic reasons for SMEs to embrace sustainable entrepreneurship include fulfilling the requirements that larger companies are imposing on their supply-chain partners, thus expanding opportunities for business partnerships with larger firms, and establishing a niche in their local communities that will be difficult for larger global companies to duplicate. Additional potential benefits of sustainable entrepreneurship for SMEs mentioned by Crals and Vereeck included a positive image and reputation; lesser dependency on depleted resources; higher motivation of employees and attractiveness for new employees; efficient production due to superior technologies and better skilled staff; superior insight in market preferences and opportunities; risk control with respect to environmental accidents, scandals, bad publicity, and so on; and lower burden from changes in environmental and social legislation. The New Zealand Business Council for Sustainable Development mentioned the following advantages of applying sustainable business practice: being more efficient and competitive; accessing the rapidly growing group of consumers looking to buy sustainable solutions; engaging in responsible entrepreneurship; increasing financial return and reducing risk for shareholders; attracting and retaining employees; improving customer sales and loyalty; growing supplier commitment; strengthening community relations; contributing to environmental sustainability; and building trust and mutual understanding through stakeholder engagement.[77]

The main problem for SMEs is "affordability," both in terms of the financial costs of implementing the instruments described elsewhere in this Guide and in terms of the time and effort required of executives, managers, and employees. Issues for SMEs mentioned by Crals and Vereeck included the risk that the sheer variety of available management systems created overlap and waste and the prohibitive cost of obtaining all

---

[76] Crals, E., and L. Vereeck. July 18, 2016. "Sustainable Entrepreneurship in SMEs—Theory and Practice." 6–7. http://inter-disciplinary.net/ptb/ejgc/ejgc3/cralsvereeck%20paper.pdf (accessed July 18, 2016).

[77] *Sustainable Business: A Handbook for Starting a Business.* New Zealand Trade and Enterprise.

of the certificates that would be necessary to signal to the outside world that the SME is serious about its commitments to sustainability.[78] A list of problems confronting SMEs with regard to sustainable development compiled by Hilton in 2000 included the following[79]:

- Lack of resources, time, and money;
- Lack of capabilities, skills, and knowledge;
- Lack of awareness of issues, risks, regulation;
- Lack of training needs analysis;
- Lack of awareness of tools and techniques;
- Lack of awareness of provisions and their benefits;
- Lack of strategic and holistic thinking;
- Lack of internal communication and integration;
- Lack of work floor staff involvement;
- Lack of flexibility and fear of change;
- Lack of external communication (networking); and
- Mistrust of other companies in groups.

Crals and Vereeck reported that SMEs in Europe had been slow to implement sustainable entrepreneurship practices and noted that while efforts had been made to support sustainable entrepreneurship among

---

[78] Crals, E., and L. Vereeck. July 18, 2016. "Sustainable Entrepreneurship in SMEs—Theory and Practice." 10–11. http://inter-disciplinary.net/ptb/ejgc/ejgc3/cralsvereeck%20paper.pdf (accessed July 18, 2016). Crals and Vereeck suggested that SMEs could use alternative means for publicizing their commitment to sustainable entrepreneurship such as publishing sustainability reports that define their strategies, goals, and activities with respect to financial, social, and environmental performance and showcase their achievements in each of those areas. See the case study of ES Tooling, a Belgian SME that positioned itself as a sustainable entrepreneur and relied on a sustainability report as an important tool in that process, in the Crals and Vereenck article at pp. 12–14.
[79] Id. at p. 11 (citing Hilton, M. 2001. "SME Support for Sustainable Development: Principles and Practice." In *European Foundation for the Improvement of Living and Working Conditions, Sustainable Development, SMEs and New Enterprises*, 25–27. Conference Report, Luxembourg: Office for Official Publications of the European Communities).

SMEs they had often been too abstract and impractical and poorly tailored to the needs of SMEs.[80] According to Crals and Vereeck support systems were general (i.e., insufficiently applicable to and appropriate for specific industries), too passive, superficial or lacking in quality, too expensive, time-consuming or inflexible, not correctly tailored to the needs of SMEs, or poorly targeted or promoted. SMEs were encouraged to pursue environmental management systems and certification; however, businesses grew disenchanted because certification alone does not guarantee significant improvements and often raises, rather than lowers, costs of production. Crals and Vereeck argued that more emphasis should be placed on teaching SMEs about strategies that are both environmentally-positive and productivity enhancing (e.g., eco-efficiency, eco-design, integrated approaches, and sustainable production).

Bergh noted that environmental and social entrepreneurs face many of the same challenges as commercial entrepreneurs including access to capital, creating efficient capital markets, leadership and organizational concerns, policy and regulatory issues, measurement and performance metrics, and access to incubators and support organizations. However, Bergh pointed to several specific challenges that environmental and social entrepreneurs must face that are not shared by their commercial counterparts, such as the ethical justification for existence, and that some of the challenges that appear at first glance to be similar to those of commercial entrepreneurs are actually based on very different root causes (e.g., access to capital is denied to social entrepreneurs because of the length of time required for their innovations to become commercially viable and policy frameworks that do not provide a climate conducive to green entrepreneurs due to government's lack of ecological awareness and willpower.[81] Looking specifically at the South African context, Bergh identified the

---

[80] Id. at p. 11.

[81] Bergh, L. July 2013. *Sustainability-Driven Entrepreneurship: Perceptions of Challenges and Obstacles in a South African Context*, 12–13. Cambridge UK: Master Thesis for MS in Sustainability Leadership (citing Linnanen, L. 2002. "An Insider's Experiences with Environmental Entrepreneurship." *Greener Management International, Greenleaf Publishing [e-journal]* 38; and Isaak, R. 2002. "The Making of the Ecopreneur." *Greener Management International [e-journal]*, pp. 38–81).

following themes of potential constraints to environmental and social entrepreneurs[82]:

- *Access to Capital*: Environmental and social entrepreneurs often have more difficulties gaining access to seed funding than commercial entrepreneurs because they are working in difficult conditions on problems that are hard to solve and hence are considered high risk ventures. There is socially responsible capital available; however, the main target of those types of investors is generally later stage. In order to gain access to private capital, environmental and social entrepreneurs need to demonstrate that they are "high impact" with potential for multiple job creation, high profit generation that contributes to GDP, rapid scaling, and financial sustainability.
- *Enabling Environment*: Statutes and regulations, as well as government service providers, are often not supportive of the special needs of environmental and social entrepreneurs. Investment and funding criteria for social enterprises is difficult to determine and legal advice is limited. Governmental departments have often been criticized for lacking the relevant resources and correct skills and incentives for assisting and supporting civil society.
- *Business Development Services*: While there has been an increase in the number of financial and specialized providers of business development services for environmental and social entrepreneurs, including incubators and accelerators, they are typically located in large urban areas and seldom communicate with one another in order to coordinate their programs. Some of the providers, while claiming they are suitable for environmental and social entrepreneurs, are uninformed about their special needs and priorities.
- *Scaling for Impact*: Support and encouragement is needed to push environmental and social entrepreneurs to scale up

---

[82] Id. at pp. 13–16.

to the point where they attract the interest of funders and investors to fully commit to the entrepreneur's mission and the markets that they are trying to serve. The path to the scale up phase needs to include partnerships with government and business and increased availability of social venture funds. Attention also needs to be paid to monitoring, measuring, evaluating, and reporting the nonfinancial impact of environmental and social entrepreneurship so that entrepreneurs, investors, and government officials have better data to rely on in making decisions.

Integrating Sustainability into Strategic and Business Processes

Companies willing to pursue sustainability need to find ways to integrate it into their strategic and business processes. [83] AkzoNobel (https://akzonobel.com/), a leading global paints and coating company and a major producer of specialty chemicals, provided an example of a sustainability framework that included three phases—invent, manage, and improve—and a set of initiatives that addressed governance, economic, environmental, and social issues:

- The invention phase of the framework focused on identifying and integrating sustainable value propositions into the company's business model. In the environmental area this may include climate change initiatives (e.g., carbon policy, energy, and greenhouse gases) and initiatives based on managing scarce resources (e.g., "cradle-to-cradle" design). In the

---

[83] See, for example, Hockerts, K. 2003. *Sustainability Innovations, Ecological and Social Entrepreneurship and the Management of Antagonistic Assets*, 154. Difo-Druck: Bamberg, who claimed to have developed an entrepreneurial process model for sustainability entrepreneurship that aimed to identify distinct phases of sustainability entrepreneurship as well as the managerial practices that go along with them, thus providing sustainability entrepreneurs with a practical road map for managing the transformation from informal sector start-up to for-profit mainstream business.

economic/governance area, initiatives may include development of eco-premium solutions and external partnerships. In the social area initiatives might focus on development of sustainability leadership and creation of talent factories.

- The management phase of the framework focused on integrating sustainability into all aspects of the value chain (i.e., market research, research and development, investment decisions, sourcing, manufacturing, and sales and marketing). Examples of potential initiatives include increased support for research and development and innovation, particularly eco-premium solutions; emphasis on functional excellence in sourcing arrangements and manufacturing; and emphasizing eco-premium solutions in sales and marketing.

- The improvement phrase of the framework focused on continued compliance and ensuring a long-term "license to operate." Major areas of emphasis include environmental management (e.g., management and reduction of emissions and waste, raw material efficiency, energy and greenhouse gases, and land remediation); product stewardship and distribution; integrity and risk management (e.g., codes of conduct, competition compliance, anti-bribery, and supply chain management); health, safety, and security management (e.g., process safety); employment practices (e.g., people development and diversity/inclusion); and community involvement.

Case Study: Pearl Automation

Pearl Automation was founded in 2014 by three former senior managers from Apple's iPod and iPhone groups. While Pearl has maintained what its founders believe to be the best parts of Apple culture, particularly the focus on innovative design and creating products that provide the highest quality user experience, they have also made a conscious decision to reject certain elements of that culture that they found to be counterproductive for engaging employees and creating and maintaining a healthy work environment that allows employees to fill as if they are seen as valued contributors.

The first thing to understand about Pearl is its focus on using technology to improve the safety of the tens of millions of older cars that are being driven without the high tech safety features that are now commonly installed on newer models. Pearl seeks to develop products that will make the roads safer, a socially responsible goal that proved to be quite appealing to the dozens of former Apple employees who joined Pearl after growing weary of spending their professional lives worrying about incremental improvements to the iPhone and the Mac. One of the co-founders explained: "Adding safety features to the cars on the road today is a way to make them more useful. We want to help people to modernize their cars without having to buy a new one." Indeed this a laudable social objective; however, the number of older cards being used by consumers who are not interested in, or able to, invest in new models makes Pearl's target market quite large and the opportunity for economic success is apparent.

Open and continuous communication with everyone in the company is an important principle for the founders, something that stands in stark contrast to an Apple culture in which access to information was closely guarded and employees were discouraged from talking with one another about their jobs. At Pearl, the founders and other managers hold weekly meetings with the entire staff to provide briefings on upcoming products, the financial health of the company and technical problems that have been identified and the solutions that the company is pursuing. Employees are even given a chance to see and hear presentations that senior managers are making to the board of directors. The guiding principle behind these practices is that everyone at the company is seen as an important contributor to the company's success and in order to be effective they need to have as much information as possible.

The founders obviously believe that a culture of openness makes the design practices that have been imported from Apple more effective. For example, Pearl's products share the same level of complexity as the ones that employees worked on at Apple and Pearl has followed Apple's lead by breaking big projects down into smaller tasks that are assigned to small teams. Each of the team members is charged with completing one or more subtasks necessary for the team to be successful, something that was referred to at Apple as assigning people to be the "directly responsible individual." This approach maximizes participation and decentralizes decision making, in sharp contrast to the tight control that Steve Jobs, and now his successors, exerted over the smallest details relating to the work the Pearl employees did at Apple. Contributing at Pearl means having a say in what problems need to be solved, something that only works if employees have access to full product design picture.

Pearl's cultural and business competencies also include a disciplined approach to engineering, a passion for elegant and efficient design and an appreciation of the need to vigorously oversee the activities of the dozens of companies in the company's supply chain. Rigorous deadlines are set and presumably circulated among everyone in the company at the weekly meetings. Communication regarding technical issues compliments the company's focus on relentless investigation of design and operating flaws, a practice that also carries over to negative feedback from customers. The founders emphasized the importance of understanding why a failure occurred as a means for getting a good grasp on the full boundaries of the problems that must be solved. Pearl also invests a lot of time and effort in testing, something that the founders believe many start-ups do not pay enough attention to.

All in all, the early steps that Pearl has taken to develop and implement its business model include a number of important elements for all potential sustainable entrepreneurs to consider:

- Pearl's founders selected a business model that emphasizes innovation and proactively targets an important social issue: minimize the risks associated with driving by making cars safer.

- Pearl's products are closely related to the actual needs and preferences of potential customers and continuous testing of prototypes ensures that customer feedback is collected and integrated into product design.
- Borrowing from their experiences at Apple, the founders have established functional excellence as a requirement of Pearl's sourcing arrangements.
- The founders have created an organizational culture in which everyone is involved in the development and implementation of sustainability practices and has an opportunity to access information about the business model and contribute to the success of the product development and commercialization process.

However, Pearl also faces several challenges in its path toward sustainable entrepreneurship. For example, while the size of the potential market for its product seems apparent, the company has yet to demonstrate its ability to execute a production and pricing strategy that ensures the product will be accessible at reasonable prices that still allow the company to enjoy margins that will support survival of the business. Another consideration is whether making it easier for drivers to keep their older vehicles on the road will slow transition to newer, more environmentally-friendly cars or wider use of mass transit solutions.

Source: "Life After Apple." *The New York Times* (January 3, 2017), B1.

About the Author

Dr Alan S. Gutterman is the Founding Director of the Sustainable Entrepreneurship Project (www.seproject.org). In addition, Alan's prolific output of practical guidance and tools for legal and financial professionals, managers, entrepreneurs, and investors has made him one of the best-selling individual authors in the global legal publishing marketplace. His cornerstone work, *Business Transactions Solution*, is an online-only product available and featured on Thomson Reuter's Westlaw, the world's largest legal content platform, which includes almost 200 book-length modules covering the entire lifecycle of a business. Alan has also authored or edited over 40 books on sustainable entrepreneurship, management, business law and transactions, international law business, and technology management for a number of publishers including Thomson Reuters, Kluwer, Aspatore, Oxford, Quorum, ABA Press, Aspen, Sweet & Maxwell, Euromoney, CCH, and BNA. Alan has over three decades of experience as a partner and senior counsel with internationally recognized law firms counseling small and large business enterprises in the areas of general corporate and securities matters, venture capital, mergers and acquisitions, international law and transactions, strategic business alliances, technology transfers, and intellectual property, and has also held senior management positions with several technology-based businesses including service as the chief legal officer of a leading international distributor of IT products headquartered in Silicon Valley and as the chief operating officer of an emerging broadband media company. He has been an adjunct faculty member at several colleges and universities, including Boalt Hall, Golden Gate University, Hastings College of Law, Santa Clara University, and the University of San Francisco, teaching classes on a diverse range of topics including corporate finance, venture capital, corporate law, Japanese business law, and law and economic development, He received his AB, MBA, and JD from the University of California at Berkeley, a DBA from Golden Gate University, and a PhD from the University of Cambridge. For more information about Alan, his publications, or the Sustainable Entrepreneurship Project, please contact him directly at alangutterman@gmail.com, and follow him on LinkedIn (https://linkedin.com/in/alangutterman/).

Index

OTHER TITLES IN THE ENTREPRENEURSHIP AND SMALL BUSINESS MANAGEMENT COLLECTION

Scott Shane, Case Western University, Editor

- *Open Innovation Essentials for Small and Medium Enterprises: A Guide to Help Entrepreneurs in Adopting the Open Innovation Paradigm in Their Business* by Luca Escoffier, Adriano La Vopa, Phyllis Speser, and Daniel Satinsky
- *The Technological Entrepreneur's Playbook* by Ian Chaston
- *Licensing Myths & Mastery: Why Most Ideas Don't Work and What to Do About It* by William S. Seidel
- *Arts and Entrepreneurship* by J. Mark Munoz and Julie Shields
- *The Human Being's Guide to Business Growth: A Simple Process for Unleashing the Power of Your People for Growth* by Gregory Scott Chambers
- *Understanding the Family Business: Exploring the Differences Between Family and Nonfamily Businesses, Second Edition* by Keanon J. Alderson

Announcing the Business Expert Press Digital Library

Concise e-books business students need for classroom and research

This book can also be purchased in an e-book collection by your library as

- a one-time purchase,
- that is owned forever,
- allows for simultaneous readers,
- has no restrictions on printing, and
- can be downloaded as PDFs from within the library community.

Our digital library collections are a great solution to beat the rising cost of textbooks. E-books can be loaded into their course management systems or onto students' e-book readers.
The **Business Expert Press** digital libraries are very affordable, with no obligation to buy in future years. For more information, please visit **www.businessexpertpress.com/librarians**. To set up a trial in the United States, please email **sales@businessexpertpress.com**.

www.ingramcontent.com/pod-product-compliance
Lightning Source LLC
Chambersburg PA
CBHW070542200326
41519CB00013B/3101